EUROPEAN COMM

EUROPEAN COMMUNITY LAW

An Introduction

Second Edition

David A O Edward CMG, QC, MA, LLB, LLD, FRSE
Judge of the Court of Justice of
the European Communities
Honorary Professor of the University of Edinburgh
(Salvesen Professor of European Institutions 1985–89)

and

Robert C Lane BA, MA, PHD
Senior Lecturer in the Europa Institute in the
University of Edinburgh

Foreword by Professor Walter van Gerven
Professor of Law, Katholieke Universiteit Leuven
Advocate-General, Court of Justice of the
European Communities 1988–94

Butterworths/Law Society of Scotland
Edinburgh
1995

United Kingdom	Butterworths a Division of Reed Elsevier (UK) Ltd, Halsbury House, 35 Chancery Lane, LONDON WC2A 1EL and 4 Hill Street, EDINBURGH EH2 3JZ
Australia	Butterworths, SYDNEY, MELBOURNE, BRISBANE, ADELAIDE, PERTH, CANBERRA and HOBART
Canada	Butterworths Canada Ltd, TORONTO and VANCOUVER
Ireland	Butterworth (Ireland) Ltd, DUBLIN
Malaysia	Malayan Law Journal Sdn Bhd, KUALA LUMPUR
New Zealand	Butterworths of New Zealand Ltd, WELLINGTON and AUCKLAND
Puerto Rico	Butterworth of Puerto Rico, Inc, SAN JUAN
Singapore	Butterworths Asia, SINGAPORE
South Africa	Butterworths Publishers (Pty) Ltd, DURBAN
USA	Butterworths Legal Publishers, CARLSBAD, California and SALEM, New Hamphire

A CIP Catalogue record for this book is available from the British Library.

ISBN 0 406 05670 6

Typeset by Phoenix Photosetting, Chatham, Kent
Printed and bound in Great Britain by
Mackays of Chatham PLC, Chatham, Kent

FOREWORD

It is very hard to improve on a good thing. When the first 'European Community Law' came out in 1991, I was thrilled to find a book of no more than 100 pages that provided a most comprehensive and fully reliable overview of Community law. The scope and scheme of this first version owed its success to the succinct chapters that in few, but well-chosen words, provided an excellent last-minute preparation for lectures and seminars. The constraint of space which the authors imposed on themselves led them to provide a very high quality introduction to an area of law that is – more often than not – treated in 500-page-plus books on all areas (general and specific) of Community law, leaving the unsuspecting first-time readers with the hopeless and not entirely untrue feeling that Community law is difficult, complex and overloaded.

Whilst it is easy to make things complicated and difficult, it is much more difficult to provide insight and guidance in simple but nevertheless correct terms. This is exactly what has been achieved by the authors, yet again, in this second edition. For obvious reasons, some fundamental changes in Community law have now been included. One cannot ignore the impact the Treaty of Maastricht has wrought nor bypass the significant developments in the case law of the European Court of Justice. All of these institutional and substantive law changes have been successfully inserted into the existing structure of the book. The qualities which made its first edition a success have been maintained. Not only is the written text extremely readable, but the detail of cases and other references under each heading (including, even, a number of decisions from national courts!) provide direct access to the nitty-gritty of Community law.

Whilst written in the first place for a UK audience, this book is at least as useful for European continental and other lawyers whether specialised in the law of the European Union or not: for the first, it provides a handy last minute reference book; for those not specialised in (or too specialised in a very limited area of) the law of the European Union, it provides a reliable first minute guide book.

I can most warmly recommend this book to all students, lecturers and practitioners for giving an insight in a complex area of the law, now made easily accessible.

WALTER van GERVEN
Leuven

20 February 1995

PREFACE

The first edition of this book was addressed primarily to a Scottish audience. But it was also received favourably outside Scotland: it has been used in law schools in continental Europe and in the United States, and it was translated into Czech and Estonian for teaching in those countries. This encouraged us and the publishers to embark upon a second edition addressed to a wider audience. We are particularly grateful for the encouragement of Professor Walter van Gerven, who has kindly written a foreword for this edition, and of Professor Sacha Prechal, who updated the first edition for use in Czech.

Our exposition of European Community law is founded on two basic beliefs. The first is that Community law must be seen as a whole in its historical context: that the institutional and substantive law are inseparable: and that a grasp of the structure of the EC Treaty is essential to a proper understanding of what it contains. The second is that the basic principles of Community law can be mastered in a relatively short time by any reasonably intelligent person who is not blinded by preconceived ideas. Community law is, after all, a new type of law, designed to deal with the problems of the late twentieth century: it affects us all, and it *ought* to be accessible.

At the cost of exceeding Professor van Gerven's ideal of 100 pages, this edition offers more complete coverage of substantive Community law as well as a child's guide to the mysteries of Maastricht and the EEA. We hope this will make the book more useful, but no less readable.

Amongst the many friends who have helped and encouraged us with this edition, we should like especially to mention Joxerramon Bengoetxea, Mark Hoskins, Elaine Whiteford and Elizabeth Willocks, who read all or substantial parts of the text; Judge Leif Sevón, who gave us indispensable linguistic assistance at the fifty-ninth minute; and Butterworths in Edinburgh. It goes without saying that we are responsible for any errors and omissions.

The law is stated as at 1 January 1995.

DAVID EDWARD
Luxembourg

ROBERT LANE
Edinburgh

March 1995

CONTENTS

Foreword   v
Preface   vii
Table of Statutes   xi
Table of Orders, Rules and Regulations   xiii
Table of Other Enactments   xv
Table of Cases   xxiii

Introduction   1

1. The Origins and Development of the European Communities and the European Union   3

2. The Institutions of the Community   15

(1) The Political Institutions   16
    (a) The European Parliament   16
    (b) The Council   19
    (c) The Commission   21
(2) The Legislative Process   25
(3) The Court of Justice   29
    (a) The Court   29
    (b) Forms of Process   33
(4) The Court of Auditors   46
(5) Other Organs   46

3. The Sources and Methods of Community Law   51

(1) The Nature and Enforcement of Community Law   55
(2) Community Legislation   60
(3) The General Principles of Community Law   64

4. The Structure and Main Provisions of the EC Treaty   70

(1) Introduction   70
(2) The Principles   70
(3) Citizenship of the Union   74
(4) Community Policies   75
    (a) The Four Freedoms   76
        (A) Free Movement of Goods: The Customs Union   76
        (B) Free Movement of Goods: Non-Tariff Barriers   80
        (C) Agriculture   86
        (D) Free Movement of Persons and Services   87

      (E) Services 97
      (F) Free Movement of Capital 100
      (G) Transport 101
  (b) Common Rules on Competition, Taxation and Approximation of
      Laws 102
      (A) The Rules on Competition 103
      (B) State Aids 121
      (C) Taxation 123
  (c) Other Common Policies 124
      (A) Economic and Monetary Union 124
      (B) Commercial Policy 127
      (C) Social Policy 128
      (D) Other Policies 134
(5) The General and Final Provisions of the EC Treaty 136

5. The Treaty on European Union 139

(1) Common Foreign and Security Policy 141
(2) Justice and Home Affairs 142
(3) Final Provisions of the Treaty on European Union 143

Appendix I—The European Economic Area 147

Appendix II—Guide to Community Sources and Materials 153

Index 159

Table of Statutes

PARA

British Nationality Act 1981 (c 61). 171

Civil Jurisdiction and Judgments Act
1982 (c 27) 124

Competition Act 1985 (c C-34)
(Canada) 223

Competition Act 1990 (Ireland) 223

Competition Laws of 1 July 1993
(Sweden) 223

Contracts (Applicable Law) Act 1990
(c 36). 124

Court of Session Act 1988 (c 36)
s 45(b). 103

Courts and Legal Services Act 1990
(c 41)
s 60 215

Crown Proceedings Act 1947 (c 44). 141

Employment Protection (Consolida-
tion) Act 1978 278

Equal Pay Act 1970 (c 41) 278

European Communities Act 1972
(c 68) 133, 136, 301
s 1(2)(k) 273
(3). 299
2(1) 136

PARA

European Communities Act 1972—*contd*
s 2(2) 148
3. 132

European Communities (Amend-
ment) Act 1986 (c 58) 28, 299

European Communities (Amend-
ment) Act 1993 (c 32) 36, 289,
299

s 2 267

European Economic Area Act 1993
(c 51). 40

European Parliamentary Elections
Act 1978 (c 10). 48

Law Reform (Miscellaneous Provisions) (Scotland) Act 1990 (c 40)
s 30 215

Legge 287/1990 (Italy). 223

Referendum Act 1975 (c 33) 17

Sex Discrimination Act 1975 (c 65) 278

Sheriff Courts (Scotland) Act 1907
(c 51)
Sch 1,
r 134 107

Sherman Act 1890 (USA). 223

Table of Orders, Rules and Regulations

PARA

Act of Adjournal (Consolidation)
1988
r 63–67 107
113–118 107
Act of Sederunt (Rules of the Court
of Session) 1994, SI 1994/1443
r 62.18–62.25 238
r 65.2–65.5......................... 107
County Court Rules
Ord 19
r 11 107
Crown Court Rules 1982, SI 1982/
1109
r 29 107

PARA

European Communities (Enforce-
ment of Community Judgments)
Order 1972, SI 1972/1590 238
Registration of Restrictive Trading
Agreements (EEC Documents)
Regulations 1973, SI 1973/950 242
Rules of the Supreme Court 1965,
SI 1965/1776
Ord 71
r 15–24 238
Ord 114
r 6 107

Table of Other Enactments

Para numbers in italics refer to Appendix 1

PARA

Act concerning the Election of the
Representatives of the Assembly
by Direct Universal Suffrage
(1976) 22, 48
Community Charter of the Fundamental Social Rights of Workers
(1989) 33, 38, 272, 274
  Preamble 272
  recital 15 272
  point 15 272
Convention for the Protection of
Human Rights and Funda-
mental Freedoms (1950) ... 2, 7, 153, 296
  art 25 7
  26 7
Convention on Jurisdiction and
Enforcement of Judgments in
Civil and Commercial Matters
(1968) 124
  Protocol 109
  art 4 109
Convention Concerning the Gradual
Elimination of Controls at
External Frontiers (the Schengen
Agreement) (1985) 228
Convention Determining the State
Responsible for Examining
Applications for Asylum
Lodged in one of the Member
States of the European
Communities (the Dublin
Convention) (1991). 228
Convention on Certain Institutions
Common to the European
Communities (1957). 14
Convention on the Law Applicable
to Contractual Obligations
(1980) 124
  Protocol 109
  art 3 109
Convention on the Mutual
Recognition of Companies,
Firms and Legal Persons (1968)..... 219
Convention on the Status of
Refugees (1951). 296
EC Council Decision
  70/243 19
  78/516 226
  86/398 232
  87/373 65
  88/591 84

PARA

EC Council Decision—*contd*
  art 2(1)–(4) 89
  3(1) 90, 104
  89/93 232
  91/619 .... 231, 248
  92/163 238
  92/521 226
  93/350 90
  93/492 64
  93/591 55
  93/662 58
  94/19 231
  94/65 118
  94/149 .... 90, 270
  94/728 19
  94/729 53
  94/783 193
  94/815 238
Decisions of 1 January 1995 (not yet
published) 59, 78, 300
EC Council (including EEC Council)
  Directive
  64/221 211
  64/223 213
  64/224 213
  64/225 219
  68/151 219
  68/360 204
  art 1............................. 203
  2–3.............................. 205
  4–7.............................. 206
  68/363 213
  71/305 195
  73/34 206
  73/148
  art 1............................. 204
  2–3.............................. 205
  4(1), (2) 206
  73/183 219
  73/239 219
  74/561 221
  74/562 221
  75/35 211
  75/117 .... 277, 278
  76/135 221
  76/207 277
  art 2(2) 277
  6................................. 277
  77/62 195
  77/91 219
  77/249 213

PARA

EC Council (including EEC Council)
Directive—*contd*

77/452	213
77/780	219
78/473	219
78/660	237
78/686	213
78/855	219
78/1026	213
79/7	277, 279
art 7(1)(a)	279
79/116	221
80/51	221
80/154	213
80/723	195
80/1263	221
82/714	221
82/891	219
83/189	193
83/349	219
84/253	219
85/3	221
85/384	213
85/432	213
86/216	221
86/378	277
86/613	277
87/540	221
88/357	219
88/361	220
89/48	215
89/646	220
89/665	195
89/666	219
89/667	219
90/364	206
90/365	206
90/366	206
90/434	219, 260
90/435	219, 260
90/463	260
90/531	195
91/439	221
91/670	221
91/671	221
91/672	221
92/6	221
92/22	221
92/24	221
92/49	219
92/51	215
92/62	221
92/121	219
93/16	213
93/36	195
93/37	195
93/38	195
93/65	221

PARA

EC Council (including EEC Council)
Directive—*contd*

93/89	221
93/96	206
93/104	271
94/45	274

EC Council (including EEC Council)
Regulation

1	126
7a	198
17/62	238, 248
art 1	229
2	243
3	238
4	242
(2)	242
5	242
9	240
(3)	232
11	238
13	238
14	238
(4)–(6)	238
15(1)	238
(2)	238, 242
(4)	238
(6)	242
16	238
17	238
19	242
(3)	244
20	242
27/62	242
99/63	242
950/68	182
1612/68	207
art 3	207
(1)	207
4	207
7–9	207
11	204
12	204
1251/70	206
1408/71	208
art 1(f)	208
2	208
12–15	208
574/72	208
1983/83	245
1984/83	245
2349/84	245
123/85	245
417/85	245
418/85	245
2137/85	219
3820/85	221
3821/85	221
2658/87	182

	PARA
EC Council (including EEC Council)	
Regulation—*contd*	
2423/88	270
4059/89	221
4087/88	245
556/89	245
4064/89	247
art 1(2), (3)	248
2(1)-(3)	248
9	248
10	248
(6)	248
22(3)	248
2913/92	182
art 3	177
(2)	177
3932/92	245
1617/93	245
3603/93	264
3604/93	264
3605/93	263
3652/93	245
40/94	196
518/94	268
519/94	268
2894/94	3
3320/94	21
EC Treaty	55, 60, 74, 112, 157, 2
Preamble	12, 128, 159, 161
art 2–7c	161
2	162, 164, 262
3	165, 281, 282
(b)	268
(d)	297
(f), (g)	224
(i), (j)	271
3a	164, 262
(1)-(3)	263
3b	166
1st para	45
2nd para	157
3rd para	155
4	44, 116
(1)	144
(2)	117, 118
4a	122
4b	119
5	140, 148, 167, 227
6	168, 207, 218
7	169
(7)	169
7a	
1st para	170
2nd para	170
7c	31
8–8e	171
8	169
(1), (2)	171

	PARA
EC Treaty—*contd*	
art 8a(1)	171, 206, 209
8b	171
8c	171
8d	171
Pt Three (art 9–130y)	172
Titles I–IV (art 9–84)	161, 173
art 9	178
(1)	174, 176
(2)	176
10	178
(1)	176
12–29	179
12	180, 181, 258
13	180
17	181
18–29	182
30–37	179
30	185, 186, 188, 189, 190, 192, 195, 196, 237
34	185, 186, 190, 196
36	186, 191, 192, 193, 196
37	197
Title II (art 38–47)	198
art 38(1), (2)	198
40(2)	198
Title III (art 48–73h)	
Ch 1 (art 48–51)	199
art 48	207
48(1)	205
(2)	207
(3)	65, 210
(4)	210
49	207
2nd para	203
51	208
Ch 2 (art 52–58)	199
art 52	212, 260
53	212
54	212
55	
1st para	210
56(1)	210
57	212
58	203, 260
Ch 3 (art 59–66)	199
art 65–66	247
66	210
73a–g	220
b(1), (2)	220
c(1), (2)	220
d	220
(3)	260
e	220
f	220
g(1), (2)	220
Title IV (art 74–84)	221
art 74	221

PARA

EC Treaty—*contd*
Title V (art 85–102)
Ch 1 (art 85–94)................... 223
art 85–90 223
85–102 161
85 .... 225, 226, 227, 228,
229, 232, 239, 243, 246,
247, 252, 9, 10
(1)............. 225, 228, 229, 232,
236, 237, 238, 239, 240,
242, 244, 245, 246, 247
(a)–(e)..................... 228
(2) 229, 239, 242, 246, 255
(3) 230, 232, 240, 241, 245
86 .... 225, 226, 227, 228, 229,
233, 234, 235, 236, 237,
238, 239, 240, 243, 244,
247, 252, 9, 10
(a)–(d)..................... 228
87 226
(1).......................... 226
88 226
89 226
(1).......................... 226
90 .... 226, 249, 9
(1)..................... 249, 250
(2)..................... 249, 251
(3)..................... 65, 249
91 .... 223, 270
92–94 .... 223, 253, 9
92 .... 254, 255
(1)–(3).................... 253
93 .... 254, 255
(1)........................ 254
(2)..................... 99, 254
(3)........................ 255
94 254
Ch 2 (art 95–99)................. 222
art 95–98 257
95 .... 181, 258
(2)........................ 258
99 259
Ch 3 (art 100–102)................ 222
art 100 .... 193, 222
100a 31, 170. 193, 222, 282
(3) 282
(4) 193
3rd para 99
100b 170
100c 222, 297
(3), (6)..................... 297
Title VI–XVII (art 102a–130y)........ 261
102a 263
103 263
(2)........................ 263
104 264
104a 264
104c 263, 264

PARA

EC Treaty—*contd*
art 104(10) 99
105–106........................ 122
105(1)–(2)..................... 265
105a(1), (2)..................... 265
106(1)–(3)..................... 122
(5) 299
107........................ 122
108........................ 264
108a(1), (3)..................... 122
109a........................ 122
109c(1), (2)..................... 122
109e(1), (2)..................... 264
109f 121
109g 265
109j 56
(1)........................ 264
(3), (4)..................... 264
109k(1)-(5)..................... 266
109l(1), (4)..................... 265
109l(5)..................... 266
113........................ 268
(1)........................ 268
(3)........................ 269
Title VIII (art 117-128) 271
117
1st para....................... 271
118
1st para....................... 271
118a........................ 271
118b 271
119 .... 161, 275, 276, 278,
279, 280
(1), (2)..................... 276
123–125..................... 271
126........................ 281
(1)-(3)..................... 282
(4) 118, 282
127..................... 218, 281
(3), (4)..................... 282
128........................ 281
(1), (3)..................... 282
(4) 283
(5)..................... 118, 282
129 .... 118, 281, 283
(1), (3), (4)..................... 282
129a........................ 281
129a(1)..................... 282
129b–129d 281
129d 118
130........................ 281
(3)........................ 283
130a–130y 281
130b 118, 283
130d, 130e 118
130r(2) 282, 283
(4) 282
130s........................ 282

PARA

EC Treaty—*contd*
art 130t 193
    130v 283
    130x–130y 282
    137 48
    138(3) 48
    138b
        2nd para 74
    138b(1) 79
    138c–138e 54
    139 49
    140 51
        3rd para 69
        4th para 69
    141 49
    142 49
    144 69
    146 56
        (2) 59
    148(1)–(3) 77
    151 60
        (3) 58
    155 . . . . 65, 66
    157(1) 61, 62, 299
        (2) 61
    158(2) 63
    160 69
    162(2) 64
    163 64
    164 . . . . 83, 152
    165
        1st para 85
        3rd para 87
        4th para 299
        (2) 87
    166
        1st para 85
        2nd para 88
        3rd para 299
    167
        1st para 85
        2nd para 85
        5th para 86
    168a 84
        (1) 90, 111
    169 . . . . 66, 97, 98, 99, 119,
                          132, 195, 254, 6
    170 . . . . 97, 6
    171 98
        (1), (2) 98
    173 . . . . 100, 101, 103, 104,
                          106, 110, 122, 144, 151,
                          256, 283, 6
        1st para 100
        2nd para 100, 101
        3rd para 101
        4th para 101
        5th para 100

PARA

EC Treaty—*contd*
art 174 102
    1st para 102
    2nd para 102
        (1) 6
    175 . . . . 103, 6
        2nd para 103
        3rd para 103
    176
        1st para 102, 103
        2nd para 102
    177 . . . . 90, 106, 107, 109,
                          110, 132, 137, 151, 240, 6
        1st para 106
        2nd para 107
        3rd para 107
    178 105
    179 104
    180 . . . . 119, 122
    181 285
    184 . . . . 110, 151
    185 113
    186 113
    188 299
        3rd para 83
    188a 116
    188b(1)–(3) 116
    188c(1)–(4) 116
    189 . . . . 142, 150, 238, 291
    189a(1) 74, 77
        (2) 74
    189b, 189c 79
    190 . . . . 129, 144
    191(3) 146
    192 238
    193–198 117
    193
        1st para 117
        2nd para 117
    194 117
    195(1)
        2nd para 117
    198a 118
        1st para 118
    198c(3) 118
    198d, 198e 119
    203–206 19
    203 53
    203(7)–(9) 53
    206(1) 116
    210 . . . . 284, 293
    215(1) 285
    215(2) 105
    216 45
    220 260
    222 196
    223(1) 286
    224 286

PARA

EC Treaty—*contd*
art 225 99
    2nd para....................... 287
   227 177
    (2) 177
   227(5)(a)–(c)..................... 177
   228 269
    (6) 112
   232 163
   235 287
   238 .... 284, 293
   239 160
   240 .... 13, 301
Annex II........................... 198
Declaration on Civil Protection,
  Energy and Tourism 281
Protocol concerning Article 119....... 280
Protocol concerning the Channel
  Islands and the Isle of Man........ 177
Protocol on Certain Provisions
  relating to Denmark 267
Protocol on Certain Provisions
  relating to the United Kingdom
  of Great Britain and Northern
  Ireland 267
Protocol on Convergence Criteria..... 264
Protocol on Social Policy......... 273, 289
art 2–3 273
Protocol on the Economic and
  Social Committee and the Committee of the Regions............. 118
Protocol on the European
  Monetary Institute................ 121
Protocol on the European System
  of Central Banks and of the
  European Central Bank.... 122, 264, 299
  art 2 265
   3 265
   7 122
   9 122
   10 122
   11 122
   16 265
   34 122
   35.1 122
   35.5 122
   35.6 122
   45–47 122
Protocol on the Excessive Deficit
  Procedure 263
Protocol on the Statute of the
  Court of Justice 83, 94, 299
  art 15 87
   17 96
   36 113
   37 96
   43 105
   47 90

PARA

EC Treaty—*contd*
art 49–54...................... 90, 111
   49........................... 111
   50........................... 111
    1st para.................... 96
    3rd para 96
   53........................... 111
   54........................... 111
    2nd para................... 111
    3rd para 111
Protocol on the Statute of the
  European Investment Bank 119
ECSC Treaty.......... 3, 9, 10, 13, 14, 55, 75,
          90, 112, 126, 163, 268,
            281, 299

Preamble 12
art 7............................. 117
  14............................ 55, 142
  18............................ 117
  20............................ 48
  28............................ 55
  31............................ 10, 83
  33............................ 101
  95............................ 112, 299
  97............................ 10, 301
EEA Treaty 5, 40, 41, 115, 252, *1, 2*
art 1............................. *2*
  6............................. *10*
  7............................. *3*
  8–27.......................... *8*
  8(2).......................... *8*
   (3)(b)....................... *8*
  13............................ *8*
  28–39......................... *8*
  36............................ *8*
  53............................ *9, 10*
  40–45......................... *8*
  54............................ *9, 10*
  56............................ *10*
  57............................ *9*
  58............................ *10*
  59............................ *9*
  60............................ *9*
  61–64......................... *9*
  90............................ *3*
  92............................ *3*
  93............................ *3*
  95(1), (3)..................... *3*
  96............................ *3*
  105........................... *7*
  106........................... *7*
  107........................... *7*
  108(1)........................ *4*
   (2) *5*
  109........................... *4*
  110........................... *4*
  111........................... *3*
   (3) *7*

PARA

EEA Treaty—*contd*
Annex XIV.......................... 9
Protocol 3.......................... 8
Protocol 4.......................... 8
Protocol 21
art 1 10
Protocol 23....................... 4, 10
art 10 10
Protocol 24......................... 10
Protocol 34......................... 7
Protocol 35......................... 6
Protocol 36......................... 3
EEC Treaty.................. 3, 11, 12, 13,
33, 38, 79, 170,
172, 299, 7
art 2 12
8c............................... 31
100a 31
106 220
130r(2) 283
206(1) 116
236 299
237 300
EFTA Surveillance Agreement............ 4
art 3(2) 7
7–9 4
31 6
32 6
34 6
36 6
37 6
Protocol 4......................... 10
Protocol 5
Statute of the Court 5
Euratom Treaty 3, 11, 13, 75, 163,
268, 281, 299
art 1 12
52ff 123
107 48
134 123
136 83
161 142
165–170 117
208 301
**Europe Agreement with Hungary
(1993)** 269
**Fourth ACP-EEC Convention of
Lomé (1989)**.............. 124, 269, 284
**Rules of Procedure of the Committee
of the Regions**................... 118
**Rules of Procedure of the
Commission** 64
Rules of Procedure of the Council........ 58
**Rules of Procedure of the Court of
First Instance**................... 90. 94
art 35 91
art 104(1), (2)...................... 113
111 95

**Rules of Procedure of the Court of
Justice**........................ 83, 94
art 29............................ 91
83(1), (2) 113
92............................. 95
**Rules of Procedure of the Economic
and Social Committee** 117
**Rules of Procedure of the EFTA
Surveillance Authority**
art 2............................. 4
**Rules of Procedure of the European
Parliament**....................... 49
rule 21–28 51
29(2) 50
53 82
54 157
159 54
Single European Act 19, 20, 28–32,
37, 46, 65, 78, 79, 84,
144, 170, 193, 261, 281,
283, 287, 288, 299
art 30(10) 294
**Statute of the Council of Europe
(1949)** 7
**Treaty amending Certain Financial
Provisions (1975)** 116
**Treaty establishing a Single Council
and a Single Commission of the
European Communities (the
Merger Treaty) (1965)** 14
**Treaty of Accession (Brussels Access-
ion Treaty) (1972)** 16, 300
**Treaty of Accession (Athens Access-
ion Treaty) (1979)** 23, 300
Treaty of Accession (1985) 27, 300
**Treaty of Accession (Corfu Access-
sion Treaty) (1994)**.............. 42, 79,
273, 300
Treaty on European Union 3, 4, 20,
36–39, 40, 46, 54,
55, 79, 93, 98, 118,
144, 157, 171, 206,
209, 220, 223, 261,
280, 281, 283, 287,
288–301
Preamble 292
art A–F........................ 288, 292
A............................. 37
C............................ 290
D............................. 46
E 290
F(1)–(2)....................... 288
F(2) 153
Title II–IV (art G–I) 37
G(A) 38
G(B)(83) 299
Title V (art J–J.11) 37, 46, 56, 288,
289, 291, 292, 294,
295, 296

PARA

Treaty on European Union—*contd*

art J–J.11............................ 294

J.................................... 294

J.1(1)–(3)........................... 294

J.1(4).............................. 294

J.2(1)-(3).......................... 294

J.3................................. 291

J.3(2).............................. 291

J.3(4).............................. 294

J.4(2)–(5).......................... 294

J.5(1), (4).......................... 294

J.6................................. 294

J.7................................. 292

J.8................................. 291

J.8(1).............................. 294

J.8(2).............................. 291

J.8(5).............................. 294

J.9................................. 291

J.11............................ 291, 292

Title VI (art K–K.9) 37, 170, 203, 288,
289, 291, 292, 295,
296, 297, 298

art K–K.9........................... 295

K.1................................. 296

PARA

Treaty on European Union—*contd*

art K.2(1) 296

K.3................................. 291

K.3(1) 295, 296

K.3(2) 291, 296

K.3(2)(c)

3rd para 292

K.4(1) 296

K.4(2), (3) 291

K.5................................. 296

K.6................................. 292

K.8................................. 292

K.8(2) 291

K.9........................... 291, 297

L............................... 93, 292

N................................... 299

(2) 39, 299

O................................... 300

P(2)................................. 37

Q............................... 36, 301

Declaration on Western European
Union........................... 294

Vienna Convention on the Law of
Treaties (1969)................... 128

Table of Cases

A

Accession to the European Convention on Human Rights, re (Opinion 2/94) pending 153
Adams v Commission (145/83) [1985] ECR 3539, [1986] 1 CMLR 506 105
Adams, R v Secretary of State for the Home Department, ex parte (C-229/94) pending. 206, 209
Administration des Douanes et Droits Indirects v Legros (C-163/90) [1992] ECR I-4625. . . . 108,
    154
Adoui and Cornuaille v Belgium (115 & 116/81) [1982] ECR 1665, [1982] 3 CMLR 631 210
Åhlström v Commission (Woodpulp) (89 etc/85) [1988] ECR 5193, [1988] 4 CMLR 901. 232
Ahmed Saeed Flugreisen v Zentrale zur Bekämpfung Unlauteren Wettbewerbs (66/88)
    [1989] ECR 803, [1990] 4 CMLR 102 . . . . 221, 225, 231
AKZO v Commission (5/85) [1986] ECR 2585, [1987] 3 CMLR 716. 64
AKZO v Commission (62/86) [1991] ECR I-3359, [1993] 5 CMLR 215 . . . . 233, 234, 235
Al-Jubail Fertiliser Company v Council (49/88) [1991] ECR I-3187, [1991] 3 CMLR 377. 153
All Weather Sports Benelux v Commission (T-38/92) [1994] ECR II-211. . . . . 144, 154
Almelo, Municipality of v IJsselmij NV (C-393/92) [1994] ECR I-1477. 251
Allen and Hanburys v Generics (UK) Ltd (434/85) [1988] ECR 1245, [1988] 1 CMLR 701 . . . 189,
    191
A M & S Europe v Commission (155/79) [1982] ECR 1575, [1982] 2 CMLR 264 . . . . 153, 158, 238
Amendment of the ECSC Treaty, re (Opinion 1/61) [1961] ECR 243 112
Amministrazione delle Finanze dello Stato v Simmenthal (106/77) [1978] ECR 629,
    [1978] 3 CMLR 623. 135
Anastasiou (Pissouri) Ltd, R v Minister for Agriculture, Fisheries and Food, ex parte
    (C-432/92) [1994] ECR I-3087. 284
Antonissen, R v Immigration Appeal Tribunal, ex parte (C-292/89) [1991] ECR I-745,
    [1991] 2 CMLR 373. 205
Aragonesa de Publicidad Exterior v Departmento de Sanidad y Securidad Social de la
    Generalitat de Cataluña (C-1 & 176/90) [1990] ECR I-4151, [1994] 1 CMLR 887. . . . 147, 167
Argyll v Distillers (OH) 1987 SLT 514, [1986] 1 CMLR 764. . . . . 139, 239
'Art Treasures', sub nom Commission v Italy (First Art Treasures Case) (7/68) [1968] ECR
    423, [1969] CMLR 1 176
'Art Treasures', sub nom Commission v Italy (Second Art Treasures Case) (48/71) [1972]
    ECR 527, [1972] ECR 699. 98
Asia Motor France v Commission (C-72/90) [1990] ECR I-218 90
Asia Motor France v Commission (T-28/90) [1992] ECR II-2285, [1992] 5 CMLR 431 . . . 103, 238
Association de Soutien aux Travailleurs Immigrés v Chambre des Employés Privés
    (C-213/90) [1991] ECR I-3507, [1993] 3 CMLR 621. . . . . 168, 207
Asteris AE v Commission (106-20/87) [1988] ECR 5515 105
Atlanta Fruit v Germany (C-465/93) pending 107
Aubertin, Criminal proceedings against (C-29 etc/94) 16 February 1995, not yet reported . . 209
Automec v Commission (T-64/89) [1990] ECR II-367, [1991] 4 CMLR 177 238
Automec v Commission (T-24/90) [1992] ECR II-2223, [1992] 5 CMLR 431 238
Automobiles Peugeot v Commission (T-23/90) [1991] ECR II-653, [1993] 5 CMLR 540 238

B

Bachmann v Belgian State (C-204/90) [1992] ECR I-249 207
'Bananas' sub nom Germany v Council (C-280/93) [1994] ECR I-4973 156
Banchero, Pretore di Genova v (C-157/92) [1993] ECR I-1085 107
'Bangladesh', sub nom European Parliament v Council and Commission (C-181 & 248/91)
    [1993] ECR I-3685, [1994] 3 CMLR 317 100
Banks v British Coal Corporation (C-128/92) [1994] ECR I-1209, [1994] 5 CMLR 30 14
Barber v Guardian Royal Exchange (292/88) [1990] ECR I-1889, [1990] 2 CMLR 513 . . . 108, 154,
    276, 279, 280

Barra v Belgium (309/85) [1988] ECR 355 108
'Bathing Water', sub nom Commission v United Kingdom (C-56/90) [1993] ECR I-4109,
 [1994] 1 CMLR 769. 97
'Battery Hens', sub nom United Kingdom v Council (131/86) [1988] ECR 905, [1988]
 2 CMLR 364 144
Bayer v Commission (C-195/91P) 15 December 1994, not yet reported 100
Bayerische HNL v Council and Commission (83 & 94/76, 4, 15 & 40/77) [1978] ECR 1209,
 [1978] 3 CMLR 566. 105
Béguelin v GL Import Export (22/71) [1971] ECR 949, [1972] CMLR 81 232
Bekaert v Procureur de la République, Rennes (204/87) [1988] ECR 2036, [1988]
 2 CMLR 655 209
Belgische Radio en Televisie v SABAM (127/73) [1974] ECR 313, [1974] 2 CMLR 238 229
Belgium v Commission (142/87) [1990] ECR I-959 . . . . 153, 253
Belgium v Humbel (263/86) [1988] ECR 5365, [1989] 1 CMLR 393 218
Benedetti v Munari (52/76) [1977] ECR 163 106
Bestuur van het Algemeen Burgerlijk Pensioenfonds v Beune (C-7/93) [1994] ECR
 I-4471. . . . . 279, 280
Bethell v Commission (246/81) [1982] ECR 2277, [1982] 3 CMLR 300 103
Beune, Bestuur van het Algemeen Burgerlijk Pensioenfonds v (C-7/93) [1994] ECR
 I-4471. . . . . 279, 280
Bilka-Kaufhaus v Weber von Hartz (170/84) [1986] ECR 1607, [1986] 2 CMLR 701 . . . . . 278, 280
Binon v Agence et Messageries de la Presse (243/83) [1985] ECR 2015, [1985] 3 CMLR 800. . 232
Blaizot v University of Liège (24/86) [1988] ECR 379, [1989] 1 CMLR 57 . . . . 154, 218
Bock v Commission (62/70) [1971] ECR 897, [1972] CMLR 160. 101
Boehringer Mannheim v Commission (45/69) [1970] ECR 769 238
Bonnamy v Council (T-179/94) 14 July 1994, not reported 46
Bonnamy v Council (C-264/94P) 13 January 1995, not yet reported 46
Bordessa, Minsterio Fiscal v (C-358 & 416/93) 23 February 1995, not yet reported 176, 200
Bouchereau, R v (30/77) [1977] ECR 1999, [1977] 2 CMLR 800 . . . . 155, 210
Bouchoucha (C-61/89) [1990] ECR I-3551, [1992] 1 CMLR 1033 212
Bourgoin v Minister for Agriculture, Fisheries and Food (CA) [1985] 3 All ER 585,
 [1986] 1 CMLR 267. 141
Brasserie de Haecht v Wilkin-Janssen (No 2) (48/72) [1973] ECR 77, [1973] CMLR 287 . 240, 246
Brasserie de Pêcheur v Germany (C-46/93) pending. 141
British Aerospace and Rover Group Holdings v Commission (C-294/90) [1992] ECR I-493 . 255
British Airways, Scandinavian Air Service and Koninklijke Luchtvaart Maatschappij
 v Commission (T-371/94) pending. 90
British American Tobacco Ltd v Commission (Philip Morris) (142 & 156/84) [1987] ECR
 4487, [1988] 4 CMLR 24. 247
Broekmeulen v Huisarts Registratie Commissie (246/80) [1981] ECR 2311. [1982]
 1 CMLR 91 106
Brown v Secretary of State for Scotland (197/86) [1988] ECR 3205, [1988] 3 CMLR 403 218
Buet v Ministère Public (382/87) [1989] ECR 1235. 192
Bulmer v Bollinger (CA) [1974] Ch 401, [1974] 2 CMLR 91. 107
Bundesanstalt für den Guterfernverkehr v Gebrüder Reiff (C-185/91) [1993] ECR I-5801 . . . 227
Bureau Européen des Unions des Consummateurs v Commission (T-37/92) [1994]
 ECR II-285. 238

C

CAM v Commission (100/74) [1975] ECR 1393 101
Camera Care v Commission (792/79R) [1980] ECR 119, [1980] 1 CMLR 334. 238
Campus Oil v Minister for Industry and Energy (Irish SC) [1984] 1 CMLR 479 107
'Cassis de Dijon', sub nom Rewe-Zentrale v Bundesmonopolverwaltung für Branntwein
 (120/78) [1979] ECR 649, [1979] 3 CMLR 494 . . . . 188, 189, 214, 217
CBEM v CLT and IPB (Telemarketing) (311/84) [1985] ECR 3261. 235
Centrafarm v Sterling Drug (15/74) [1974] ECR 1147, [1974] 2 CMLR 480 . . . . 231, 237
Charmasson v Minister for Economic Affairs and Finance (48/74) [1974] ECR 1383,
 [1975] 2 CMLR 208. 198

'Chernobyl', sub nom European Parliament v Council (70/88) [1990] ECR I-2041, [1992]
    1 CMLR 91 . . . . 79, 101
Chomel v Commission (T-123/89) [1990] ECR II-131 154
CILFIT v Ministero della Sanità (283/81) [1982] ECR 3415, [1983] 1 CMLR 472 . . . . 107, 130, 132
Cinéthèque v Fédération National des Cinemas Français (60-61/84) [1985] ECR 2605,
    [1986] 1 CMLR 365. 189
CIRFS v Commission (C-313/90) [1993] ECR I-1125 256
CNTA v Commission (74/74) [1975] ECR 533, [1977] 1 CMLR 171. 154
Codorniu v Council (C-309/89) [1994] ECR I-1853 151
Coloroll Pension Trustees Ltd v Russell (C-200/91) [1994] ECR I-4389 280
Commercial Solvents v Commission (6 & 7/73) [1974] ECR 223, [1974] 1 CMLR 309 . . . 235, 238
Commerzbank, R v Inland Revenue Commissioners, ex parte (C-330/90) [1993] ECR I-4017,
    [1993] 3 CMLR 357. 260
Commission v BASF (PVC) (C-137/92P) [1994] ECR I-2555. . . . . 45, 64, 102, 111
Commission v Belgium (149/79) [1980] ECR 3881, [1981] 2 CMLR 413; [1982] ECR 1845,
    [1982] 3 CMLR 539. 210
Commission v Belgium (293/85) [1988] ECR 305, [1986] 1 CMLR 594 . . . . 97, 218
Commission v Belgium (C-374/89) [1991] ECR I-367 167
Commission v Belgium (C-2/90) [1992] ECR I-4431, [1993] 1 CMLR 365. . . . . 176, 189
Commission v Belgium (C-211/91) [1992] ECR I-6757 217
Commission v Belgium (C-37/93) [1993] ECR I-6295 210
Commission v Belgium (C-47/93) [1994] ECR I-1593, [1994] 3 CMLR 711. 218
Commission v Council (ERTA) (22/70) [1971] ECR 263, [1971] CMLR 335 . . . . 100, 150, 282, 284
Commission v Council (Generalised Tariff Preferences) (45/86) [1987] ECR 1493, [1988]
    2 CMLR 131 . . . . 102, 144, 287
Commission v Council (Titanium Dioxide) (C-300/89) [1991] ECR I-2867, [1993]
    3 CMLR 359 144
Commission v Council (Waste Disposal) (C-155/91) [1993] ECR I-939 144
Commission v Denmark (Returnable Bottles) (302/86) [1988] ECR 4607, [1989] 1 CMLR
    619 189
Commission v Denmark (Storebælt) (C-243/89) [1993] ECR I-3353 195
Commission v France (167/73) [1974] ECR 359 271
Commission v France (68/76) [1977] ECR 515, [1977] 2 CMLR 161. 198
Commission v France (Tourist Guides) (C-154/89) [1991] ECR I-659. 217
Commission v France (Maritime Transport) (C-381/93) [1994] ECR I-5145. 216
Commission v Germany (Kohlgesetz) (70/72) [1973] ECR 813, [1974] CMLR 741 255
Commission v Germany (Insurance and Co-Insurance) (205/84) [1986] ECR 3755, [1987]
    2 CMLR 69 . . . . 201, 217, 219
Commission v Germany (Reinheitsgebot) (178/84) [1987] ECR 1227, [1988] 1 CMLR 780 . . . 192
Commission v Greece (240/86) [1988] ECR 1835 97
Commission v Greece (127/87) [1988] ECR 3333 284
Commission v Greece (132/88) [1990] ECR I-1567. 195
Commission v Greece (C-45/91) [1992] ECR I-2525. 195
Commission v Greece (C-120/94R) [1994] ECR I-3037 . . . . 113, 286
Commission v Greece (C-120/94) pending 286
Commission v Ireland (Irish Souvenirs) (113/80) [1981] ECR 1625, [1982] 1 CMLR 706 . 189, 191
Commission v Ireland (45/87R) [1987] ECR 783 195
Commission v Ireland (45/87) [1988] ECR 4929. 195
Commission v Italy (First Art Treasures Case) (7/68) [1968] ECR 423, [1969] CMLR 1 176
Commission v Italy (24/68) [1969] ECR 193, [1971] CMLR 611 180
Commission v Italy (Second Art Treasures Case) (48/71) [1972] ECR 527, [1972] CMLR 699 . 98
Commission v Italy (154/85) [1987] ECR 2717 97
Commission v Italy (194/88R) [1988] ECR 5647. 195
Commission v Italy (3/88) [1989] ECR 4035 212
Commission v Italy (C-139/92) [1993] ECR I-4707. 193
Commission v Italy (Public Supply Contracts) (C-362/90) [1992] ECR I-2353, [1994]
    3 CMLR 1 97
Commission v Luxembourg and Belgium (Gingerbread) (2-3/62) [1962] ECR 425, [1963]
    CMLR 199. 198

Commission v Netherlands (96/81) [1982] ECR 1791 167
Commission v United Kingdom (170/78) [1980] ECR 417, [1980] 1 CMLR 716; [1983] ECR 2265, [1983] 3 CMLR 512 258
Commission v United Kingdom (Pasteurised Milk) (261/85) [1988] ECR 547, [1988] 2 CMLR 11 192
Commission v United Kingdom ('Dim-Dip Headlamps') (60/86) [1988] ECR 3921, [1988] 3 CMLR 437 193
Commission v United Kingdom (C-246/89R) [1989] ECR 3125 113
Commission v United Kingdom (Bathing Water) (C-56/90) [1993] ECR I-4109, [1994] 1 CMLR 769 97
Compagnie Commercial de l'Ouest v Administration des Douanes (C-78-83/90) [1992] ECR I-1847 167
Conegate v HM Customs and Excise (121/85) [1986] ECR 1007, [1986] 1 CMLR 739 192
Confédération Nationale des Producteurs des Fruits et Légumes v EEC Council (16-17/62) [1962] ECR 471, [1963] CMLR 160 151
Consten & Grundig v EEC Commission (56 & 58/64) [1966] ECR 299, [1966] CMLR 418 ... 232, 237, 239
Corbeau, Criminal proceedings against (C-230/91) [1993] ECR I-2533 250
Cornelius Kramer (3, 4 & 6/76) [1976] ECR 1279, [1976] 2 CMLR 440 284
Cooperativa Co-Frutta v Amministrazione delle Finanze dello Stato (193/85) [1987] ECR 2085 257
Cooperative Verenigung 'Suiker Unie' v Commission (40 etc/73) [1975] ECR 1663, [1976] 1 CMLR 295 .... 234, 235
Corsica Ferries Italia v Corpo dei Piloti del Porto de Genova (C-18/93) [1994] ECR I-1783 .... 167, 168, 216, 217, 221, 234
Costa v ENEL (6/64) [1964] ECR 585, [1964] CMLR 425 .... 107, 197, 212
Council v European Parliament (34/86) [1986] ECR 2155, [1986] 3 CMLR 94 53
Cowan v Trésor Public (186/87) [1989] ECR 195, 1990] 2 CMLR 613 216
Criminal proceedings against Aubertin (C-29 etc/94) 16 February 1995, not yet reported ... 209
Criminal proceedings against Corbeau (C-230/91) [1993] ECR I-2533 250
Criminal proceedings against Keck and Mithouard (C-267-8/91) [1993] ECR I-6097 .... 87, 132, 187, 188
Criminal proceedings against Meng (C-2/91) [1993] ECR I-5751 227
Criminal proceedings against Ohra Schadeverzekeringen (C-245/91) [1993] ECR I-5851.... 227
Criminal proceedings against Prantl (16/83) [1984] ECR 1299, [1985] 2 CMLR 238 187
Crotty v An Taoiseach (Irish SC) [1987] 2 CMLR 666 28

D

Daily Mail, R v HM Treasury and Commissioners of Inland Revenue, ex parte (81/87) [1988] ECR 5483, [1988] 3 CMLR 713 212
Dassonville, Procureur du Roi v (8/74) [1974] ECR 837, [1974] 2 CMLR 436 .... 187, 217
Defrenne v Belgium (80/70) [1971] ECR 445 279
Defrenne v SABENA (No 2) (43/75) [1976] ECR 455, [1976] 2 CMLR 98 .... 108, 154, 278
Dekker v Stichting Vormingscentrum voor Jong Volwassenen Plus (177/88) [1990] ECR I-3941 .... 277, 278
Delimitis v Henninger Bräu (C-234/89) [1991] ECR I-935, [1992] 5 CMLR 210 .... 45, 246
Denkavit v Minister fur Ernährung (251/78) [1979] ECR 3369, [1980] 3 CMLR 513 193
Department of Health and Social Security v Barr and Montrose Holdings Ltd (C-355/89) [1991] ECR I-3479, [1991] 3 CMLR 325 177
Deutsche Grammophon v Metro (78/70) [1971] ECR 487, [1971] CMLR 631 196
Diatta v Land Berlin (267/83) [1985] ECR 567, [1986] 2 CMLR 164 204
'Dim-Dip Headlamps', sub nom Commission v United Kingdom (60/86) [1988] ECR 3921, [1988] 3 CMLR 437 193
Dirección General de Defensa de la Competencia v Asociación Española de Banca Privada (C-67/91) [1992] ECR I-4785 242
Distillers v Commission (30/78) [1980] ECR 2229, [1980] 3 CMLR 121 242
Dona v Mantero (13/76) [1976] ECR 133, [1976] 2 CMLR 578 206
Donckerwolcke v Procureur de la République (41/76) [1976] ECR 1921, [1977] 2 CMLR 535 .... 169, 178

Doughty v Rolls Royce (CA) [1992] 1 CMLR 1045 148
Draft Convention on the Physical Protection of Nuclear Materials, re the (Ruling 1/78
    [1978] ECR 2151, [1979] 1 CMLR 131 284
Driessen en Zonen v Minister van Verkeer en Waterstaat (C-13-16/92) [1993] ECR I-4751,
    [1994] 2 CMLR 141 79
Du Pont de Nemours v Unita Sanitaria di Carrera (21/88) [1990] ECR I-889 195
Duke v GEC Reliance Ltd (HL) [1988] AC 618, [1988] 1 CMLR 719 148
'Dyestuffs', sub nom ICI v Commission (48/69) [1972] ECR 619, [1972] CMLR 557 232

E

EEA Agreement, re the (Opinion 1/91) [1991] ECR I-6079, [1992] 1 CMLR 245 .... 112, 133
EEA Agreement, re the (No 2) (Opinion 1/92) [1993] ECR I-1061, [1992] 2 CMLR 217 284
Elliniki Radiophonia Tiléorasi v Dimotiki Etairia Pliroforissis (260/89) [1991] ECR I-2925,
    [1994] 4 CMLR 540 .... 153, 234, 235, 250
Emerald Meats v Commission (C-106 & 317/90 & 129/91) [1993] ECR I-209, [1994]
    1 CMLR 505 105
Emmott v Minister for Social Welfare and Attorney General (C-208/90) [1991] ECR I-4269 . 139
Enderby v Frenchay Health Authority (C-127/92) [1993] ECR I-5535 278
ENU v Commission (C-107/91) [1993] ECR I-599 103
Equal Opportunities Commission, R v Secretary of State for Social Security, ex parte
    (C-9/91) [1992] ECR I-4297 279
'ERTA', sub nom Commission v Council (22/70) [1971] ECR 263, [1971] CMLR 335 ... 150, 282,
                                                                                  284
'European Development Fund', sub nom European Parliament v Council (C-316/91)
    [1994] ECR I-625, [1994] 3 CMLR 149 .... 100, 144
European Parliament v Council (13/83) [1985] ECR 1513, [1986] 1 CMLR 138 .... 103, 221
European Parliament v Council (Chernobyl) (70/88) [1990] ECR I-2041, [1992] 1 CMLR
    91 .... 79, 101
European Parliament v Council (Students) (C-295/90) [1992] ECR I-4193, [1992] 3 CMLR
    281 .... 102, 144, 206
European Parliament v Council (C-65/90) [1992] ECR I-4593 79
European Parliament v Council (C-181 & 248/91) [1993] ECR I-3685 57
European Parliament v Council and Commission (Bangladesh) (C-181 & 248/91) [1993]
    ECR I-3685, [1994] 3 CMLR 317 79
European Parliament v Council (European Development Fund) (C-316/91) [1994] ECR
    I-625, [1994] 3 CMLR 149 .... 100, 144
European Parliament v Council (C-388/92) [1994] ECR I-2067 .... 79, 102
European Parliament v Council (Waste Removal) (C-187/93) [1994] ECR I-2857 144
Europemballage and Continental Can v Commission (6/72) [1973] ECR 215, [1973]
    CMLR 199 .... 225, 247

F

F, Mr and Mrs v Belgium (7/75) [1975] ECR 679, [1975] 2 CMLR 442 208
Faccini Dori v Recreb (C-91/92) [1994] ECR I-3325 .... 141, 148
Factortame, R v Secretary of State for Transport, ex parte (No 1) (C-213/89) [1990] ECR
    I-2433, [1990] 3 CMLR 1 139
Factortame, R v Secretary of State for Transport, ex parte (HL) [1990] 2 AC 55, [1989]
    3 CMLR 1; [1991] 1 AC 603, [1990] 3 CMLR 375 .... 136, 139
Factortame, R v Secretary of State for Transport, ex parte (No 2) (C-221/89) [1991]
    ECR I-3905, [1991] 3 CMLR 589 201
Factortame, R v Secretary of State for Transport, ex parte (No 3) (C-48/93) pending 141
Farrauto v Bau-Berufsgenossenschaft Wuppertal (66/74) [1975] ECR 157, [1976] 2 CMLR
    334 154
Fédération Charbonnière de Belgique v High Authority (8/55) [1954-56] ECR 292 155
FEDESA, R v Minister for Agriculture, Fisheries and Food, ex parte (331/88) [1990]
    ECR I-4023, [1991] 1 CMLR 507 .... 144, 153, 155
Filtrona Española v Commission (T-125/89) [1990] ECR II-393, [1990] 4 CMLR 832 100
Finanzamt Köln-Altstadt v Schumacker (C-279/83) 14 February 1995, not yet reported 207

Finnegan v Clowney Youth Training Programme (HL) [1990] 2 AC 407, [1990] 2 CMLR
859 148
Fiskano v Commission (C-135/92) [1994] ECR I-2885 153
Fisscher v Voorhuis Hengelo (C-128/93) [1994] ECR I-4583 280
Foglia v Novello (No 1) (104/79) [1980] ECR 745, [1981] 1 CMLR 45 107
Foglia v Novello (No 2) (244/80) [1981] ECR 3045, [1982] 1 CMLR 585 107
Ford Werke v Commission (228-9/82) [1984] ECR 1129, [1984] 1 CMLR 649 238
Foster v British Gas (C-188/89) [1990] ECR I-3313, [1990] 2 CMLR 833 148
Foto-Frost v Hauptzollamt Lübeck-Ost (314/85) [1987] ECR 4199, [1988] 3 CMLR 57 107
France v Commission (102/87) [1988] ECR 4067 253
France v Commission (366/88) [1990] ECR I-3571, [1992] 1 CMLR 205 150
France v Commission (202/88) [1991] ECR I-1223 249
France v Commission (C-327/91) [1994] ECR I-3641 .... 100, 126
France v Commission (C-41/93) [1994] ECR I-1829 .... 144, 193
France v United Kingdom (141/78) [1979] ECR 2923, [1980] 1 CMLR 697 97
Francovich and Bonifaci v Italy (C-6 & 9/90) [1991] ECR I-5357, [1993] 2 CMLR 66 141,
148, 278
Frederiksen v European Parliament (T-106/92) 2 February 1995, not yet reported 100
Funke v France (ECHR) [1993] 1 CMLR 897 153

G

Gallaher, R v Secretary of State for Health, ex parte (C-11/92) [1993] ECR I-3545, [1994]
3 CMLR 179 193
Garden Cottage Foods Ltd v Milk Marketing Board (HL) [1984] AC 130, [1983] 3 CMLR 43. 239
Garland v British Rail Engineering Ltd (12/81) [1982] ECR 359, [1982] 1 CMLR 696 276
Garland v British Rail Engineering Ltd (HL) [1983] 2 AC 751, [1982] 2 CMLR 402 ..... 107, 136
Gaston Schul v Inspecteur der Invoerrechten en Accijnzen (15/81) [1982] ECR 1409,
[1982] 3 CMLR 229 .... 163, 184
Gebhard v Consiglio dell' Ordine degli Avvocati e Procuratori di Milano (C-55/94)
pending 213
'Generalised Tariff Preferences', sub nom Commission v Council (45/86) [1987] ECR 1493,
[1988] 2 CMLR 131 .... 102, 144, 287
Germany v Commission (84/82) [1984] ECR 1505 254
Germany v Council (C-359/92) [1994] ECR I-3681 222
Germany v Council (Bananas) (C-280/93) [1994] ECR I-4973 156
Gibraltar, Government of v Council (C-298/89) [1993] ECR I-3605, [1994] 3 CMLR 425 151
Gibson v Lord Advocate (OH) 1975 SC 136, [1975] 1 CMLR 563 136
'Gingerbread', sub nom Commission v Luxembourg and Belgium (2-3/62) [1962] ECR 425,
[1963] ECR 199 198
Gøttrup-Klim v Dansk Landbrugs Grovvareselskab (C-250/92) 15 December 1994,
not yet reported 198, 246
Gourmetterie van den Burg (C-169/89) [1990] ECR I-2143 193
Government of Gibraltar v Council (C-298/89) [1993] ECR I-3605, [1994] 3 CMLR 425 151
Grad v Finanzamt Traunstein (9/70) [1970] ECR 825, [1971] CMLR 1 146
Granaria v Hoofdproduktschap voor Akkerbouwprodukten [1979] ECR 623, [1979]
3 CMLR 124 102
Grandes Distilleries Peureux v Directeur des Services Fisceaux (86/78) [1979] ECR 897,
[1980] 3 CMLR 337 197
Gravier v Ville de Liège (298/83) [1986] ECR 610, [1985] 3 CMLR 1 218
Griffin v South West Water (Ch D) [1995] IRLR 15 148
Grimaldi v Fonds des Maladies Professionnelles (322/88) [1989] ECR 4407, [1991]
2 CMLR 265 .... 149, 151
Groener v Minister for Education (379/87) [1989] ECR 3967, [1990] 1 CMLR 401 207
Groenveld v Produktschap voor Vee en Vlees (15/79) [1979] ECR 3409, [1981] 1 CMLR
207 190
Grogan, Society for the Protection of Unborn Children v (C-159/90) [1991] ECR I-4685,
[1991] 3 CMLR 849 .... 153, 216
Gül v Regierungspräsident Düsseldorf (131/85) [1986] ECR 1573, [1987] 1 CMLR 501 204

Gullung v Conseil de l'ordre des avocats du barreau de Colmar et de Savergne (292/86)
 [1988] ECR 111, [1988] 2 CMLR 57 217
Gutmann v Euratom Comission (18 & 35/65) [1966] ECR 103. 153
GVL v Commission (7/82) [1983] ECR 483, [1983] 3 CMLR 645 238

H

Habermann-Beltermann v Arbeiterwohlfahrt Bezirksverband (C-421/92) [1994] ECR
 I-1657, [1994] 2 CMLR 681 148
Haegemann v Belgian State (181/73) [1974] ECR 449, [1975] 1 CMLR 515 284
'Hag II', sub nom SA-CNL Sucal NV v HAG GV AG (C-10/89) [1990] ECR I-3711,
 [1990] 3 CMLR 571. . . . . 132, 196
Haim v Kassenzahnärtzliche Vereinigung Nordrhein (C-319/92) [1994] ECR I-428,
 [1994] 2 CMLR 169. 214
Hauer v Land Rheinland-Pfalz (44/79) [1979] ECR 3727, [1980] 3 CMLR 42. . . . . 153, 158
Hauptzollamt Hamburg v Bollmann (40/69) [1970] ECR 69, [1970] CMLR 141 145
Hauptzollamt Mainz v Kupferberg (104/81) [1982] ECR 3641, [1983] 1 CMLR 1 284
Hencke v Hauptzollamt Emmerich [1971] ECR 743. 154
Henn and Darby v DPP (HL) [1981] AC 850, [1980] 2 CMLR 166 107
Hertz v Dansk Arbejdsgiverforening (179/88) [1990] ECR I-3979. 277
Hilti v Commission (T-30/89) [1991] ECR II-1439 235
HM Customs and Excise v Schindler (C-275/92) [1994] ECR I-1039, [1995] 1 CMLR 4 . . 176, 217
Hoechst v Commission (46/87 & 227/88) [1989] ECR 2859, [1991] 4 CMLR 410 . . . . 153, 238
Hoffmann-La Roche v Centrafarm (107/76) [1977] ECR 957, [1977] 2 CMLR 334 107
Hoffmann-La Roche v Commission (85/76) [1979] ECR 461, [1979] 3 CMLR 211 . . 153, 234, 235
Höfner v Macrotron (C-41/90) [1991] ECR I-1979, [1993] 4 CMLR 306. . . . . 226, 234, 249
Holdijk (141-43/81) [1982] ECR 1299, [1983] 2 CMLR 635 190
Holleran v Thwaites (Ch D) [1989] 2 CMLR 917. 239
Hopkins v National Power (QBD) [1994] 1 CMLR 147 139
Hopkins v National Power (C-18/94) pending. 139
Hugin Kassaregister v Commission (22/78) [1979] ECR 1869, [1979] 3 CMLR 345 231
Hünermund v Landesapothekerskammer Baden-Württemberg (C-292/92) [1993]
 ECR I-6787. 187
Hurd v Jones (44/84) [1986] ECR 29, [1986] 2 CMLR 1 167

I

Ianelli e Volpi v Meroni (74/76) [1977] ECR 557, [1977] 2 CMLR 688. 185
ICI v Commission (Dyestuffs) (48/69) [1972] ECR 619, [1972] CMLR 557 232
IGAV v ENCC (94/74) [1975] ECR 699 181
IHT Internationale Heiztechnik v Ideal Standard (C-9/93) [1994] ECR I-2789 196
Imperial Chemical Industries Ltd v Commission (48/69) [1972] ECR 619, [1972] CMLR
 557 154
Inno v ATAB (13/77) [1977] ECR 2115, [1978] 1 CMLR 283 227
'Insurance and Co-Insurance', sub nom Commission v Germany (205/84) [1986] ECR 3755,
 [1987] 2 CMLR 69. . . . . 201, 217, 219
International Chemical Corporation v Amministrazione delle Finanze dello Stato (66/80)
 [1981] ECR 1191, [1983] 2 CMLR 593 . . . . 110, 132
Internationale Handelsgesellschaft mbH v Einfuhr- und Vorratsstelle für Getreide
 und Futtermittel (11/70) [1970] ECR 1125, [1972] CMLR 255. 153
Interzuccheri v Ditta Rezzano e Cavassa (105/76) [1977] ECR 1029 258
'Irish Souvenirs', sub nom Commission v Ireland (113/80) [1981] ECR 1625, [1982]
 1 CMLR 706 . . . . 189, 191

J

Jenkins v Kingsgate (Clothing Productions) Ltd (96/80) [1981] ECR 911, [1981] 2 CMLR
 24 278
Johnson v Chief Adjudication Officer (C-410/92) 6 December 1994, not yet reported. 139

Johnston v Chief Constable of the RUC (222/84) [1986] ECR 1651, [1986] 3 CMLR 240 . . . . . 139, 153, 277

K

Kaur v Lord Advocate (OH) 1981 SLT 322, [1980] 3 CMLR 79 209
Keck and Mithouard, Criminal proceedings against (C-267-8/91) [1993] ECR I-6097 . . . 87, 132, 187, 188
Kempf v Staatssecretaris van Justitie (139/85) [1986] ECR 1741, [1987] 1 CMLR 764 200
Keurkoop v Nancy Kean Gifts (144/81) [1982] ECR 2853, [1983] 2 CMLR 47 237
Kincardine and Deeside District Council v Forestry Commissioners (OH) 1992 SLT 1180,
    [1994] 2 CMLR 869 139
Kirkees Municipal Borough Council v Wickes Building Supplies Ltd (HL) [1993] AC 227 . . 141
'Kohlgesetz', sub nom Commission v Germany (70/72) [1973] ECR 813, [1974] CMLR 741 . . 255
Kolpinghuis Nijmegen, Officier van Justitie v (80/86) [1987] ECR 3969, [1989] 2 CMLR 18 . 148, 154
Konstantinidis v Stadt Altensteig (C-168/91) [1993] ECR I-1191, [1993] 3 CMLR 401 . . . . 96, 153
Kramer, Cornelius (3, 4 & 6/76) [1976] ECR 1279, [1976] 2 CMLR 440 284
Kraus v Land Baden-Württemberg (C-19/92) [1993] ECR I-1663 . . . . 96, 214
Krohn v Commission (175/84) [1986] ECR 753, [1987] 1 CMLR 745 105

L

La Cinq v Commission (T-44/90) [1992] ECR II-1, [1992] 4 CMLR 449 238
Ladbroke Racing (Deutschland) GmbH v Commission (T-74/92) 24 January 1995, not yet
    reported 103, 238
Lagauche, Procureur du Roi v (C-46/90 & 93/91) [1993] ECR I-I-5267 . . . . 87, 249
Lair v Universität Hannover (39/86) [1988] ECR 3161, [1989] 3 CMLR 545 218
Langnese-Iglo & Schöller v Commission (T-24 & 28/92R) [1992] ECR II-1839 235
L'Oréal v De Nieuwe (31/80) [1980] ECR 3775, [1981] 2 CMLR 235 244
La Pyramide (C-378/93) [1994] ECR I-3999 107
Lancome v Etos (99/79) [1980] ECR 2511, [1981] 2 CMLR 264 240
Lawrie Blum v Land Baden-Württemberg (66/85) [1986] ECR 2121, [1987] 3 CMLR 389 210
Legros, Administration des Douanes et Droits Indirects v (C-163/90) [1992] ECR I-4625 . . . 108, 154
Leonesio v Ministry of Agriculture and Forestry (93/71) [1972] ECR 287, [1973] CMLR 343 . 145
Levin v Staatssecretaris van Justitie (53/81) [1982] ECR 1035, [1982] 2 CMLR 454 . . . . . . 200, 205
Leyland DAF v Automotive Products (Ch D and CA) [1994] BCLC 245 239
Litster v Forth Dry Dock Ltd (HL) 1989 SC 96, [1989] 2 CMLR 194 148
Lorenz v Germany (120/73) [1973] ECR 1471 254
Luisi and Carbone v Ministero del Tesoro (286/82 & 26/83) [1984] ECR 377, [1985]
    3 CMLR 52 . . . . 216, 220
Lütticke v EEC Commission (48/65) [1966] ECR 19, [1966] CMLR 378 97
Luxembourg v European Parliament (230/81) [1983] ECR 255, [1983] 2 CMLR 726 . . . . 150, 167
Luxembourg v European Parliament (213/88 & C-39/89) [1991] ECR I-5643, [1994]
    1 CMLR 351 150

M

M v Home Office (HL) [1993] 3 All ER 537 139
McDonald v Secretary of State for Scotland (2nd Div) 1994 SLT 692 139
Macarthys Ltd v Smith (CA) [1979] 3 All ER 325, [1979] 3 CMLR 44 136
Magnavision v General Optical Council (QBD) [1987] 2 CMLR 262 107
'Maize Seeds', sub nom Nungesser v Commission (258/78) [1982] ECR 2015, [1983]
    1 CMLR 278 232
Manghera, Pubblico Ministero v (59/75) [1976] ECR 91, [1976] 1 CMLR 557 197
Marcel Rochas v Bitsch (1/70) [1970] ECR 515, [1971] CMLR 104 240
Marchandise (C-332/89) [1991] ECR I-1027 187

'Maritime Transport', sub nom Commission v France (C-381/93), 5 October 1994,
    not yet reported 216
Marleasing v La Comercial Internacional de Alimentación (106/89) [1990] ECR I-435,
    [1992] 1 CMLR 305. 148
Marshall v Southampton and South West Hampshire Area Health Authority (No 1)
    (152/84) [1986] ECR 723, [1986] 1 CMLR 768 .... 148, 278
Marshall v Southampton and South West Hampshire Area Health Authority (No 2)
    (C-271/91) [1993] ECR I-4367, [1993] 3 CMLR 293 139
Meilicke v ORGA Meyer (C-83/91) [1992] ECR I-4871 107
Meng, Wolf, Criminal proceedings against (C-2/91) [1993] ECR I-5751. 228
Merci Convenzionali Porto di Genova v Siderurgica Gabrielli ((C-179/90) [1991]
    ECR I-5889, [1994] 4 CMLR 422. .... 168, 234, 250
Meroni v High Authority (9/56) [1957-58] ECR 133 64
Methot, Ministère Public v (98/86) [1987] ECR 809, [1988] 1 CMLR 411 194
Metro-SB-Großmärkte v Commission (26/76) [1977] ECR 1875, [1978] 2 CMLR 1. 232
Michelin v Commission (322/81) [1983] ECR 3461, [1985] 1 CMLR 282. ...... 153, 233, 234, 235
Ministère Public v Methot (98/86) [1987] ECR 809, [1988] 1 CMLR 411. 194
Ministre des Affaires Economiques v Fromagerie Franco-Suisse 'Le Ski' (Belgian Cour de
    Cassation) [1972] CMLR 330 141
Ministre du commerce extérieur v Société Alivar (French Conseil d'Etat) [1984] Rec Dalloz
    128 141
Ministerio Fiscal v Bordessa (C-358 & 416/93) 23 February 1995, not yet reported 176, 220
Misset v Council (152/85) [1987] ECR 223. 100
Moat and TAO/AFI v Commission (T-78/91) [1991] ECR II-1387 90
Molkerei-Zentrale Westfalen/Lippe GmbH v Hauptzollamt Paderborn (28/67) [1968]
    ECR 187. 130
Monckton v Lord Advocate (OH) 5 May 1994, not yet reported 36
Monin Automobiles (No 1) (C-386/92) [1993] ECR I-2049 107
Monin Automobiles (No 2) (C-428/93) [1994] ECR I-1707 107
Moroni v Firma Collo GmbH (C-110/91) [1993] ECR I-6591 280
Morson and Jhanjan v Netherlands (35-36/82) [1982] ECR 3723, [1983] 2 CMLR 221 209
Mulder v Council and Commission (C-104/89) [1992] ECR I-3061. 105
Mulder v Minister for Agriculture and Fisheries (120/86) [1988] ECR 2321, [1989] 2
    CMLR 1. 154
Municipality of Almelo v IJsselmij NV (C-393/92) [1994] ECR I-1477 251

N

National Union of Public Employees v Grampian Regional Council (OH) 11 March 1993,
    not yet reported 139
Neath v Hugh Steeper Ltd (C-152/91) [1993] ECR I-6935. 280
Nederlandse Bankvereniging v Commission (T-138/89) [1992] ECR II-2181, [1993]
    5 CMLR 436 238
Netherlands v Reed (59/85) [1986] ECR 1283, [1987] 2 CMLR 448 .... 204, 207
Nold v Commission (4/73) [1974] ECR 491, [1974] 2 CMLR 338 .... 153, 158
Nungesser v Commission (Maize Seeds) (258/78) [1982] ECR 2015, [1983] 1 CMLR 278 232

O

Officier van Justitie v Kolpinghuis Nijmegen (80/86) [1987] ECR 3969, [1989] 2 CMLR 18 .. 148,
                                                                                  154
Officier van Justitie v van den Hazel (111/76) [1977] ECR 901, [1980] 3 CMLR 12. 198
Ordre des avocats au Barreau de Paris v Klopp (107/83) [1984] ECR 2971, [1985] 1 CMLR
    99 212
Ohra Schadeverzekeringen, Criminal proceedings against (C-245/91) [1993] ECR I-5851 ... 227
Orkem v Commission (374/87) [1989] ECR 3283, [1991] 4 CMLR 502 .... 153, 238
Otto v Postbank (C-60/92) [1993] ECR I-5683. .... 153, 242

P

Parti Ecologiste 'Les Verts' v European Parliament (294/83) [1986] ECR 1339, [1987] 2 CMLR 343 .... 94, 100

'Pasteurised Milk', sub nom Commission v United Kingdom (261/85) [1988] ECR 547, [1988] 2 CMLR 11... 192

Patrick v Ministre des Affaires Culturelles (11/77) [1977] ECR 1199, [1977] 2 CMLR 523. . . . 214

'Perfume', sub nom Procureur de la République v Giry et Guerlain (253/78 & 1-3/79) [1981] ECR 2327, [1981] 2 CMLR 99 244

Petrogal v Correia Simoes (C-39/92) [1993] ECR I-5659 240

Petroni v ONPTS (24/75) [1975] ECR 1149 208

Pharmon v Hoechst (19/84) [1985] ECR 2281, [1985] 3 CMLR 775 196

'Philip Morris', sub nom British American Tobacco Ltd v Commission (142 & 156/84) [1987] ECR 4487, [1988] 4 CMLR 24 247

Pickstone v Freemans (HL) [1989] AC 66, [1988] 3 CMLR 221 148

Pinna v Caisse d'Allocations Familiales de la Savoie (41/84) [1986] ECR 1................. 31

Piraiki-Patraiki v Commission (11/82) [1985] ECR 207, [1985] 2 CMLR 4 101

Plaumann v EEC Commission (25/62) [1963] ECR 95, [1964] CMLR 29.................. 101

Postbank v Commission (T-353/94) pending 242

Prantl, Karl, Criminal proceedings against (16/83) [1984] ECR 1299, [1985] 2 CMLR 238. . . . 187

Pretore di Genova v Banchero (C-157/92) [1993] ECR I-1085...................... 107

Pretore di Salò v Persons Unknown (14/86) [1987] ECR 2545 106

Procurator Fiscal, Elgin v Cowie and Wood (J) 1991 SLT 401, [1990] 3 CMLR 445.......... 107

Procureur de la République v Giry et Guerlain (Perfume) (253/78 & 1-3/79) [1981] ECR 2327, [1981] 2 CMLR 99 244

Procureur de la République v Waterkeyn (314-16/81 & 83/82) [1982] ECR 4337, [1983] 2 CMLR 145... 98

Procureur du Roi v Dassonville (8/74) [1974] ECR 837, [1974] 2 CMLR 436 .... 187, 217

Procureur du Roi v Lagauche (C-46/90 & 93/91) [1993] ECR I-5267 .... 87, 249

Procureur du Roi v Royer (48/75) [1976] ECR 497, [1976] 2 CMLR 614 205

Prodiforma v Commission (T-116/89) [1990] ECR II-843 238

Pronuptia de Paris v Schillgalis (161/84) [1986] ECR 353, [1986] 1 CMLR 414 232

Pubblico Ministero v Manghera (59/75) [1976] ECR 91, [1976] 1 CMLR 557............... 197

Pubblico Ministero v Ratti (148/78) [1979] ECR 1629, [1980] 1 CMLR 96.......... 133, 148, 193

Publishers Association v Commission (C-360/92P) 17 January 1995, not yet reported . . 111, 231

Punto Casa v Sindaco del Commune di Capena (C-69 & 258/93) [1994] ECR I-2355........ 187

'PVC', sub nom Commission v BASF (C-137/92P) [1994] ECR I-2555 .... 45, 64, 102, 111

R

R v Bouchereau (30/77) [1977] ECR 1999, [1977] 2 CMLR 800.................... 155, 210

R v Bow Street Magistrates, ex parte Noncyp (QBD) [1988] 3 CMLR 84 192

R v HM Treasury and Commissioners of Inland Revenue, ex parte Daily Mail (81/87) [1988] ECR 5483, [1988] 3 CMLR 713 212

R v Immigration Appeal Tribunal, ex parte Antonissen (C-292/89) [1991] ECR I-745, [1991] 2 CMLR 373.. 205

R v Immigration Appeal Tribunal and Singh, ex parte Secretary of State for the Home Department (C-370/90) [1992] ECR I-4265, [1992] 3 CMLR 358................. 204, 209

R v Inland Revenue Commissioners, ex parte Commerzbank (C-330/90) [1993] ECR I-4017, [1993] 3 CMLR 357... 260

R v International Stock Exchange of Great Britain and Ireland, ex parte Else (CA) [1993] 1 All ER 420, [1993] 2 CMLR 677 107

R v Kirk (63/83) [1984] ECR 2689, [1984] 3 CMLR 522 153

R v London Borough Transport Committee, ex parte Freight Transport Association (HL) [1992] 1 CMLR 5... 107

R v Minister for Agriculture, Fisheries and Food, ex parte FEDESA (331/88) [1990] ECR I-4023, [1991] 1 CMLR 507 .... 144, 153, 155

R v Minister for Agriculture, Fisheries and Food, ex parte Anastasiou (Pissouri) Ltd (C-432/92) [1994] ECR I-3087.. 284

R v Secretary of State for Employment, ex parte Equal Opportunities Commission (HL)
[1995] 1 AC 1, [1994] 1 All ER 910 . . . . 136, 139, 141, 278
R v Secretary of State for the Foreign and Commonwealth Office, ex parte Rees-Mogg
(QBD) [1994] 1 All ER 457, [1993] 3 CMLR 101 36
R v Secretary of State for Health, ex parte Gallaher (C-11/92) [1993] ECR I-3545,
[1994] 3 CMLR 179 193
R v Secretary of State for Home Affairs, ex parte Tombofa (CA) [1988] 2 CMLR 609 209
R v Secretary of State for the Home Department, ex parte Adams (C 229/94) pending 206,
                                                                                          209
R v Secretary of State for the National Heritage, ex parte Continental Television (QBD)
[1993] 2 CMLR 333 139
R v Secretary of State for Social Security, ex parte Equal Opportunities Commission
(C-9/91) [1992] ECR I-4297 279
R v Secretary of State for Transport, ex parte Factortame (No 1) (C-213/89) [1990]
ECR I-2433, [1990] 3 CMLR 1 139
R v Secretary of State for Transport, ex parte Factortame (HL) [1990] 2 AC 55, [1989]
3 CMLR 1; [1991] 1 AC 603, [1990] 3 CMLR 375 . . . . 136, 139
R v Secretary of State for Transport, ex parte Factortame (No 2) (C-221/89) [1991]
ECR I-3905, [1991] 3 CMLR 589 201
R v Secretary of State for Transport, ex parte Factortame (No 3) (C-48/93) pending 141
R v Thompson (7/78) [1978] ECR 2247, [1979] 1 CMLR 47 176
R v Tymen (269/80) [1981] ECR 3079, [1982] 2 CMLR 111 139
Ratification of the Maastricht Treaty, re (Bundesverfassungsgericht) [1994] 1 CMLR 57 36,
                                                                                          267
Ratification of the Maastricht Treaty, re (Conseil Constitutionnel) [1993] 3 CMLR 345 36
Ratification of the Maastricht Treaty, re (Tribunal Constitucional) [1994] 3 CMLR 101 36
Ratti, Pubblico Ministero v (148/78) [1979] ECR 1629, [1980] 1 CMLR 96 . . . . 133, 148, 193
Raulin v Minister for Education and Science (C-357/89) [1992] ECR I-1027, [1994]
1 CMLR 227 218
Ravintoloitsijain Liiton Kustannus Oy Restamark v Helsingen Piiritullikamari (E-1/91)
16 December 1994 . . . . App.I, 6
'Returnable Bottles', sub nom Commission v Denmark (302/86) [1988] ECR 4607,
[1989] 1 CMLR 619 189
'Reinheitsgebot', sub nom Commission v Germany (178/84) [1987] ECR 1227, [1988]
1 CMLR 780 192
Rewe Handelsgesellschaft Nord v Hauptzollamt Kiel (158/80) [1981] ECR 1805,
[1982] 1 CMLR 449 144
Rewe-Zentrale v Bundesmonopolverwaltung für Branntwein (Cassis de Dijon) (120/78)
[1979] ECR 649, [1979] 3 CMLR 494 . . . . 188, 189, 214, 217
Rewe-Zentralfinanz v Landwirtschaftskammer (4/75) [1975] ECR 843, [1977] 1 CMLR
599 192
Rewe-Zentralfinanz and Rewe-Zentral v Landwirschaftskammer für das Saarland (33/76)
[1976] ECR 1989, [1977] 1 CMLR 533 139
Reyners v Belgium (2/74) [1974] ECR 63, [1974] 2 CMLR 305 . . . . 169, 210, 212
Rhône-Poulenc v Commission (Polypropylene) (T-1/89) [1991] ECR II-867 232
Rinner-Kühn v FWW Spezial-Gebäudereinigung (171/88) [1989] ECR 2743 278
Roquette Frères v Council (138/79) [1980] ECR 3333 79
Roquette Frères v Hauptzollamt Geldern (C-228/92) [1994] ECR I-1445 107
Rothmans v Ministère des Finances (French Conseil d'Etat) [1993] 1 CMLR 253 141
Roujansky v Council (T-584/93) [1994] ECR II-585 46
Roujansky v Council (C-253/94P) 13 January 1995, not yet reported 46
Royer, Procureur du Roi v (48/75) [1976] ECR 497, [1976] 2 CMLR 614 205
RTE, BBC and ITP v Commission (T-69, 70 & 76/89) [1991] ECR II-485, 535 and 575,
[1991] 4 CMLR 586, 669 and 745 . . . . 235, 237
RTE and ITP v Commission (C-241/91P) pending 237
Ruckdeschel v Hauptzollamt Hamburg-St Annen (117/76 & 16/77) [1977] ECR 1753,
[1979] 2 CMLR 445 156
Rush Portuguesa v Office National de l'Immigration (C-113/89) [1990] ECR I-1417 203
Rutili v Minister of the Interior (36/75) [1975] ECR 1219, [1976] 1 CMLR 140 210

S

SA CNL-Sucal NV v HAG GF AG (Hag II) (C-10/89) [1990] ECR I-3711, [1990] 3 CMLR 571 .... 132, 196
SACE v Ministero delle Finanze (33/70) [1970] ECR 1213, [1971] CMLR 123 180
Sacchi, Giuseppe (155/73) [1974] ECR 409, [1974] 2 CMLR 177 .... 176, 216
Säger v Dennemeyer (C-76/90) [1991] ECR I-4221 .... 216, 217
Samenwerkende Elektriciteits-Produktiebedrijven v Commission (C-36/92P) [1994] ECR I-1911 238
San Giorgio v Amministrazione delle Finanze dello Stato (199/82) [1983] ECR 3595 139
Schindler, HM Customs and Excise v (C-275/92) [1994] ECR I-1039, [1995] 1 CMLR 4 .. 176, 217
Schillgalis, Pronuptia de Paris v (161/84) [1986] ECR 353, [1986] 1 CMLR 414 232
Schlüter v Hauptzollamt Lörrach (9/73) [1973] ECR 1135 155
Scholtz v Opera Universitaria di Cagliari (C-419/92) [1994] ECR I-505, [1994] 1 CMLR 873 . 210
Schoppenstedt v Council (5/71) [1971] ECR 975 105
Schul, Gaston v Inspecteur der Invoerrechten en Accijnzen (15/81) [1982] ECR 1409, [1982] 3 CMLR 229 .... 163, 184
Schumacker, Finanzamt Köln-Altstadt v (C-279/93) 14 February 1995, not yet reported 207
Scottish Salmon Growers Association v EFTA Surveillance Authority (E-2/94) pending App.I,6
Sevince v Staatssecretaris van Justitie (C-192/89) [1990] ECR I-3461, [1992] 2 CMLR 57 284
Simmenthal, Amministrazione delle Finanze dello Stato v (106/77) [1978] ECR 629, [1978] 3 CMLR 623 135
Singh, R v Immigration Appeal Tribunal and Singh, ex parte Secretary of State for the Home Department (C-370/90) [1992] ECR I-4265, [1992] 3 CMLR 358 .... 204, 209
Sirena v Eda (40/70) [1971] ECR 69, [1971] CMLR 260 237
SNUPAT v High Authority (32, 33/58) [1959] ECR 127 64
Sociaal Fonds voor de Diamantarbeiders v Indiamex (37-38/73) [1973] ECR 1609, [1976] 2 CMLR 222 182
Società Italiana Vetro v Commission (Flat Glass) (T-68 & 77-78/89) [1992] ECR II-1403, [1992] 5 CMLR 302 .... 225, 236
Société civile agricole de Centre d'insémination de la Crespelle v Coopérative d'élevage et d'insémination artificielle de département de la Mayenne (C-323/93) [1994] ECR I-5077 .... 167, 193, 236, 250
Société de Vente de Ciments et Bretons v Kerpen et Kerpen (319/82) [1983] ECR 4173, [1985] 1 CMLR 511 239
Société des Producteurs de Maïs v Administration des Douanes (112/83) [1985] ECR 719 .. 107
Société les Commissionnaires Réunis v Receveur des Douanes (80 & 81/77) [1978] ECR 927 131
Société Technique Minière v Maschinenbau Ulm (56/65) [1966] ECR 235, [1966] CMLR 357 .... 232, 239
Society for the Protection of Unborn Children v Grogan (C-159/90) [1991] ECR I-4685, [1991] 3 CMLR 849 .... 153, 216
Sotgiu v Deutsche Bundespost (152/73) [1974] ECR 153 207
Spotti v Freistaat Bayern (C-272/92) [1993] ECR I-5185, [1994] 3 CMLR 629 207
Star Fruit v Commission (247/87) [1989] ECR 291, [1990] 1 CMLR 733 97
Stauder v Ulm (29/69) [1969] ECR 419, [1970] 1 CMLR 112 153
Steenhorst-Neerings v Bedrijfsvereniging voor Detailhandel, Ambachten en Huisvrouwen (C-335/91) [1993] ECR I-3475 .... 139, 154
Steymann v Staatssecretaris van Justitie (196/87) [1988] ECR 6159, [1989] 1 CMLR 449 .... 200, 206
Stichting Collectieve Antennevoorziening Gouda v Commissariat voor de Media (C-288/89) [1991] ECR I-4007 .... 216, 217
Stichting Sigarettenindustrie v Commission (240/82) [1985] ECR 3831 242
Stoke-on-Trent City Council v B & Q plc (Ch D) [1990] 3 CMLR 31 136
Stoke-on-Trent City Council v B & Q plc (C-169/91) [1992] ECR I-6635, [1993] 1 CMLR 426. 187
'Storebælt', sub nom Commission v Denmark (C-243/89) [1993] ECR I-3353 195
'Students', sub nom European Parliament v Council (C-295/90) [1992] ECR I-4193, [1993] 2 CMLR 281 .... 102, 144, 206

T

Tankstation 't Heukske and Boermans (C-401-2/92) [1994] ECR I-2199. 187
Tedeschi v Denkavit Commerciale (5/77) [1977] ECR 1555, [1978] 1 CMLR 1 193
'Telemarketing', sub nom CBEM v CLT and IBP (311/84) [1985] ECR 3261 235
Telemarsicabruzzo v Circostel (C-320/90) [1993] ECR I-393 107
Ten Oever v Stichting Bedrijfspensioenfonds voor het Glazenwassers- en Schoonaakbedrijf
    (C-109/91) [1993] ECR I-4879. 280
Tetrapak v Commission (T-51/89) [1990] ECR I-309, [1991] 4 CMLR 344. . . . . 225, 237,
                                                                                          240, 247
Tetrapak v Commission (No 2) (T-83/91) 6 October 1994, not yet reported 238
Thieffry v Conseil de l'ordre des avocats à la Cour de Paris (71/76) [1977] ECR 765,
    [1977] 2 CMLR 373. 214
Thijssen v Controledienst voor Verzekering (C-42/92) [1993] ECR I-4047. 210
Thompson, R v (7/78) [1978] ECR 2247, [1979] 1 CMLR 47 176
'Titanium Dioxide' sub nom Commission v Council (C-300/89) [1991] ECR I-2867,
    [1993] 3 CMLR 359. 144
Toepfer v EEC Commission (106-7/63) [1965] ECR 405, [1966] CMLR 111 101
Töpfer v Commission (112/77) [1978] ECR 1019 154
Torfaen Borough Council v B & Q plc (145/88) [1989] ECR 3851, [1990] 1 CMLR 357. 187
'Tourist Guides', sub nom Commission v France (C-154/89) [1991] ECR I-659 217
Transocean Marine Paint Association v Commission (17/74) [1974] ECR 1063,
    [1974] 2 CMLR 459. 153
TV10 v Commissariat voor de Media (C-23/93) [1994] ECR I-4795 . . . . 176, 217
TWD Textilwerke Deggendorf v Germany (C-188/92) [1994] ECR I-833. 256

U

UNECTEF v Heylens (222/86) [1987] ECR 4097, [1989] 1 CMLR 901 . . . . 153, 214
Union Départmentale des Syndicats CGT de l'Aisne v Conforama (C-312/89) [1991]
    ECR I-997. 187
United Brands v Commission (27/76) [1978] ECR 207, [1978] 1 CMLR 429. . . . . 231, 234
United Kingdom v Commission (C-274/94) pending 90
United Kingdom v Council (Battery Hens) (131/86) [1988] ECR 905, [1988] 2 CMLR 364 . . . 144
United Kingdom v Council (C-84/94) pending 271
Unger v Bestuur der Bedrijfsvereniging voor Detailhandel en Ambachten (75/63)
    [1964] ECR 177, [1964] CMLR 319. 200

V

Vaasen-Goebbels v Bestuur van het Beambtenfonds voor het Mijnbedrijf (61/65) [1966]
    ECR 261. 106
Van Binsbergen v Bestuur van de Bedrijfsvereniging voor de Metaalnijverheid (33/74)
    [1974] ECR 1299, [1975] 1 CMLR 298 217
Van der Hulst's Zonen v Produktschap voor Siergewassen (51/74) [1975] ECR 79,
    [1975] 1 CMLR 236. 198
Van Duyn v Home Office (41/74) [1974] ECR 1337, [1975] 1 CMLR 1 . . . . 148, 211
Van Gend en Loos v Nederlandse Tariefcommissie (26/62) [1962] ECR 1, [1963] CMLR
    105 . . . . 107, 133, 171
Van Munster v Rijksdienst voor Pensioenen (C-165/91) [1994] ECR I-4461. 167,
                                                                                              208
Vandemoortele v Commission (C-172/89) [1990] ECR I-4677 153
Vander Elst v Office des Migrations Internationales (C-43/93) [1994] ECR I-3803. 203
Vereniging van Vlaamse Reisbureaus v Sociale Dienst van de Plaatslijke en Gewestelijke
    Overheidsdiensten (311/85) [1987] ECR 3801, [1989] 4 CMLR 213 227
Vereniging Veronica Omroep Organisatie v Commissariat voor de Media (C-148/91)
    [1993] ECR I-487. 217
Viciano v Commission (T-72/89) [1990] ECR II-57. 104
Viho Europe BV v Commission (T-102/92) 12 January 1995, not yet reported 232

Vlassopoulou v Ministerium für Justiz, Bundes- und Europaangelegenheiten
   Baden-Württemberg (C-340/89) [1991] ECR I-2357, [1993] 2 CMLR 221 214
Völk v Vervaecke (5/69) [1969] ECR 295, [1969] CMLR 723. 232
Volvo v Veng (238/87) [1988] ECR 6211, [1989] 4 CMLR 122. 237
Von Colson and Kamann v Land Nordrhein-Westfalen (14/83) [1984] ECR 1891,
   [1986] 2 CMLR 430. . . . . 148, 277
Vroege v NCIV Instituut voor Volkshuisvesting (C-57/93) [1994] ECR I-4541 . . . . 108, 280

W

Wachauf v Germany (5/88) [1989] ECR 2609, [1991] 1 CMLR 328 . . . . 153, 158
Wagner Miret v Fondo de Garantía Salarial (C-334/92) [1993] ECR I-6911 . . . . 141, 148
'Waste Disposal', sub nom Commission v Council (C-155/91) [1993] ECR I-939 144
'Waste Removal', sub nom European Parliament v Council (C-187/93) [1994] ECR I-2857 . . 144
Waterkeyn, Procureur de la République v (314-16/81 & 83/82) [1982] ECR 4337, [1983]
   2 CMLR 145 98
Webb v EMO Air Cargo Ltd (C-32/93) [1994] ECR I-3567, [1994] 2 CMLR 729 277
Weiser v Caisse Nationale des Barreaux Francais (C-37/89) [1990] ECR I-2395 156
Wendelboe v LJ Music (19/83) [1985] ECR 457. 126
Wilhelm v Bundeskartellamt (14/68) [1969] ECR 1, [1969] CMLR 100. . . . . 153, 232
Wirth v Landeshauptstadt Hannover (C-109/92) [1993] ECR I-6447 218
Wöhrmann v EEC Commission (31 & 33/62) [1962] ECR 501, [1963] CMLR 152 110
'Woodpulp', sub nom Åhlström v Commission (89 etc/85) [1988] ECR 5193, [1988]
   4 CMLR 901 232
World Trade Organisation, re the (Opinion 1/94) 15 November 1994, not yet reported 112,
                                                                                        163, 268, 269, 284

X

X v Commission (C-404/92P) [1994] ECR I-4737 153

Z

Zuckerfabriken Süderdithmarschen und Soest v Hauptzollämter Itzehoe und Paderborn
   (143/88 & C-92/89) [1991] ECR I-415, [1993] 3 CMLR 1 107
Zwartveld (C-2/88 Imm) [1990] ECR I-3365, [1990] 3 CMLR 457 45

INTRODUCTION

1. 'European law'. Since the 1939–45 war numerous institutions and bodies have been set up in Europe with confusingly similar titles. Some of these are explained in the following chapter. There are now at least four fields of law commonly described as 'European law':
- the law of the European Convention on Human Rights;
- the law of the European Communities;
- the law of the European Union; and
- the law of the European Economic Area.

This book is concerned primarily with the law of the European Communities, which is really a 'subset' of the law of the European Union.

2. The European Convention on Human Rights (ECHR); the Commission and Court of Human Rights. The European Convention on Human Rights (ECHR) was drawn up in 1950 under the auspices of the Council of Europe, which was established in 1949 and now has 33 member states. The European Commission and Court of Human Rights are institutions of the Council of Europe, established under the Convention. They sit in Strasbourg and adjudicate only upon alleged violations of the Convention. They are *not* institutions of the European Communities, the European Union or the European Economic Area. The ECHR, although binding upon the United Kingdom as a signatory state, has not been incorporated into, and forms no part of, United Kingdom law. It is not, as such, enforceable by the British courts.

3. European Community law. European Community law is the body of law created by or under three international treaties:
- the Treaty of Paris (1951) establishing the European Coal and Steel Community (ECSC); and
- the two Treaties of Rome (1957) establishing the European Economic Community (EEC) and the European Atomic Energy Community (EAEC or Euratom). The EEC was renamed the 'European Community' (the 'EC') by the Treaty on European Union (the 'Maastricht Treaty'), signed in 1992 and which came into force on 1 November 1993.

Although they share common institutions and principles the three Communities are legally distinct. The terms 'the Community' and 'Community law' may refer to any one of the Communities and its law, but have also been used to signify the three Communities and their common legal order taken together. In practice, except for specialists, 'Community law' has meant the law of the EEC, now the EC. Community law is part of United Kingdom law and is enforceable in British courts.

4. The European Union. The Maastricht Treaty absorbed the three Communities into a new constitutional superstructure – 'the European Union'. At the same time it created other features of Union law which are not part of, and are of an entirely different character from, Community law.

Apart from Community law, the law of the European Union is not part of the law of the United Kingdom.

5. The European Economic Area. The European Economic Area (EEA) was created in 1994 by a treaty between, on the one hand, the Community and its member states, and, on the other, six member states of the European Free Trade Association (EFTA). At the time of writing the EEA is undergoing change as a result of three of the EFTA states acceding to the European Union at the beginning of 1995. The law of the EEA forms part of Community law, and so in turn part of the law of the United Kingdom.

6. Scope and scheme of this book. This book falls into five chapters. The first chapter contains a brief account of the origins of the European Communities and their development down to the creation of the European Union and its enlargement to the present fifteen member states. The second chapter deals with the Community institutions and their functions. This chapter covers the jurisdiction of, and proceedings before, the Court of Justice. The third chapter deals with the sources of Community law and the methods of interpretation and application. The fourth chapter offers an overview of the structure, main provisions and substantive law of the EC Treaty. The final chapter considers the machinery and law of the European Union.

1. THE ORIGINS AND DEVELOPMENT OF THE EUROPEAN COMMUNITIES AND THE EUROPEAN UNION

7. Post-war co-operation; the Council of Europe. In the aftermath of the 1939–45 war a number of bodies and institutions were set up to promote European reconciliation and economic recovery and to avoid the risks of further conflicts between the nations of Europe. In the early years the United Kingdom played an active part in this process, particularly in setting up the Council of Europe in 1949[1]. The United Kingdom was one of the first states to ratify the European Convention on Human Rights, promulgated by the Council of Europe, and to recognise the compulsory jurisdiction of the Court of Human Rights[2].

8. Economic and political co-operation; differences of approach. All the organisations of which, at that time, the United Kingdom became a member were based upon traditional methods of intergovernmental negotiation and co-operation. But there were many who believed that these traditional methods were inadequate to solve the structural problems of the European economies and provide lasting political cohesion. In particular the division of Germany and the Berlin crisis underlined the need to bind the new Federal Republic of Germany more firmly into the political structure of western Europe.

9. The Schuman Declaration. On 9 May 1950, in a statement which has come to be known as the 'Schuman Declaration'[3], the Foreign Minister of France, M Robert Schuman, announced that:

'the French government proposes to take action immediately on one limited but decisive point. It proposes to place Franco-German production of coal and steel as a whole under a common higher authority within the framework of an organisation open to the participation of the other countries of Europe'.

This led to the Treaty of Paris of 18 April 1951 establishing the European Coal and Steel Community (the 'ECSC Treaty'), of which the signatory states

---

1 See the Statute of the Council of Europe, signed in London on 5 May 1949 (TS 51 (1949); Cmnd 7778).
2 See the Convention for the Protection of Human Rights and Fundamental Freedoms (the 'European Convention on Human Rights', or 'ECHR') (TS 71 (1953); Cmnd 8969), and in particular arts 25, 26. Parliament has never acted to incorporate the ECHR into law and British courts are not bound to take notice of it. But it may, or must, be applied by them as part of the general principles of Community law when applying that law; see para 153 below.
3 The Schuman Declaration repays careful study. Originally drafted by Jean Monnet, it contains the seeds of nearly all the ideas which have gone into the making of the European Communities. The text may be found in *Selection of Texts concerning Institutional Matters of the Community from 1950 to 1982*, published by the European Parliament.

were 'the original Six' – Belgium, Germany, France, Italy, Luxembourg and the Netherlands. The United Kingdom was invited to take part but declined to do so.

10. The European Coal and Steel Community (ECSC). The essential feature of the European Coal and Steel Community was the creation of a new entity (a 'Community') with international legal personality and autonomous institutions in which the member states pooled their sovereignty for limited but defined purposes. The production and distribution of coal and steel were brought under the control of a High Authority with supranational powers, including the power to make legally binding 'decisions' and 'recommendations'. The other institutions of the Community were a Common Assembly with supervisory powers, representing the peoples of the states brought together in the Community; a Special Council of Ministers, whose powers were partly legislative and partly consultative, representing the member states; and a Court of Justice whose function was to 'ensure that in the interpretation and application of this Treaty . . . the law is observed'[1]. The ECSC Treaty was concluded for a period of 50 years[2].

11. The Messina Conference and the Treaties of Rome (EEC and Euratom). The setting up of the ECSC was followed by abortive attempts to establish a European Defence Community and a European Political Community. In 1955 an intergovernmental conference of the original Six (in which, although sending observers, the United Kingdom again declined to take part) met at Messina under the chairmanship of the Belgian foreign minister M Paul-Henri Spaak. This led to the two Treaties of Rome of 25 March 1957 establishing amongst the Six the European Economic Community (the EEC Treaty) and the European Atomic Energy Community (the EAEC or Euratom Treaty).

12. The three Communities and their political aims. The immediate purpose of the EEC was to establish a 'common market' for all forms of economic activity[3], whilst that of Euratom was to create 'the conditions necessary for the speedy establishment and growth of nuclear industries'[4]. But it is fundamental to an understanding of the Communities and their law to appreciate that from the outset the treaties had longer-term political aims. The Schuman Declaration referred to 'common foundations of economic development as a first step towards a European federation'; the Preamble of the ECSC Treaty refers to 'a broader and deeper Community among peoples long divided by bloody conflicts' and that of the EEC Treaty to a determination of its signatories 'to lay the foundations of an ever closer union among

---

1 ECSC Treaty, art 31. The provisions regarding the institutions of the ECSC are to be found in arts 7-45.
2 Ibid, art 97.
3 EEC Treaty, art 2.
4 Euratom Treaty, art 1.

the peoples of Europe'[1]. The aim of the treaties was to achieve political ends through economic means. Coal and steel were, at the time, in the words of the Schuman Declaration 'the basic elements of industrial production', and atomic energy, then in its infancy, was seen as the principal future source of energy. It was believed that the bringing of coal and steel and atomic energy, as well as economic activity generally, under common rules and common institutions would lead to economic interdependence and, eventually, to the political integration of the member states. Subsequent events were to prove that economic, not to speak of political, integration would be more difficult to achieve than the immediate and short-term aims of the treaties.

13. The institutions of the Communities. The EEC and Euratom Treaties, both concluded for an unlimited period[2], followed the same general scheme as the ECSC Treaty in establishing a Community with legal personality and four autonomous institutions to exercise the powers conferred upon the Communities by the member states. As before, the institutions included an Assembly representing the peoples, a Council representing the member states and a Court of Justice. The institution equivalent to the High Authority of the ECSC was, however, called the Commission; its powers were more limited and it was ranked after the Assembly and the Council in order of precedence.

14. The merging of the institutions. Under a convention signed at the same time as the Treaties of Rome, a single Assembly and a single Court of Justice were established for all three Communities[3]. In 1967, by a treaty known as the Merger Treaty[4], a single Council was established and the ECSC High Authority and the EEC and Euratom Commissions were merged into a single body to be known as the Commission. Nevertheless, although they have common institutions, the three Communities remain legally distinct and the powers and functions of the institutions depend upon the terms of the treaty under which they act. In particular, when acting under the ECSC Treaty, the Commission enjoys the more extensive powers conferred upon the High Authority[5]. In what follows, 'the Community' refers, according to context, either to the three Communities collectively or to the EC, formerly the EEC.

15. First United Kingdom application for membership; the Luxembourg Compromise. In August 1961, during the premiership of Mr Harold Macmillan, the United Kingdom applied to join the Community. Owing to the attitude of President de Gaulle of France, the application was rejected in January 1963. President de Gaulle also became dissatisfied with

1 As to the legal relevance of the Preambles to the treaties, see paras 128ff and 161 below.
2 EEC Treaty, art 240; Euratom Treaty, art 208.
3 Convention of 25 March 1957 on Certain Institutions Common to the European Communities.
4 (Brussels) Treaty of 8 April 1965 establishing a Single Council and a Single Commission of the European Communities.
5 See eg Case C-128/92 *Banks v British Coal Corpn* [1994] ECR I-1209, [1994] 5 CMLR 30.

the workings of the Community, and in 1965 France adopted 'the policy of the empty chair', absenting herself from meetings of the Council and effectively bringing the legislative machinery of the Community to a standstill. The crisis was resolved by the so-called 'Luxembourg Compromise'[1], which, although it had no legal status and was little more than an agreement to disagree, had the political effect of allowing any member state to veto any legislative proposal which it conceived to affect its 'very important interests'. It also altered the balance between the institutions which had been intended by the Treaty[2].

16. United Kingdom accession. In May 1967, under the premiership of Mr Harold Wilson, the United Kingdom applied a second time, again unsuccessfully, to join the Community, but a third application under the premiership of Mr Edward Heath was successful. A Treaty of Accession was signed in Brussels on 22 January 1972[3] between the six member states and the four applicant states of Denmark, Ireland, Norway and the United Kingdom. Following a 'no' vote in a national referendum, Norway did not deposit instruments of ratification. On 1 January 1973 the United Kingdom, with Denmark and Ireland, became member states subject to transitional arrangements which expired at the end of 1977.

17. Renegotiation and referendum. The accession of the three new member states was followed almost immediately by the world oil crisis and the fall of Mr Heath's government. The government of Mr Wilson sought to 'renegotiate' the terms of entry. Some concessions were made which involved no amendment to the treaties. Thereafter, in the only national referendum in United Kingdom history[4], a substantial majority voted, in effect, in favour of continued membership of the Community.

18. Progress and setbacks. During the late 1960s and 1970s various attempts were made to make more effective progress towards economic, monetary and political union. The Community was successful in expanding its activities into new fields, such as regional, social and environmental policy. But completion of the common market through legislation, the procedures for which were hampered by the Luxembourg Compromise, made little progress. Some steps were, however, taken to improve the workings and accountability of the institutions and to promote political and monetary co-operation.

---

1 For the text of the Luxembourg Compromise (or Luxembourg Accords), see Bull EC 3-1966, pp 9 ff.
2 See paras 30 and 78 below.
3 For the text of the 1972 Accession Treaty and on accession generally see para 300 below.
4 There have been three 'regional' referenda: the 1973 referendum in Northern Ireland on whether the province should remain part of the United Kingdom, and the 1979 devolution referenda in Scotland and Wales. The Community referendum (see The Referendum Act 1975, c 33) took place on 5 June 1975.

19. Budgetary reform. In 1970 the Assembly, which had come to be known as the European Parliament[1], was given greater powers in relation to the Community budget[2], and the system under which Community revenue was raised by financial contributions from the member states was replaced by a system known as 'own resources'[3]. Under this system, the Community budget is financed almost entirely[4] from agricultural levies, customs duties and a percentage of the value added tax levied by the member states.

20. Political co-operation; the 'European Council'. The early 1970s saw the beginnings of the process of political co-operation in the field of foreign policy, and of regular meetings of the heads of state and government of the member states known as 'summits' or, since 1974, as meetings of the 'European Council' (not to be confused with the Council of Europe or the Council of Ministers)[5]. The European Council increasingly assumed overall policymaking authority, although it had neither legal status in the framework of the Community nor any power to take binding decisions. Its existence was first recognised by the Single European Act[6], and re-affirmed subsequently by the Maastricht Treaty[7].

21. The European Monetary System. In 1978 a Resolution of the European Council[8] established the European Monetary System (EMS), including a mechanism for stabilising exchange rates (the Exchange Rate Mechanism, or ERM) and a new unit of monetary value (the European Currency Unit, or ECU) based on a 'basket' of values of national currencies[9]. The EMS was established alongside, but independent of, the Community. The pound sterling has always been part of the basket comprising the ECU. The United Kingdom joined the Exchange Rate Mechanism in 1990, but following serious disruption of the currency markets ('black Wednesday') left it in 1992.

---

1 The Assembly had been called 'the Parliament' in normal and sometimes official usage since 1962; see Assembly resolution of 30 March 1962 (JO 1962, p 1045). By virtue of the Single European Act (see paras 28ff below), art 3(1), the name of the institution was changed formally (although in a roundabout way) to 'the European Parliament'.
2 See the EC Treaty, arts 203-206 as amended; see para 53 below.
3 See Council Decision 70/243 on the Replacement of Financial Contributions from the Member States by the Communities' Own Resources, JO L94, 28.4.70, p 19 (S Edn 1970 (I) p 224); now replaced by Council Decision 94/728, OJ L293, 12.11.94, p 9.
4 There are minor sources of Community revenue, such as tax upon the income of Community employees, income from the sale of publications, investment income, competition fines and the sale of property, but these are insignificant in relation to the budget as a whole.
5 The original 'constitution' of the European Council was laid down at the Paris Summit of 1974; see Bull EC 12-1974, pp 7 ff.
6 See para 29 below.
7 See para 46 below.
8 Bulletin EC 12-1978, pp 10 ff; Cmnd 7419.
9 The value of the ECU is now fixed by Regulation 3320/94, OJ L350, 31.12.94, p 27, and varies relative to a national currency with currency fluctuations. One ECU is now worth about 80 pence.

22. Direct elections to the Parliament. 1979 saw the first direct elections to the European Parliament[1], which until then had consisted of nominees of the parliaments of the member states. Although the Parliament had, since 1973 (chiefly at the instigation of its British members), begun to call the Commission more effectively to account by parliamentary questions, it remained a consultative assembly unwilling to use the two draconian powers conferred upon it by the treaties: the power to reject the budget prepared by the Commission and approved by the Council[2] and the power to force the resignation of the Commission as a body[3]. It first made use of its power in relation to the budget in 1980, thereby complicating a financial situation already fraught by demands of the United Kingdom for a reduction in her financial contribution and by the impending accession of Greece. Since direct elections the Parliament has also edged closer to using its power in relation to the Commission[3].

23. Greek accession. On 1 January 1981 Greece became the tenth member state, subject to transitional arrangements which expired at the end of 1985[4].

24. The Genscher-Colombo Plan; the Solemn Declaration of Stuttgart. The Parliament began to press for radical reform of the institutional machinery of the Community with a view, *inter alia*, to its being given an equal if not predominant part in the process of legislation. In 1983 the European Council responded with the Solemn Declaration of Stuttgart on European Union. This was a watered-down version of the 'Genscher-Colombo Plan'[5], a proposal originally put forward in 1981 by the German and Italian governments for a 'European Act' which would progressively transform the Community into a new entity to be called 'European Union'.

25. The Draft Treaty on European Union; the Fontainebleau Summit. The Parliament in the meanwhile employed experts to draft a new proposal for comprehensive reform in the form of a 'Draft Treaty establishing the European Union'[6]. This was approved by a substantial, but not absolute, majority of the members of the Parliament in February 1984. Then, in June 1984, a meeting of the European Council (the Fontainebleau Summit) settled the long-running dispute about the United Kingdom's financial contribution and set up an *ad hoc* Committee (the Dooge or Spaak II Committee) 'to make suggestions for the improvement of the

---

1 Act concerning the Election of the Representatives of the Assembly by Direct Universal Suffrage, OJ L278, 8.10.76, p 10.
2 See para 53 below.
3 See para 69 below.
4 For the text of the Greek Accession Treaty and on accession generally see para 300 below.
5 For the texts see (1983) 20 CML Rev 685.
6 For the text see OJ C77, 19.3.84, p 33. This draft Treaty is often referred to as the 'Spinelli Treaty' because it was based upon a proposal from the veteran Italian politican Altiero Spinelli.

operation of European cooperation in both the Community field and that of political, or any other, cooperation'[1].

26. The Delors Commission; the Cockfield White Paper; the Milan Summit; the Luxembourg Conference. The Dooge Committee reported in March 1985 and proposed that an intergovernmental conference be convened 'to negotiate a draft European Union Treaty . . . guided by the spirit and method of the draft Treaty voted by the European Parliament'[2]. In the meanwhile, a new Commission under the presidency of M Jacques Delors had taken office in January 1985. Shortly thereafter Lord Cockfield, the Commissioner with responsibility for the internal Community market, produced his White Paper[3] identifying the remaining barriers to trade within the Community and proposing a timetable for their elimination over the lifetime of two Commissions – that is, by the end of 1992 (hence, the '1992 Programme'). Despite British, Danish and Greek opposition, the European Council at its meeting in June 1985 (the Milan Summit) resolved to convene a conference for the purpose of implementing both the Dooge recommendations and the Cockfield White Paper[4]. The conference met in Luxembourg and Brussels during the autumn of 1985.

27. Spanish and Portuguese accession. The conference included the participation of Spain and Portugal, which formally acceded to membership of the Community on 1 January 1986, so bringing the number of member states to twelve, subject to transitional arrangements which expired at the end of 1993[5].

28. The Single European Act. The outcome of the conference convened as a result of the Milan Summit was a new Treaty known as the 'Single European Act'[6], so called because it dealt with a number of separate matters in a single treaty. The Single European Act was signed on 17 and 28 February 1986, and after some delay waiting upon Irish ratification[7], came into force on 1 July 1987.

29. Treaty amendment and political co-operation. The Single European Act formally recognised the existence of the European Council, although it assigned no powers or functions to it. It provided for a number of amend-

---

1 For the text see Bull EC 6-1984, p 11.
2 For the Interim and Final Reports of the Dooge Committee, see *European Union*, 14th Report of the Select Committee on the European Communities (HL Paper (1984-85) no 226), pp 21, lxvi.
3 *Completing the Internal Market*, White Paper from the Commission to the European Council, COM(85) 310.
4 For the text, see Bull EC 6-1985, p 15.
5 For the text of the Spanish and Portuguese Accession Treaty and on accession generally see para 300 below.
6 For the text, see OJ L169, 29.6.87, p 1. The Single European Act was incorporated into United Kingdom law by the European Communities (Amendment) Act 1986, c 58.
7 See *Crotty v An Taoiseach* [1987] 2 CMLR 666 (Irish SC).

ments to the founding treaties, and gave institutional form to the machinery of political co-operation in the field of foreign policy. The machinery of European Political Co-operation (EPC) was established parallel to, but not as part of, the institutional machinery of the Community.

30. Majority voting under the Single European Act. The Single European Act amended the EEC Treaty so as to create greater opportunity for legislative decisions to be taken by qualified majority vote in the Council and involve the Parliament more closely in certain aspects of the legislative process[1]. The Single European Act contained no reference to the Luxembourg Compromise[2] and neither recognised, nor provided any machinery for, the exercise of any right of veto. The risk of any such right being exercised was in any event reduced by allowing a measure of 'variable geometry', which eased the political process of agreement, but created new difficulties for the lawyer in ascertaining the law to be applied.

31. 'Variable geometry'. Before the Single European Act it was a general principle of Community law that it be applied uniformly throughout all the member states. So, Community legislation which provided, without objective justification, different rules to be applied in different member states was declared to be unlawful[3]. New provisions in the Single European Act[4] implicitly recognised that Community law could be applied differently, at different times, in different member states. This scheme is usually called 'variable geometry' or 'multi-speed' integration. There is a presumption that whilst integration and the rules giving effect to it may proceed more rapidly as amongst some member states, all member states will eventually catch up and Community rules will apply uniformly thereafter. Latterly the terms have been applied to situations whereby some member states enjoy in one sphere or another a right of permanent derogation from Community rules.

32. Implementation of the Cockfield White Paper; 1992. The Single European Act also provided the legislative mechanisms necessary to implement the recommendations of the Cockfield White Paper[5]. The legislative programme envisaged by the White Paper for the completion of the internal market was largely achieved by the end of 1992[6].

33. The Social Charter. The Commission became concerned that implementation of the internal market as proposed by the White Paper would

---

1 See paras 79–80 below.
2 It is understood that throughout the negotiations leading to the Single European Act no mention was made of the Luxembourg Compromise, as to which see paras 15 above and 78 below.
3 See eg Case 41/84 *Pinna v Caisse d'Allocations Familiales de la Savoie* [1986] ECR 1.
4 EEC Treaty, arts 8c and 100a (now EC Treaty, arts 7c and 100a).
5 See para 170 below. As to the Cockfield White Paper, see para 26 above.
6 See paras 170, 193, 195 and 259 below.

have serious social repercussions which were not sufficiently addressed by the EEC Treaty. Accordingly, it put forward a Community Charter of Fundamental Social Rights of Workers (the Social Charter), which was adopted by eleven of the member states – the United Kingdom opposing – in December 1989. The Social Charter has no legal force; it was intended as a blueprint for the adoption by the Community of legislation in the social sphere[1].

34. European Monetary Union. Commitment to eventual realisation of economic and monetary union (EMU) within the Community was reconfirmed at the Hanover Summit of the European Council in 1988, which charged a committee chaired by the President of the Commission, Jacques Delors, to study the matter. The Delors Committee reported in 1989[2], identifying three 'stages' necessary for the achievement of EMU. An intergovernmental conference was convened in December 1990 to consider incorporation of the 'Delors Plan' into the treaties.

35. European Political Union. Some member states were unwilling to proceed to EMU without an extension of Community competences and enhancement of the democratic accountability of its institutions. Accordingly, a parallel intergovernmental conference was convened in December 1990 to consider these issues and those of foreign affairs, defence and collective security.

36. The Treaty on European Union (the 'Maastricht Treaty'). Whilst there was little interaction between the two conferences, the deliberations resulted in a single treaty, the Treaty on European Union (TEU), signed at Maastricht (hence, the 'Maastricht Treaty') on 2 February 1992[3]. Following legal challenges to ratification in four member states, including the United Kingdom[4], referenda in three (two in Denmark[5]) and constitutional amendments in three, the TEU came into force on 1 November 1993. It is concluded for an unlimited period[6].

---

1 See paras 272-274 below.
2 For the text see *Report of the Committee for the Study of Economic and Monetary Union*, 1989; summarised in Bull EC 4-1989, p 8.
3 For the text see OJ C191, 29.1.92, p 1; Cmnd 1934.
4 *R v Secretary of State for the Foreign and Commonwealth Office*, ex parte *Rees-Mogg* [1994] 1 All ER 457; [1993] 3 CMLR 101 (QBD); see also *Monckton v Lord Advocate*, judgment of the Outer House of the Court of Session of 5 May 1994, not yet reported. Rather more sophisticated challenges were mounted in France (see the judgment of the *Conseil Constitutionnel* of 9 April 1992, [1993] 3 CMLR 345), in Spain (see the opinion of the *Tribunal Constitucional* of 1 July 1992, [1994] 3 CMLR 101) and in Germany (see the judgment of the *Bundesverfassungsgericht* of 12 October 1993, [1994] 1 CMLR 57). The Treaty on European Union is given effect in the UK by the European Communities (Amendment) Act 1993, c 32.
5 In a June 1992 referendum the Danes voted narrowly against ratification of the treaty, but following a series of undertakings given to Denmark at a meeting of the European Council in December 1992 (the Edinburgh Summit) which involved no alterations to the treaty, a second referendum in May 1993 produced a vote comfortably in favour of Danish ratification.
6 TEU, art Q.

37. European Union. The Treaty on European Union created the 'European Union', which consists essentially of three so-called pillars: the central pillar is the existing Communities and their law (as amended significantly by the Maastricht Treaty)[1]. The two other pillars comprise provisions on common foreign and security policy[2] and provisions on co-operation in the fields of justice and home affairs[3]. The three pillars 'support' the over-arching constitutional order of the Union. The latter two pillars, like European Political Co-operation under the Single European Act[4], extend the areas in which the member states undertake to pursue common action, but are subject only to the legal order of the Union, not to that of the Community. So, although the Union is 'founded on' the Communities[5] and is served by the Community institutions[6], its non-Community competences are not subject to the democratic and judicial control inherent in the Community system. They remain, in effect, intergovernmental treaty obligations amongst the member states[7]. They were not incorporated into United Kingdom law and are not enforceable in British courts[8].

38. Amendment to the EEC Treaty. The TEU amended the treaties founding the Communities in a number of significant respects. Chief amongst these amendments are the following. Recognising its pre-eminence amongst the three Communities and the conferral upon it of new competences in areas which are not primarily economic, the EEC was renamed the 'European Community' ('EC')[9]. Citizenship of the Union was created[10]. The Community is committed to achievement of Economic and Monetary Union (EMU) by 1999[11]. It undertakes to develop a social policy within the framework of the 1989 Social Charter (although the United Kingdom will play no part in this)[12]. A number of changes were made to the institutional (especially in relation to the Parliament[13]) and judicial mechanisms of the Community. And the principle of subsidiarity was introduced, as such, into Community law[14].

39. Future amendment. It was anticipated that the peculiar constitutional structure of the European Union would require adjustment. There were also

1 TEU, Titles II-IV.
2 Ibid, Title V.
3 Ibid, Title VI.
4 See para 29 above. The TEU, art P(2), repealed the provisions of the Single European Act dealing with EPC, which were subsumed into the more sophisticated provisions of the TEU on common foreign and security policy.
5 TEU, art A.
6 See paras 290-291 below.
7 On Titles V and VI of the TEU, see paras 294-298 below.
8 See para 289 below.
9 TEU, art G(A).
10 See para 171 below.
11 See paras 262–267 below.
12 See paras 273–274 below.
13 See paras 79, 81 below.
14 See para 157 below.

a number of contentious issues upon which the conferences failed to reach agreement. The TEU therefore provides that a subsequent intergovernmental conference is to be convened in 1996 in order to consider further revisions[1].

40. The European Economic Area (EEA). Unconnected but contemporaneous with the process leading up to the TEU, the seven member states of the European Free Trade Area (EFTA)[2] had sought closer economic relations with the Community. As a result, on 2 May 1992, an agreement was signed between the EEC, the ECSC (but not Euratom) and the Community member states on the one part and each of the EFTA states on the other designed to create a European Economic Area (EEA)[3]. In a December 1992 referendum the Swiss voted against ratification. Following ratification by the two Communities, all Community member states[4] and all the EFTA states except Switzerland, the EEA Agreement (as amended in order to take account of the Swiss refusal to join[5]) entered into force, and the EEA came into being, on 1 January 1994.

41. Purpose and scope of the EEA. The purpose of the EEA Treaty is to create, in effect, a sophisticated free trade regime, combined with provisions on the free movement of persons, services and capital, within the area of the EC and EFTA, except Switzerland. It therefore replicates, although less profoundly, the aims of the Community. The EEA Treaty creates its own institutions charged with overseeing the development of the EEA. It will be considered more fully below[5].

42. Austrian, Finnish and Swedish accession. In June 1994 a fourth accession treaty was signed in Corfu (hence, the 'Corfu Accession Treaty') between the European Union, its member states and four EEA member states: Norway, Austria, Finland and Sweden[6]. Referenda were held in each of the applicant states. The Austrians, Finns and Swedes voted in favour of accession, but in November 1994 Norwegians voted, for a second time, not to join. Following ratification by Austria, Finland and Sweden and by all existing member states, the treaty entered into force on 1 January 1995, so bringing the number of member states to the present fifteen. Adjustment to the Treaties necessitated by the failure of Norway to ratify were made by the

---

1 TEU, art B, 1st para and art N(2).
2 Ie Austria, Finland, Iceland, Liechtenstein, Norway, Sweden and Switzerland. The EFTA was formed in 1960 as an alternative to, and less profound system of economic integration than, the Community. The UK was a founding member of EFTA, but left it in 1973 upon accession to the Community.
3 For the text see OJ L1, 3.1.94, p 3.
4 For United Kingdom ratification see the European Economic Area Act 1993, c 51.
5 See Appendix I.
6 For the text of the Corfu Accession Treaty and on accession generally see para 300 below.

Council by authority of the Corfu Treaty. Transitional arrangements for the three new member states expire for the most part in 1998.

43. Recapitulation. The European Union, which came into being in November 1993, now comprises fifteen member states. The Union rests upon three 'pillars', the central one of which is the three Communities and their law. Of the three Communities, the EC (before November 1993, the EEC) is pre-eminent. The Community institutions provide the institutional framework of the Union, but their powers under the Community treaties are of an entirely different character from those under the non-Community pillars of the Union. The Community (but not the European Union) and its fifteen member states belong to the European Economic Area (EEA); the law of the EEA applies throughout its territory, including the Community.

2.   THE INSTITUTIONS OF THE COMMUNITY

44. The institutions. There are five Community 'institutions' properly so-called: the European Parliament (the Assembly), the Council, the Commission, the Court of Justice and the Court of Auditors[1]. The EC Treaty also establishes a number of other 'organs' (the Economic and Social Committee, the European Investment Bank and the Committee of the Regions) and provides for the establishment of further organs to regulate the proposed economic and monetary union. Other bodies have been created by Community legislation to develop and supervise aspects of the work of the Community.

45. The institutions generally. All Community institutions are required to act within the limits of the powers conferred upon them by the Treaty[2]. Each has adopted Rules of Procedure, and failure to comply with them may render their conduct unlawful[3]. The institutions have a duty of loyalty to co-operate fully, where appropriate, with national authorities in order to assist in the implementation of Community rules[4]. The seats of the institutions, to be determined by agreement amongst the member states[5], were finally fixed at a meeting of the European Council (the Edinburgh Summit) in 1992[6].

46. The European Council. The European Council is not formally recognised in the EC Treaty and is not a Community institution. It was first recognised by the Single European Act, which assigned to it no specific powers or functions. The Treaty on European Union now provides:

> 'The European Council shall bring together the Heads of State or of Government of the Member Sates and the President of the Commission. They shall be assisted by the Ministers of Foreign Affairs of the Member States and by a Member of the Commission. The European Council shall meet at least twice a year, under the chairmanship of the Head of State or of Government of the Member State which holds the Presidency of the Council'.[7]

The European Council, meetings of which are sometimes called 'Summits', is 'to provide the Union with the necessary impetus for its development and shall define the general political guidelines thereof'[8]. It is further charged with responsibility for defining the principles of and general guidelines for

---

1 EC Treaty, art 4.
2 Ibid, art 3b, para 1.
3 See eg Case C-137/92P *Commission v BASF* (PVC) [1994] ECR I-2555.
4 Case C-2/88 Imm *Zwartveld* [1990] ECR I-3365, [1990] 3 CMLR 457; Case C-234/89 *Delimitis v Henninger Bräu* [1991] ECR I-935, [1992] 5 CMLR 210.
5 EC Treaty, art 216.
6 Decision of the Representatives of the Governments of the Member States on the Location of the Seats of the Institutions, OJ C341, 23.12.92, p 1.
7 TEU, art D. As to presidency of the Council, see para 59 below.
8 Ibid, art D.

the common foreign and security policy pursued under Title V of the TEU[1] and has a supervisory role in Community progress towards economic and monetary union[2]. It is not otherwise mentioned in the treaty texts. It is not competent as such to adopt legally binding acts[3] and it plays no part in the formal legislative machinery of the Community. The heads of State and government could however, if constituted as the Council of Ministers, undertake the legislative functions assigned by the treaties to the Council[4].

47. Plan of this part. It is proposed first to describe the composition, membership and general responsibilities of the three 'political institutions' (the Parliament, the Council and the Commission) and then the legislative process in which they are, to a greater or lesser degree, involved. This is followed by a description of the two 'supervisory institutions', the Court of Justice and the Court of Auditors, and thereafter of the other organs.

(1) THE POLITICAL INSTITUTIONS

(a) The European Parliament

48. Membership of the Parliament. Each of the founding treaties provides that the Parliament

> 'shall consist of representatives of the peoples of the States brought together in the Community, [and] shall exercise the powers conferred upon it by this Treaty'[5].

The members of the Parliament ('MEPs') are elected by direct universal suffrage for a fixed five-year term[6]. The treaties require the adoption of a uniform voting procedure[7], but this has not yet been achieved, and the voting system still varies from member state to member state. There are at present 626 MEPs[8]. Their numbers are broadly proportionate to the population size

---

1 See para 294 below.
2 See para 263 below.
3 Case T-584/93 *Roujansky v Council* [1984] ECR II-585 and Case T-179/94 *Bonnamy v Council*, order of 14 July 1994, unreported; appealed unsuccessfully as Case C-253/94P *Roujansky v Council* and Case C-264/94P *Bonnamy v Council*, orders of 13 January 1995, not yet reported.
4 See paras 56 and 75-78 below.
5 EC Treaty, art 137; ECSC Treaty, art 20 (which makes reference to '*supervisory* powers'); Euratom Treaty, art 107 ('*advisory and supervisory* powers').
6 Act concerning the Election of the Representatives of the Assembly by Direct Universal Suffrage, OJ L278, 8.10.76, p 10. MEPs from Austria, Finland and Sweden are appointed from amongst national parliaments until such time as direct elections are held in each of those member states, which must be before the end of 1996; Corfu Accession Treaty, art 31.
7 EC Treaty, art 138(3).
8 Act concerning the Election of the Representatives of the Assembly by Direct Universal Suffrage, OJ L278, 8.10.76, p 10 as amended.

of the member states with a weighting in favour of the smaller states, ranging from six for Luxembourg to eighty-seven each for France, Italy and the United Kingdom and to ninety-nine for Germany[1].

49. Parliamentary procedures. The Parliament adopts its own rules of procedure[2]. Except where otherwise provided in the treaty the Parliament acts by an absolute majority of votes cast[3]. However, many important matters involving the participation of the Parliament require a positive vote by a majority of its members (ie, at present at least 314 votes). Frequently the Parliament finds itself unable to act simply because it fails to muster the necessary number of votes. Preliminary work is done by the standing parliamentary committees, of which there are currently twenty. They are becoming increasingly influential in the process of legislation and now work very closely with the services of the Council and of the Commission. The committees report to the plenary session of the Parliament, which is required to meet annually[4], but in practice sits for one week in every four from October to July.

50. Political groups. MEPs sit not as national deputies but in transnational 'political groups'. The incentive to form political groups (which must include a minimum number of MEPs[5]) is that appointment to parliamentary committees, speaking time and disbursement of funding is on a political group basis. At present there are nine political groups[6] plus some two dozen 'non-attached' MEPs. By far the largest is the European Socialists Group with 221 seats, which includes sixty-two Labour and one Social Democratic and Labour MEPs from the United Kingdom[7].

51. Organisation. The President and officers of the Parliament are elected from amongst its members[8], and in practice hold office for two-and-a-half years. Much of the work of organisation is undertaken by the 'Bureau', con-

---

1 Ibid. Under the European Parliamentary Elections Act 1978, c 10 as amended, the eighty-seven United Kingdom MEPs are further subdivided into seventy-one from England, eight from Scotland, five from Wales (all representing single constituencies) and three from Northern Ireland (a single multi-member constituency).
2 EC Treaty, art 142. The present Rules of Procedure were adopted on 15 September 1993; they are not published in the Official Journal but are available from the Parliament.
3 Ibid, art 141.
4 Ibid, art 139.
5 A political group must have at least twenty-nine MEPs if all from one member state, twenty-three if from two, eighteen if from three and fourteen if from four or more; Rules of Procedure, rule 29(2), as amended.
6 Ie, European Socialists, European People's Party (Christian Democrats), European Liberal Democratic and Reformist, European United Left, Forza Europa, European Democratic Alliance, Greens, European Radical Alliance, Europe of Nations (Co-ordination Group).
7 The other UK MEPs sit in the following groups: eighteen Conservative and one Ulster Unionist in the European Peoples' Party; two Liberal Democrats in the Liberal Democratic and Reformist Group; two Scottish Nationalists in the European Radical Alliance; and one Democratic Unionist in the Non-Attached Group.
8 EC Treaty, art 140.

sisting of the President and the fourteen Vice-Presidents, assisted by the five Quaestors (the 'officers' of the Parliament) and by the 'Conference of Presidents', consisting of the President and the chairmen (sic) of the political groups[1]. The seat of the Parliament is in Strasbourg, but its General Secretariat is in Luxembourg and its committees meet in Brussels.

52. Powers of the Parliament. The principal powers of the Parliament fall into three broad categories. First, it enjoys a degree of political control over the Commission[2]. Second, it plays an (increasingly) important role in the adoption of Community legislation[3]. And third, it has significant powers in relation to the Community budget.

53. Powers with respect to the budget. The budgetary procedure under the treaties involves an intricate process of power sharing amongst the Parliament, the Council and the Commission[4]. Ultimately it is the President of the Parliament who declares the budget to be finally 'adopted'[5]. The Parliament may reject the budget outright by a two-thirds vote cast by a majority of its members[6]. It has now done so on three occasions, leading to temporary financial paralysis. It may not, however, increase the total amount of the budget beyond the 'maximum rate of increase' set by the Commission in areas of non-compulsory spending unless the alteration is agreed between the Council and the Parliament[7]. Within the constraints of the Treaty, the budgetary procedure is governed by an agreement amongst the three institutions[8].

54. General supervisory powers. Since the entry into force of the Treaty on European Union the Parliament has power to establish temporary Committees of Inquiry to investigate alleged contraventions of or maladministration in the implementation of Community law[9]. It is to appoint an Ombudsman with powers to investigate allegations of maladministration in the activities of the Community institutions other than the judicial activities

---

1 See generally Rules of Procedure, rules 21-28.
2 See para 69 below.
3 See paras 79-81 below.
4 EC Treaty, art 203.
5 Ibid, art 203(7). In Case 34/86 *Council v European Parliament* [1986] ECR 2155, [1986] 3 CMLR 94, the Court of Justice struck down the Parliament's adoption of the 1986 budget as premature and unlawful.
6 EC Treaty, art 203(8).
7 Ibid, art 203(9). 'Compulsory expenditure' describes those areas of the Community budget in which there is a legal obligation to dispense Community funds; the vast majority is in the agricultural sector. 'Non-compulsory expenditure' encompasses areas in which there is discretion.
8 See the Interinstitutional Agreement of 29 October 1993 on budgetary discipline and improvement of the budgetary procedure, OJ C331, 7.12.93, p 1, which is a revision of a 1988 agreement. See also Council Decision 94/729, OJ L293, 12.11.94, p 14 on budgetary discipline.
9 EC Treaty, art 138c.

of the Court of Justice[1]. Any citizen of the Union or any natural or legal person within its jurisdiction may address a petition to the Parliament on any matter of Community activity which affects him directly[2].

(b) The Council

55. Name and function of the Council. The EC Treaty and the Treaty on European Union refer to 'the Council'. Following the entry into force of the Treaty on European Union it renamed itself 'the Council of the European Union'[3]. But it is more commonly known as the Council of Ministers. It is the ultimate legislative organ of the Community, except (a) under the ECSC Treaty where the Commission can take legislative decisions, the assent of the Council being required only for certain purposes[4], and (b) where the EC Treaty requires recourse to the co-decision procedure with the Parliament[5]. It also has significant powers in relation to the two non-Community pillars of the Union[6].

56. Composition of the Council. In terms of the EC Treaty,

'The Council shall consist of a representative of each Member State at ministerial level, authorized to commit the government of that Member State'[7].

The original intention was that the Council should be a 'college of delegates', acting as a single autonomous Community institution in which each member state would be represented by a minister specially appointed for the purpose. In practice the Council has become more like a traditional forum for intergovernmental negotiation, and its composition depends upon the subject matter under discussion. So, for a matter relating to economic and monetary policy, the Council consists of the national Ministers of Finance ('Ecofin'); for a matter relating to agriculture, of the Ministers of Agriculture; and so on. As a (small) step towards greater regional influence in Community decision making, and owing to pressure from the German *Länder* and the Belgian autonomous communities, the Treaty was amended by the Treaty on European Union so as to allow a member state to be represented by ministers from regional government, so long as they are empowered to bind the member state[7]. The 'senior' body is the General Affairs

---

1 EC Treaty, art 138e; Rules of Procedure, rule 159.
2 Ibid, art 138d.
3 Council Decision 93/591, OJ L281, 16.11.93, p 18. The Treaty provides no authority for the Council to do so.
4 ECSC Treaty, arts 14 and 28.
5 See para 81 below.
6 See para 291 below.
7 EC Treaty, art 146.

Council or Council of Foreign Ministers, which takes decisions on matters of foreign and security policy under Title V of the Treaty on European Union and on Community matters of general importance, such as institutional affairs, preparation of European Council summits and 'Group of Seven' meetings, and residual matters not fitting clearly into other government portfolios. For certain decisions in the area of economic and monetary union the Council is required to meet as heads of State and government[1]. Whatever its composition, all decisions are taken in name of the Council as such.

57. The member states meeting in the Council. Some provisions of the Treaty provide for decisions to be taken by the 'common accord of the governments of the Member States'. Where this applies, or where the member states wish to co-operate from time to time on a matter outwith Community and European Union competences, representatives of the fifteen governments meet using the facilities of the Council but adopt such measures as decisions of the representatives of the member states, sometimes adding the words 'meeting in the Council' (*au sein du Conseil*)[2].

58. Organisation. The Council has its own Secretariat-General under the direction of a Secretary-General, consisting of six Directorates-General and a Legal Service. It has its seat in Brussels, and adopts its own rules of procedure[3].

59. Presidency of the Council. The Presidency of the Council is held for six months at a time by each member state in strict rotation[4]. Continuity is now sought under a system by which the officials of the last two, the current and the next two Presidencies work together[5]. The powers of the Presidency are significant, since the President controls the agenda of Council meetings. Member states have been criticised for arranging the legislative programme of the Council in a manner which best suits their (or their governments') interests.

60. COREPER. The EC Treaty recognises the existence of a committee consisting of the permanent representatives (ambassadors) of the member states (commonly called COREPER)[6], permanently based in Brussels. COREPER is

---

1 EC Treaty, art 109j; see paras 264, 266 below.
2 See eg Cases C-181 & 248/91 *European Parliament v Council* [1993] ECR I-3685.
3 EC Treaty, art 151(3); for the present Rules of Procedure see Decision 93/662, OJ L304, 10.12.93, p 1.
4 EC Treaty, art 146(2). The order of rotation (from 1 January 1995) is fixed by a (not yet published) Council Decision of 1 January 1995, thus: France, Spain, Italy, Ireland, Netherlands, Luxembourg, United Kingdom, Austria, Germany, Finland, Portugal, France, Sweden, Belgium, Spain, Denmark, Greece.
5 Since the officials from the last and next Presidency - and *a fortiori* the last and next but one - are generally of lower grade than those who took part or will take part in substantive business, continuity may be more effectively assured through the day-to-day working relationship of the Council Secretariat-General, COREPER and the Commission.
6 EC Treaty, art 151; the title COREPER comes from *COmité des REprésentants PERmanents*.

'responsible for preparing the work of the Council and for carrying out the tasks assigned to it by the Council'[1]. Much of the preparatory work of the Council is done by committees or working groups of national civil servants. A number of decisions of the Council are, for practical purposes, taken by COREPER and formally adopted by the Council[2].

(c) The Commission

(A) THE COMMISSION PROPERLY SO-CALLED

61. The Commission and its services. The Commission is not, as frequently suggested, the civil service or bureaucracy of the Community. It is an autonomous political institution consisting of twenty members 'chosen on the grounds of their general competence and whose independence is beyond doubt'[3]. The Commissioners must be 'completely independent in the performance of their duties' and 'neither seek nor take instructions from any government or from any other body'[4]. 'Each Member State undertakes . . . not to seek to influence the members of the Commission in the performance of their tasks'[4]. Much of the work of the Commission is carried out, and some administrative decisions are taken in the name of the Commission, by the Commission's 'services' – that is, by the officials employed by the Commission[5].

62. Membership of the Commission. The EC Treaty provides that

'the Commission must include at least one national of each of the Member States, but may not include more than two members having the nationality of the same State'[6].

In practice, each of the larger member states (Germany, Spain, France, Italy and the United Kingdom) nominate two Commissioners and the remainder one each. In the United Kingdom, the convention is that its nominees include one politician, or person with political experience, from the ruling majority party and the other from the opposition. Similar conventions apply in some of the other large member states. From January 1995 appointment to the

---

1 EC Treaty, art 151.
2 The Council agenda is divided into 'A points', upon which agreement has been reached in COREPER and only the formality of a Council decision is required, and 'B points', which require debate in the Council. Some B points are dealt with by written procedure without a meeting, whilst others are 'false B points' (where in reality there is no dispute but one or more delegations require, for domestic political reasons, to go through the motions of recording their points of view in the minutes).
3 EC Treaty, art 157(1).
4 Ibid, art 157(2).
5 See paras 70-72 below.
6 EC Treaty, art 157(1).

Commission is for a five-year term (previously it was four) and its members are subject as a body to the approval of the Parliament[1].

63. Presidency of and appointment to the Commission. Prior to 1995 the President of the Commission was selected by a process of horse trading amongst the member states, and he had little influence in its eventual composition. A new procedure introduced by the Treaty on European Union applied for the first time to the appointment of the Commission which took office in January 1995. By it, the President is first nominated by 'common accord' of the governments of the member states and in consultation with the Parliament[2]. Thereafter the governments select the other members in consultation with the President-nominate. The proposed Commission is then subject as a body to a vote of approval by the Parliament[3].

64. Collegiality. In taking decisions the Commission acts by simple majority[4] and as a 'college', there being no scope for overt opposition or dissent on the part of individual Commissioners. No legislative power may be delegated by the Commission, but the power to adopt legally binding administrative acts in the name of the Commission may be delegated to an individual Commissioner[5] and, in certain cases, administrative competences may be delegated to other bodies, but only within a framework of very tightly defined checks and balances[6]. The Commission adopts its own rules of procedure[7].

65. Powers and functions as regards subordinate legislation. The EC Treaty provides that 'the Commission shall . . . exercise the powers conferred on it by the Council for the implementation of the rules laid down by the latter'[8]. Whilst the Commission alone enjoys very little autonomous legislative authority under the Treaty[9], it is often empowered by Council regulations to enact delegated legislation in the implementation and administration of a broad legislative programme. This is particularly so in the fields of agriculture[10] and competition[11]. By virtue of the Single European Act, the Council is

---

1 See para 63 below.
2 EC Treaty, art 158(2). The practical operation of 'common accord' was illustrated by the appointment of the present Commission, when the United Kingdom government vetoed the nomination as President of Mr Jean-Luc Dehaene, so resulting in the eventual and unanimous nomination of M Jacques Santer.
3 EC Treaty, art 158(2).
4 Ibid, art 163.
5 Case 5/85 *AKZO v Commission* [1986] ECR 2585, [1987] 3 CMLR 716.
6 Case 9/56 *Meroni v High Authority* [1957–58] ECR 133; Cases 32, 33/58 *SNUPAT v High Authority* [1959] ECR 127.
7 EC Treaty, art 162(2); for the present Rules of Procedure see Decision 93/492, OJ L230, 11.9.93, p 15. The Rules of Procedure are binding and contrary practice does not cause them to fall into desuetude; see Case C-137/92P *Commission v BASF* (PVC) [1994] ECR I-2555.
8 EC Treaty, art 155.
9 See eg arts 48(3) and 90(3).
10 See para 198 below.
11 See paras 238-252 below.

empowered to confer upon the Commission wide-ranging powers for the implementation of acts of the Council[1]. The Council has adopted legislation setting out the framework of procedure for exercising these implementing powers through the establishment of committees[2] – 'comitology'.

66. Enforcement powers and functions. Under the EC Treaty it is the duty of the Commission to 'ensure that the provisions of this Treaty and the measures taken by the institutions pursuant thereto are applied'[3]. To this end the Commission is empowered to raise actions before the Court of Justice against member states for failing in an obligation imposed by Community law[4].

67. The Commission and the EEA. The Commission is charged by the Treaty creating the European Economic Area (EEA) with its enforcement within the territory of the Community. Commission powers under the EEA Treaty are discussed below[5].

68. Responsibilities of the Commissioners. Each Commissioner is assigned one or more 'portfolios' – that is, responsibility for one or more areas of Community activity. The responsible Commissioner may, and frequently does, issue statements or make speeches on aspects of Commission policy falling within his portfolio, and such statements and speeches are a valuable guide, particularly in the field of competition policy, to the way in which the Commission is likely to apply Community law.

69. Accountability to the Parliament. The Commission is politically accountable to the Parliament in three ways. First, the membership of the Commission is subject to Parliamentary approval[6]. Second, the Parliament has the power, by a two-thirds majority of votes cast and an absolute majority of its members, to pass a motion of censure upon the Commission, in which event the Commission must resign as a body[7]. Although use of this power has been attempted on a number of occasions, most recently in 1992, it has, as yet, never been exercised. (Individual Commissioners may be compulsorily retired by the Court of Justice on grounds of 'serious misconduct'[8].) Third, the Commission is required to reply orally or in writing to questions

---

1 EC Treaty, art 145.
2 Decision 87/373, OJ L197, 18.7.87, p 33. There are three main types of committee: the regulatory committee, whose positive approval is required before a proposal can be implemented; the management committee, whose positive approval is not required but whose adverse opinion has suspensive effect until the matter has been considered by the Council; and the advisory committee, which must be consulted but whose opinion is not binding.
3 EC Treaty, art 155.
4 Ibid, art 169; see paras 97–99 below.
5 See Appendix I.
6 See para 63 above.
7 EC Treaty, art 144.
8 Ibid, art 160.

put to it by the Parliament or by its members[1]. The Commission's replies to such questions are another valuable guide in ascertaining the legislative policy of the Commission and to its thinking on points of existing Community law. The members of the Commission and the Council are entitled to be given the opportunity to be heard by the Parliament[2], and the speeches made on these occasions may again be a guide to the policy aspects of law-making. Parliamentary answers and speeches may also be helpful in assessing the prospects of Community legislation being enacted and, if so, on what time scale.

(B) THE SERVICES OF THE COMMISSION

70. Internal organisation of the Commission. In general, the Commission's services are organised under Directorates-General (under Directors-General), which are divided into Directorates (under Directors) and further subdivided into Units (under Heads of Unit). There are at present twenty-three Directorates-General, each of which is responsible for a general area of policy - for example, external relations (DG I), competition (DG IV) and agriculture (DG VI)[3]. The responsibilities of the Directorates-General do not necessarily correspond to the portfolios of the Commissioners, two or more of whom may be responsible for aspects of the work of a single Directorate-General. Conversely, one Commissioner may have responsibility for more than one Directorate-General. Subject to that, the Directorates-General of the Commission may be compared with United Kingdom ministries, the Commissioner being analogous to the Minister and the Directorate-General to the Permanent Secretary. There are a number of services, offices and task forces outwith the structure of the Directorates-General.

71. The Secretariat-General. The duties of the Secretariat-General correspond roughly to those of the Cabinet Office in the United Kingdom. It is responsible for the preparation of the agenda and administration of the Commission and has overall responsibility for relations between the Commission on the one hand and the other Community institutions and the member states on the other.

72. The Legal Service. The function of the Legal Service is to give independent legal advice to the Commission and its services. The Commission relies heavily upon its advice, especially in matters of enforcement of Treaty obligations, and the opinion of the Legal Service must be sought upon, and is attached to, all Commission proposals. It is organised, under a Director-General, in 'teams' (*équipes*), each of which is responsible for giving advice

1 EC Treaty, art 140, 3rd para.
2 Ibid, art 140, 4th para.
3 Directorates-General are designated by Roman numerals, Directorates by capital letters and Units by Arabic numerals. So, for example, regional aids fall within the responsibility of DG IV E 3, being Unit 3 (regional aids) of Directorate E (state aids) of DG IV (competition).

on a particular area or areas of the law. The Commission is normally represented before the European Court of Justice by a member of the relevant team acting as agent for the Commission. Both the Secretariat-General and the Legal Service are represented as of right at all Commission meetings.

(2) THE LEGISLATIVE PROCESS

73. Forms of Community legislation. The Community institutions are competent to adopt legislation in a number of forms which produce different legal effects[1]. The legislative process does not vary depending upon the form of legislation.

74. Initiation of legislation. Under the EC Treaty it is normally the exclusive prerogative of the Commission to make proposals for legislation, in the sense that the machinery of legislation can normally be set in motion only by the submission of a proposal by the Commission to the Council. A proposal is developed by the responsible Directorate-General under the authority of its Commissioner and in consultation with other services of the Commission as necessary. The Directorate-General will also, whenever desirable, obtain help and advice from experts from the member states (whether from the national administration or from the private sector), from professional or trade union organisations (for example the *Union des Industries de la Communauté Européenne* (UNICE) and the European Trade Union Confederation (ETUC)), and from a variety of other sources[2]. When the file is ready, the draft proposal is submitted by the responsible Commissioner or Commissioners to the Commission itself and there approved, with or without amendment. In practice, amendments at Commission level can be very extensive, reflecting the many political cross-currents which run through it. Once a proposal has been submitted to the Council, the Commission may, and frequently does, amend it, *inter alia* in the light of an advisory opinion of the Parliament. The Commission may alter a proposal at any time until the Council has acted[3], and the Council may amend the proposal only by unanimity[4]. The Commission therefore remains 'master of the text' virtually throughout. Since the entry into force of the Treaty on European Union the Parliament may request that the Commission introduce legislation[5], but the Commission need not comply with the request.

---

1 See paras 142ff below.
2 The Commission is more open than most United Kingdom ministries to discussion of proposed or possible legislation with interested persons and bodies. Indeed, the Commission must often rely upon the expertise of interested groups in technical matters, thus creating an unusual degree of co-operation between the public authority and those who are affected by its acts and decisions. Direct contact with the responsible officials is often welcomed rather than shunned.
3 EC Treaty, art 189a(2).
4 Ibid, art 189a(1).
5 Ibid, art 138b, 2nd para.

75. Powers of the Council. As noted above[1], the powers conferred upon the Commission by the ECSC Treaty are considerably greater than those of the Commission under the EC or Euratom Treaties. Consequently, the powers and functions of the Council under the ECSC Treaty are more limited than under the EC and Euratom Treaties. In what follows here, only the powers and functions of the Council in relation to legislation under the EC Treaty are considered[2].

76. Legislative procedure in the Council. The Council is the principal, and in most cases the ultimate, legislative organ of the Community. Hence the saying 'the Commission proposes, the Council disposes', which expresses the nature of the relationship between the two institutions in the promulgation of law: the Commission proposes but cannot enact; the Council cannot enact without a Commission proposal[3]. The Treaty normally specifies, depending upon the article(s) of the Treaty under which the institutions act, the form of legislation and the procedure to be followed. The procedure varies with the role afforded the Parliament, usually being one of consultation (advisory opinions), co-operation, co-decision, or assent[4]. The Treaty may also require consultation with the Economic and Social Committee and/or the Committee of the Regions[5]. Failure of the Council to carry out the procedure specified in the treaty is a ground for annulment of a legislative act[6].

77. Voting in the Council. Except where the treaty specifies otherwise, decisions of the Council are taken by simple majority[7]. In a few very important areas, the treaty requires unanimity; in such cases, abstentions are not counted[8]. Unanimity is also required to amend a Commission proposal[9]. But many Treaty articles require decision by 'qualified majority', the votes of the member states being weighted by reference to their population sizes[10].

---

1 See para 13 above.
2 The Council is empowered by the TEU to act in the areas of foreign and security policy and justice and home affairs, ie, the two non-Community pillars of the European Union. But when it does so it follows special rules and procedures; see para 291 below.
3 There are exceptions to this: first, where an institution adopts legislation by virtue of express Treaty authority which bypasses normal procedures, and second, legislation adopted by the European Central Bank within its spheres of competence; see para 122 below.
4 See paras 79–81 below.
5 See paras 117, 118 below.
6 As to the annulment of legislative acts, see paras 100ff below.
7 EC Treaty, art 148(1).
8 Ibid, art 148(3).
9 Ibid, art 189a(1).
10 Ibid, art 148(2), under which the United Kingdom has a weight of ten out of the Council total of eighty-seven. Sixty-two votes are required for the Council to act by qualified majority, or sixty-two votes cast by at least ten members where the Council is acting other than upon a proposal from the Commission; conversely, twenty-six votes are required to block the adoption of legislation.

78. The 'veto'. As noted above[1], the operation of the treaty rules on voting were distorted by the Luxembourg Compromise, which was said to allow any member state to 'veto' a proposal which it considered to affect its 'very important interests' even in areas in which the Treaty allowed for majority voting. From a strictly legal point of view no right of veto has ever existed except, of course, where the treaty requires unanimity in the Council. Since the signing of the Single European Act, majority voting has again become the rule. Recourse to the Luxembourg Compromise has fallen into disuse and there seems to be little enthusiasm to resuscitate it. However, the final negotiation of the Corfu Accession Treaty produced an agreement within the European Council known as the 'Ioannina Compromise'. A Council Decision giving effect to it[2] provides that, although the Treaty requires sixty-two Council votes to adopt an act by qualified majority (or, conversely, twenty-six votes to block it), in a case where a proposed measure is opposed by member states representing twenty-three to twenty-five Council votes, the Council will 'do all in its power' to reach a satisfactory solution which can be adopted by at least sixty-five votes. It remains to be seen how the Ioannina Compromise will operate in practice. The question will be addressed again at the 1996 intergovernmental conference[3].

79. Powers of the Parliament. A number of articles of the founding treaties provide that, before acting, the Council must consult the Parliament. The opinion thus obtained is not binding upon the Council; it is advisory only. But the Court of Justice held that the requirement to consult the Parliament, far from being a mere formality,

> 'reflects at Community level the fundamental democratic principle that the peoples should take part in the exercise of power through the intermediary of a representative assembly'[4].

The Court has also held that the Council is required to re-consult the Parliament if the Commission has amended a draft proposal, or the Council itself intends to amend it, and the resulting text departs substantially from the text upon which the Parliament has already been consulted (except where the amendments correspond essentially to the wishes of the Parliament itself)[5]. Even where the Treaty does not require consultation the Commission will urge the Council to consult the Parliament in important matters. Nevertheless, the right of the Parliament to be consulted gave it

---

1 See para 15 above.
2 Decision of 29 March 1994, OJ C105, 13.4.94, p 1 as amended by Decision of 1 January 1995, OJ C1, 1.1.95, p 1.
3 See the Joint Declaration (No 8) attached to the Corfu Accession Treaty on institutional procedures.
4 Case 138/79 *Roquette Frères v Council* [1980] ECR 3333 at 3360. See also Case 70/88 *European Parliament v Council* ('Chernobyl') [1990] ECR I-2041, [1992] 1 CMLR 91.
5 Case C-65/90 *European Parliament v Council* [1992] ECR I-4593; Cases C-13-16/92 *Driessen en Zonen v Minister van Verkeer en Waterstaat* [1993] ECR I-4751, [1994] 2 CMLR 141; Case C-388/92 *European Parliament v Council* [1994] ECR I-2067.

only a minor role in the legislative process and led to criticism of a 'democratic deficit' in the Community system. This led eventually to an increase in the Parliament's legislative functions. There are now four distinct procedures by which the Parliament is involved in Community legislation[1]:

- *consultation* (*advisory opinions*), as described above;
- *co-operation procedure*, instituted by the Single European Act[2];
- *co-decision procedure*, instituted by the Treaty on European Union[3]; and
- *assent*, whereby, in a small number of areas, the positive approval of the Parliament is required before action can be taken.

80. Co-operation procedure. Under the co-operation procedure, following submission of a proposal for legislation from the Commission to the Council, the Council must adopt a 'common position' by qualified majority, which it submits to the Parliament. If the Parliament approves the common position or does nothing within three months, the Council may adopt the proposal into law. If the Parliament, by an absolute majority of MEPs, proposes amendments to or rejects the common position, then the Council may override the Parliament only by unanimity. Failing unanimity in the Council, the Commission must re-submit the proposal 'taking account' of the Parliament's proposed amendments. The proposal may then be adopted by the Council by qualified majority vote.

81. Co-decision procedure. Under the co-decision procedure, the same path is followed until a point at which the Parliament amends or rejects the Council's common position. If the Parliament rejects the common position or the Council refuses to accept its amendments, a Conciliation Committee must be convened, composed of representatives of the Council and fifteen MEPs. The Committee seeks to reconcile the opposing views of the two institutions. If it approves a joint text, it may be adopted by a qualified majority vote in the Council and by simple majority vote in the Parliament; if either of the institutions fails to approve the joint text, the proposal cannot be adopted. If the Committee fails to adopt a joint text, the Council may re-confirm its common position by majority vote, in which case the proposal is adopted unless the Parliament rejects it by an absolute majority of MEPs. So, in areas where the co-decision procedure applies the Parliament now enjoys a power of veto. Because it allows for a degree of parity between the Council and the Parliament, measures adopted by the co-decision procedure are, uniquely, acts not of the Council but of 'the European Parliament and the Council'.

82. The legal base. The Treaty article which empowers the institutions to legislate (the 'legal base' for the legislation) specifies the procedure to be

---

1 EC Treaty, art 138b(1).
2 Now provided in EC Treaty, art 189c. The term 'co-operation' was used in the EEC Treaty but was abandoned with the entry into force of the TEU.
3 EC Treaty, art 189b; nor does the term 'co-decision' appear in the Treaty, having been abandoned in the later drafts of the TEU.

followed. Since this affects the Parliament's power to influence the outcome, the Parliament has become active in challenging legislation before the Court of Justice on the ground that it was adopted upon an incorrect legal base[1].

(3) THE COURT OF JUSTICE

(a) The Court

83. Function and jurisdiction of the Court of Justice. Under the founding treaties the function of the Court of Justice is to

'ensure that in the interpretation and application of this Treaty the law is observed'[2].

The Court is not, however, a court of general jurisdiction. The nature and extent of its jurisdiction, and the conditions for its exercise, are laid down in the treaties. Further detailed provisions are found in the Statutes of the Court (contained in Protocols to the treaties, one for each), in the Rules of Procedure, which the Court adopts subject to approval of the Council[3], and in a number of supplementary statutes, protocols and regulations. The most relevant of these are gathered together in *Selected Instruments relating to the Organisation, Jurisdiction and Procedure of the Court*, published by the Court. It has its seat in Luxembourg.

84. The Court of Justice and the Court of First Instance. In order to ease the workload of the Court of Justice the Single European Act amended the founding treaties so as to empower the Council, upon a request from the Court of Justice, to 'attach' to it a court with first instance jurisdiction in certain forms of action[4]. This Court, styled the 'Court of First Instance', was established in 1989[5]. The term 'Court of Justice' may therefore refer either to the Court of Justice as a Community institution, in which case it includes the Court of First Instance, or to the Court of Justice as a judicial body separate, and with distinct jurisdiction, from the Court of First Instance. Since the

---

1 See para 144 below. For this reason the Parliament always examines draft legislation upon which it is consulted for 'validity and appropriateness' of the legal base; Rules of Procedure, rule 53.
2 EC Treaty, art 164. The English and the essentially identical Irish and Finnish versions are less illustrative of the function of the Court than other language versions: the Court 'ensures the respect of law' (French, Dutch, Italian, Greek, Spanish, Portuguese), 'ensures the protection of law' (German), or 'safeguards law and justice' (Danish and Swedish) in the interpretation and application of the Treaty. The Euratom Treaty, art 136 is in identical terms, and the ECSC Treaty, art 31 is similar.
3 EC Treaty, art 188, 3rd para; for the present Rules of Procedure see OJ L176, 4.7.91, p 7.
4 EC Treaty, art 168a.
5 Decision 88/591, OJ L319, 25.11.88, p 1; the text was subsequently amended substantially and was reproduced, as amended, at OJ C215, 21.8.89, p 1.

Court of First Instance was created, cases brought before the Court of Justice are numbered 'C-...' (for *Cour de Justice*) and those brought before the Court of First Instance 'T-...' (*Tribunal de premier instance*) to distinguish between them.

85. Membership of the Court of Justice. The Court of Justice consists of fifteen judges[1] assisted by nine Advocates-General[2]. The Treaties provide that

> 'The judges and Advocates-General shall be chosen from persons whose independence is beyond doubt and who possess the qualifications required for appointment to the highest judicial offices in their respective countries or who are jurisconsults of recognized competence; they shall be appointed by common accord of the Governments of the Member States for a term of six years'[3].

In practice, each member state nominates one judge[4]. Five of the Advocates-General are nominated by the larger member states, and three by the smaller member states in rotation[5]. Half of the judges and half of the Advocates-General come up for renewal every three years[6]. Except for the Advocates-General from the smaller member states, appointment is renewable.

86. The President of the Court. The President of the Court of Justice is elected by the judges themselves from amongst their number[7]. The term of office is three years, which is renewable[7]. The President presides over deliberations in which he takes part, is responsible for the business and administration of the Court and represents the Court before other institutions, the member states and the outside world. He is also competent, sitting alone, to determine applications to the Court for interim or interlocutory measures and certain appeals from the Court of First Instance[8].

87. Collegiality; Chambers. Except where the President can act alone, the Court always acts as a college, sitting either in plenary session (the whole Court), for which the quorum is nine judges[9], or in Chambers. The Treaty provides that the Court may form Chambers of three, five or seven judges[10]. At present the judges, excluding the President, are divided into two

---

1 EC Treaty, art 165, 1st para.
2 Ibid, art 166, 1st para, which provides that there will be nine Advocates-General until October 2000, thereafter eight; see note 5 below.
3 Ibid, art 167, 1st para.
4 In the past, when there has been an uneven number of member states, an additional judge, nominated by one of the five larger member states (Germany, France, Spain, Italy and the UK), has been appointed to ensure an uneven number of judges.
5 The ninth Advocate-General (Mr Antonio La Pergola) – see note 2 above – was the additional judge from October 1994 (see previous note) until the accession of three new member states in January 1995 made an additional judge unnecessary.
6 EC Treaty, art 167, 1st and 2nd paras.
7 Ibid, art 167, 5th para.
8 See paras 96, 112, 113 below.
9 Statute of the Court of Justice, art 15 as amended.
10 EC Treaty, art 165(2).

Chambers of seven judges (of whom five sit in any given case), each subdivided into two Chambers of three or four judges (of whom three will sit). A 'small plenary' (*petit plenum*) consists of eleven judges[1]. Each case is assigned by the President to a Judge Rapporteur who presents a preliminary report (*rapport préalable*) to the Court[2]. The Court then decides whether the case should be assigned to a Chamber or kept before the Court in full or 'small' plenary. Where a member state or a Community institution so requests, a case must be heard by the whole Court[3]. All judgments are published as judgments of the Court, and no dissenting opinions are expressed or published.

88. The Advocates-General. The function of the Advocates-General, of whom one is assigned to each case, is 'acting with complete impartiality and independence, to make, in open court, reasoned submissions on cases brought before the Court of Justice, in order to assist the Court in the performance of the task assigned to it...'[4]. One of the Advocates-General is designated each year by his colleagues to act as First Advocate-General. The Advocates-General are not advocates; they are, in the fullest sense, members of the court and rank with the judges in order of appointment. Although the analogy is not exact, the opinion delivered by the Advocate-General can be likened to the judgment of a single judge at first instance, to be followed by a compulsory and definitive appeal – the judgment of the Court. In comparison with the relative terseness of a judgment of the Court, the opinions of the Advocates-General are similar in style to the opinions or judgments of United Kingdom judges and, although not binding upon the Court, they are a source of Community law and may be the best guide to the reasoning of the Court. Opinions are published with the judgment of the Court.

89. Composition of the Court of First Instance. The Court of First Instance consists of fifteen judges[5] 'whose independence is beyond doubt and who possess the ability required for appointment to judicial office'[6]. The method and term of appointment and the election and powers of the President are the same as those of the Court of Justice[7]. There is no separate office of Advocate-

---

1 The small plenary is now used for cases which might have been devolved to a Chamber but might also raise issues of principle with which a Chamber would feel unable to deal, so making it necessary to reopen the case before the plenary; this happened, for example, in Cases C-46/90 & 93/91 *Procureur du Roi v Lagauche* [1993] ECR I-5267 and Cases C-267-8/91 *Criminal Proceedings against Keck and Mithouard* [1993] ECR I-6097. For the criteria for the allocation of cases to Chambers see Decision of the Court of 25 January 1995, not yet published.

2 The Judge Rapporteur is also responsible for producing a second, more substantial report, the 'Report for the Hearing', which outlines the facts of the case and the arguments of the parties. Until 1994 the Report for the Hearing was published with the judgment of the Court. It is now generally available only in the language of proceedings (para 91 below) and directly from the Court; see Appendix II.

3 EC Treaty, art 165, 3rd para.

4 Ibid, art 166, 2nd para.

5 Decision 88/591 (para 84 above), art 2(1).

6 EC Treaty, art 168a(3).

7 Ibid; Decision 88/591, art 2(2).

General, but one of the judges may be called upon to perform the task of Advocate-General in a given case[1]. The Court normally sits in Chambers of three, or exceptionally five, judges, but may sit in plenary session[2].

90. Jurisdiction of the Court of First Instance. According to the EC Treaty, the Court of First Instance can be assigned 'jurisdiction to hear and determine at first instance . . . certain classes of action or proceeding [other than those] referred for a preliminary ruling under article 177'[3]. All classes of action not expressly assigned to the Court of First Instance remain within the jurisdiction of the Court of Justice. The jurisdiction originally conferred on the Court of First Instance covered only staff cases[4], certain matters involving coal and steel production governed by the ECSC Treaty, and actions for annulment of Community acts raised by a natural or legal person in the field of competition[5] – areas in which a substantial amount of fact finding and/or complex economic analysis may be required. In 1993 and in 1994 this jurisdiction was extended to include any action brought by natural or legal persons against an act of a Community institution[6]. The Court of First Instance has its own Rules of Procedure[7]. The two Courts share common services (such as translation and interpretation), but each has its own Registrar and Registry. The Statute of the Court of Justice provides for the situation where an action is raised before the wrong court[8] or the same issue is raised before both courts[9]. Judgments of the Court of First Instance are open to appeal to the Court of Justice on points of law only[10].

91. Languages. Written and oral pleadings may be in any of the eleven official languages of the Community[11] or in Irish[12]. Unless the Court authorises

---

1 Decision 88/591, art 2(3). This occurs rarely; at the time of writing a judge of the Court of First Instance has acted as Advocate-General in only four cases.
2 Decision 88/591, art 2(4). Hitherto the Court of First Instance has sat in Chambers of five judges for competition, state aids, anti-dumping and ECSC cases, but this has recently changed in the light of increased workload; for the criteria for the allocation of cases amongst Chambers see Decision of the Court, OJ C304, 29.10.94, p 14. It is only very rarely that the Court sits in plenary session.
3 EC Treaty, art 168a(1); on art 177 see paras 106-110 below.
4 See para 104 below.
5 Decision 88/591, art 3(1). On annulment of Community acts see paras 100ff below.
6 Ibid, as amended by Decision 93/350, OJ L144, 16.6.93, p 21 (as amended in turn by Decision 94/149, OJ L66, 10.3.94, p 29).
7 For the present Rules of Procedure see OJ L136, 30.5.91, p 1 as amended.
8 Statute of the Court of Justice, art 47. See eg Case C-72/90 *Asia Motor France v Commission* [1990] ECR I-2181; Case T-78/91 *Moat and TAO/AFI v Commission* [1991] ECR II-1387.
9 Statute of the Court of Justice, art 47. This arises where, for example, a Community act is challenged by both a member state (and so, at present, within the jurisdiction of the Court of Justice) and an affected natural or legal person (within that of the Court of First Instance); see eg Case C-274/94 *United Kingdom v Commission* (pending) and Case T-371/94 *British Airways, Scandinavian Air Services and Koninklijke Luchtvaart Maatschappij v Commission* (pending), both cases challenging Decision 94/653, OJ L254, 30.9.94, p 73 by which the Commission authorised substantial French aid to Air France.
10 EC Treaty, art 168a(1) and Statute of the Court of Justice, arts 49-54; see para 111 below.
11 See para 126 below.

otherwise, pleadings must be conducted in the 'language of the case', which is either (a) chosen by the applicant, (b) the language or one of the languages of a defendant member state, or (c) the language of the referring national court, depending upon the form of action. An intervening member state[1] may use its own language irrespective of the language of the case[2]. Judgments are formally delivered in the language of the case, and that text constitutes the only authentic version of the judgment. However, in present practice the working language of the courts is French, and most judgments are drafted and agreed in French. The French text of a judgment ought therefore to be consulted if, as sometimes happens, the meaning of the English text is not clear. Opinions of the Advocate-General are written and delivered in his native language.

92. Reporting. Judgments of the Court of Justice and of the Court of First Instance are reported officially in the European Court Reports, which exist in all eleven official languages. They are also reported in a number of private series of reports. A guide to reports of the Court may be found in Appendix II.

93. The Court of Justice and the Treaty on European Union. The scope of the jurisdiction of the Court of Justice extends to all three Community treaties and some provisions of the Treaty on European Union. Other provisions of the TEU, however, are expressly excluded from the Court's jurisdiction[3].

(b) Forms of Process

94. Forms of action before the court. According to the Court of Justice,

> 'the Treaty established a complete system of legal remedies and procedures designed to permit the Court of Justice to review the legality of measures adopted by the institutions'.[4]

The available forms of process also make it possible to test the lawfulness of the conduct of the member states. However, each of the forms of process before the Court of Justice (and before the Court of First Instance where that Court has jurisdiction) is distinct, and is subject to rules which are set out in some detail in the Treaty, the Statute of the Court and the Rules of Procedure. As the Court is not a court of general jurisdiction, it cannot create new forms of process.

---

12 Rules of Procedure of the Court of Justice, art 29; Rules of Procedure of the Court of First Instance, art 35.
1 See para 96 below.
2 Rules of Procedure of the Court of Justice, art 29; Rules of Procedure of the Court of First Instance, art 35. The Community institutions enjoy no such privilege as they are irrebuttably presumed to be able, and so required, to plead in all twelve languages.
3 TEU, art L; see para 292 below.
4 Case 294/83 *Parti Ecologiste 'Les Verts' v European Parliament* [1986] ECR 1339 at 1365, [1987] 2 CMLR 343 at 371.

95. Forms of process. The available forms of process are, principally, direct actions, references for preliminary rulings, appeals from the Court of First Instance, and opinions. The Court cannot decline jurisdiction when properly seized of a case. However, where the action has been raised before the wrong court[1] or where it is clear that the Court has no jurisdiction or the action is manifestly inadmissible[2], the Court may dispose of it by reasoned order without proceeding to judgment.

96. Parties and interveners. Strictly speaking there are 'parties' only in direct actions before either court and in appeals taken to the Court of Justice: the person(s) bringing the action (or the appeal) and those against whom it is brought. In such actions member states and Community institutions have the right to be heard, and other persons who can show a sufficient interest may in certain cases apply to be heard, as interveners[3]. In references for preliminary rulings, the parties to the main action before the national court, member states and Community institutions are entitled to be heard. Persons other than a member state or a Community institution must be represented by a lawyer entitled to practise before a court of a member state[4], except that, in references, those entitled to appear before the referring national court may appear before the Court of Justice[5].

97. Direct actions: the action for failure to fulfil an obligation (articles 169 and 170). The action for failure to fulfil an obligation is an action brought against a member state by the Commission under article 169 or by another member state under article 170 of the Treaty[6]. The purpose of the action is to have it declared that the defendant member state has failed to fulfil an obligation incumbent upon it under Community law. The action may be raised for virtually any failure to comply with a Treaty obligation[7], be it one of omission – for example failure to implement a directive within the prescribed time limit or failure to implement it properly – or of commission – for

---

1 See para 90 above.
2 Rules of Procedure of the Court of Justice, art 92; Rules of Procedure of the Court of First Instance, art 111.
3 Statute of the Court of Justice, art 37. Interveners are limited to supporting the submissions of one or another of the parties. A person whose application to intervene before the Court of First Instance is refused may appeal that decision to the Court of Justice by way of summary procedure; Statute of the Court of Justice, art 50, 1st and 3rd paras.
4 Statute of the Court of Justice, art 17.
5 So, if (as in the UK) national rules of procedure permit it, party litigants may appear before the Court in person; for examples of this see Case C-168/91 *Konstantinidis v Stadt Altensteig* [1993] ECR I-1191, [1993] 3 CMLR 401; Case C-19/92 *Kraus v Land Baden-Württemberg* [1993] ECR I-1663.
6 Enforcement by another member state under art 170 has not proved a popular form of action, and has been carried to the stage of judgment only once: Case 141/78 *France v United Kingdom* [1979] ECR 2923, [1980] 1 CMLR 6. However, member states intervene (see para 96 above) from time to time in support of (or against) the Commission in an action raised under art 169 against another member state.
7 Except where the Treaty provides other means of enforcement in specific areas; see para 99 below.

example the enactment or enforcement of national legislation or the implementation of national policy in a manner incompatible with Community
law.

Although many proceedings under article 169 follow a complaint to the
Commission, a complainant cannot force the Commission to launch or, once
launched, to continue enforcement proceedings[1]. Settlement can be, and
often is, reached between the Commission and the defendant member state.
Having seised the Court, the Commission may, but need not, withdraw the
action[2]. Unless the action is formally withdrawn, the Court will proceed to
judgment.

The full procedure under article 169 falls into the following stages:
- the administrative phase:
  - investigation by the Commission;
  - the formal letter of complaint (*lettre de mise en demeure*) identifying an
    alleged breach and inviting the member state to submit observations;
  - the 'reasoned opinion' (*avis motivé*), a reasoned statement identifying
    the alleged breach and allowing the member state a reasonable time in
    which to remedy it[3].
- the judicial phase:
  - written procedure;
  - oral procedure, including the opinion of the Advocate-General;
  - judgment of the Court declaring the defendant member state to be in
    breach of its obligations or finding that there has been no breach.

There may then follow a procedure for imposition of sanctions[4].

The purpose of the administrative phase is to identify the alleged breach
and to enable the defendant member state to explain why there is no breach
or, if the breach is admitted, to remedy it. The Commission cannot therefore
raise during the judicial phase any point upon which the defendant member
state has not had the opportunity to comment during the administrative
phase. The function of the Court during the judicial phase is to ensure that
the Commission has complied with procedural propriety throughout the
administrative phase[5] and to decide whether, in the circumstances disclosed
during the administrative phase, it has established the existence of the
breach.

---

1 Case 48/65 *Lütticke v EEC Commission* [1966] ECR 19, [1966] CMLR 378; Case 247/87 *Star Fruit v Commission* [1989] ECR 291, [1990] 1 CMLR 733.
2 The Commission may legitimately elect to proceed in order to obtain a clarification of the law from the Court of Justice or to establish authoritatively the basis of any civil liability which the member state may incur; see eg Case 240/86 *Commission v Greece* [1988] ECR 1835; Case 154/85 *Commission v Italy* [1987] ECR 2717.
3 As to what is reasonable time see Case 293/85 *Commission v Belgium* [1988] ECR 305, [1986] 1 CMLR 594; Case C-56/90 *Commission v United Kingdom* (Bathing Water) [1993] ECR I-4109, [1994] 1 CMLR 769.
4 See para 98 below.
5 The Court may raise this question of its own motion; see eg Case C-362/90 *Commission v Italy* (Public Supply Contracts) [1992] ECR I-2353, [1994] 3 CMLR 1.

98. Force of the declaration; sanctions (article 171). The Treaty provides that

'If the Court of Justice finds that a Member State has failed to fulfil an obligation under this Treaty, the State shall be required to take the necessary measures to comply with the judgment of the Court of Justice'[1].

A declaration under article 169 that a member state has failed to fulfil an obligation under the Treaty has the force of *res judicata* and 'is a prohibition having the full force of law on the competent national authorities against applying a national rule recognized as incompatible with the Treaty and . . . an obligation on them to take all appropriate measures to enable Community law to be fully applied. . .'[2]. Even if the legislative or administrative authorities of the member state fail to take appropriate action, its courts are bound if possible to enforce the Court's judgment, and not the offending national rule[3]. The Treaty provides no other sanction for a member state's failure to comply with Treaty obligations, and, until the Treaty on European Union, it provided no sanction for failure to comply with a declaratory judgment of the Court. No member state has, as yet, openly defied such a judgment, although there has been considerable delay in compliance in some cases. The EC Treaty as now amended empowers the Commission to raise a further action against a defaulting member state specifying the financial penalty which it considers appropriate. If the Court finds that the member state has not complied with its judgment, it may impose a lump sum or penalty payment upon it[4]. This power of sanction has not, as yet, been invoked.

99. Analogous enforcement provisions. The Treaty has other provisions whereby the Commission may raise enforcement proceedings against a member state in a manner similar to, but bypassing the administrative phase of, article 169. This applies where a member state fails to comply with a Commission decision in the area of state aids[5], derogates from internal market legislation[6] or adopts national measures in the event of internal disturbance or war[7]. In the event of a member state failing in its duty to avoid excessive government deficits, the Treaty provides other, specific enforcement procedures and recourse to article 169 is in part expressly ousted[8].

100. Direct actions: the action of annulment (article 173). The action of annulment is an action to annul (quash or, in Scotland, reduce) a legislative

---

1 EC Treaty, art 171(1).
2 Case 48/71 *Commission v Italy* (the Second Art Treasures Case) [1972] ECR 527 at 532, [1972] CMLR 699 at 708.
3 Cases 314-16/81 and 83/82 *Procureur de la République v Waterkeyn* [1982] ECR 4337, [1983] 2 CMLR 145.
4 EC Treaty, art 171(2).
5 Ibid, art 93(2); see para 254 below.
6 Ibid, art 100a(4), 3rd para; see para 89 below.
7 Ibid, art 225; see para 286 below.
8 Ibid, art 104c(10); see para 263 below.

or administrative act of one of the Community institutions. Its purpose is to deprive the act in question of legal effect. The act in question may be any measure adopted by any Community institution which has legal effects[1]. There is a two-month time bar[2], which is rigorously enforced. The grounds of action are:

- lack of competence;
- infringement of an essential procedural requirement;
- infringement of the Treaty or of any rule of law relating to its application; and
- misuse of powers[3].

The first two grounds relate to matters 'prior to the act' in the sense that the relevant question is whether the necessary enabling powers had been conferred upon the institution before it acted or whether the institution, in proceeding to act, complied with all relevant procedural rules. The third ground relates to matter 'inherent in the act' in the sense that the relevant question is whether, in form and content as enacted, the act is lawful. The fourth ground (*détournement de pouvoir* in French administrative law) applies where, although the act appears to be the lawful act of a competent authority, that authority's power has in truth been exercised for a purpose other than that for which it was conferred[4].

101. Title and interest. The action of annulment may be raised

- as of right, without need to demonstrate interest, by the Commission, the Council or a member state (the 'privileged applicants')[5];
- by the Parliament or the European Central Bank where the act in question infringes their prerogatives ('semi-privileged applicants')[6]; and

---

1 EC Treaty, art 173, 1st para. Although the Treaty refers only to review of (joint) acts of the European Parliament and the Council and acts of the Council, the Commission, the European Parliament and the European Central Bank, the Court of Justice has held (eg Case 294/83 *Parti Ecologiste 'Les Verts' v European Parliament* [1986] ECR 1339, [1987] 2 CMLR 343) that an act of *any* Community institution or body must be reviewable, so long as it is capable of producing the requisite legal effects. Acts adopted by the member states meeting in the Council (see para 57 above) are not subject to review under art 173; Cases C-181 & 248/91 *European Parliament v Council and Commission* (Bangladesh) [1993] ECR I-3685, [1994] 3 CMLR 317. As to whether an act produces legal effects see Case 22/70 *Commission v Council* (ERTA) [1971] ECR 263, [1971] CMLR 335; Case C-319/91 *European Parliament v Council* [1994] ECR I-625; Case C-327/91 *France v Commission* [1994] ECR I-3641, [1994] 5 CMLR 517.

2 EC Treaty, art 173, 5th para. For the method of computing this and other similar time limits see Case 152/85 *Misset v Council* [1987] ECR 223; Case T-125/89 *Filtrona Española v Commission* [1990] ECR II-393, [1990] 4 CMLR 832; Case C-195/91P *Bayer v Commission*, judgment of 15 December 1994, not yet reported.

3 EC Treaty, art 173, 2nd para.

4 See eg Case T-106/92 *Frederiksen v European Parliament*, judgment of 2 February 1995, not yet reported.

5 EC Treaty, art 173, 2nd para. 'Member state' here means central government; regional or local governments are not recognised to be privileged applicants.

6 Ibid, art 173, 3rd para. The implicit right of the Parliament to protect its prerogatives had been recognised by the Court of Justice in Case C-70/88 *European Parliament v Council* ('Chernobyl') [1990] ECR I-2041, [1992] 1 CMLR 91 and was codified in art 173 by the Treaty on European Union.

- subject to rigorous proof of title and interest (*locus standi*), by an affected natural or legal person ('non-privileged applicants')[1].

A non-privileged applicant is entitled to raise an action for annulment of any act of which he is personally the addressee. Otherwise he must show that the act has legal effects and that it affects him both directly and individually[2]. An applicant is 'directly' affected where there is no room for discretion, or no real likelihood of its exercise, in applying the act to him[3]. He is 'individually' affected where the act 'individualises' him in the same way as its actual addressee, either because of characteristics specific to him or because of factual circumstances which distinguish his situation from that of everyone else[4]. Generally these are very difficult tests to meet[5]; however, the position of natural and legal persons is protected by the availability of other processes[6]. All actions of annulment raised by non-privileged applications fall now within the jurisdiction of the Court of First Instance.

102. Annulment. A Community act found to be unlawful is annulled by declaration of the Court (ie, declared 'void')[7]. The effect is, in principle, to deprive the act of all legal effect, past, present and future. The institution which enacted it is required to take all necessary measures to comply with the judgment of the Court[8]. Prior to such declaration the act is presumed to be valid and must be given full force and effect[9], unless the Court has suspended its operation by interim order[10] or the act is tainted with such serious and manifest defects as to render it 'non-existent'[11]. The Court may however limit the temporal effect of annulment. Having annulled an act, it may 'if it considers this necessary' (eg, in the interests of legal certainty or legitimate expectation[12]) declare all or some of its provisions to be operative[13].

---

1 EC Treaty, art 173, 4th para. The rules as to title and interest are less strict under the ECSC Treaty, art 33.
2 EC Treaty, art 173, 4th para.
3 See eg Case 62/70 *Bock v Commission* [1971] ECR 897, [1972] CMLR 160; Case 11/82 *Piraiki-Patraiki v Commission* [1985] ECR 207, [1985] 2 CMLR 4.
4 Case 25/62 *Plaumann v EEC Commission* [1963] ECR 95, [1964] CMLR 29; Cases 106-7/63 *Toepfer v EEC Commission* [1965] ECR 405, [1966] CMLR 111; Case 100/74 *CAM v Commission* [1975] ECR 1393; Case 11/82 *Piraiki-Patraiki*, above.
5 In recent years the Court has been more generous in accepting *locus standi* in the areas of state aids, anti-dumping and competition legislation; see paras 256, 270 and 238 below.
6 See para 110 below.
7 EC Treaty, art 174, 1st para.
8 Ibid, art 176, 1st para.
9 Case 101/78 *Granaria v Hoofdproduktschap voor Akkerbouwprodukten* [1979] ECR 623, [1979] 3 CMLR 124.
10 See para 113 below.
11 Case C-137/92P *Commission v BASF* (PVC) [1994] ECR I-2555.
12 See eg Case 45/86 *Commission v Council* (Generalised Tariff Preferences) [1987] ECR 1493, [1988] 2 CMLR 131; Case C-295/90 *European Parliament v Council* (Students) [1992] ECR I-4193, [1992] 3 CMLR 281; Case C-388/92 *European Parliament v Council* [1994] ECR I-2067. Although art 174 refers only to regulations, in the *Students* case the Court exercised its declaratory power in relation to a directive. On legal certainty and legitimate expectation, see para 154 below.
13 EC Treaty, art 174, 2nd para.

Annulment of an offending act does not deprive persons who have suffered consequential injury of the right to raise an action seeking damages[1].

103. Direct actions: the action for failure to act (article 175). In British terms the action under article 175 of the Treaty for failure to act is comparable to a writ of *mandamus* or, in Scotland, a petition for an order requiring the specific performance of a statutory duty[2]. The purpose of the action is to compel a Community institution (here including the European Central Bank) to do something which, under Community law, it is legally bound to do. The action is admissible only if the institution has first been called upon to act[3]. The rules as to title and interest are essentially the same as those applying to the action of annulment, except that the privileged applicants are the Community institutions, so including the Parliament and technically the Court of Auditors. A natural or legal person must show that the institution had a duty to 'address an act to him' – ie, take a decision which, if unfavourable, he could have attacked under article 173[4]. It is a most difficult action successfully to pursue, and this has occurred only rarely[5]. An institution found by the Court to have failed in a duty under the Treaty is required to take the necessary measures to comply with the judgment[6].

104. Direct actions: staff cases (article 179). Relations between a Community institution and its servants are governed by the Staff Regulations, and any dispute arising therefrom falls within the jurisdiction of the Court of First Instance[7] which acts, in effect, as an employment appeal tribunal. Staff disputes must be raised by means of this process, and not under article 173 if the case relates to a matter covered by the Staff Regulations[8]. Judgments in staff cases are now reported separately from the main reports of the Court[9].

105. Direct actions: the action of damages or indemnity (articles 178 and 215(2)). As it has developed so far[10], the action for damages or indemnity

---

1 EC Treaty, art 176, 2nd para; see para 105 below.
2 Court of Session Act 1988, c 36, s 45(b).
3 EC Treaty, art 175, 2nd para.
4 Ibid, art 175, 3rd para. See Case 246/81 *Bethell v Commission* [1982] ECR 2277, [1982] 3 CMLR 300.
5 Case 13/83 *European Parliament v Council* [1985] ECR 1513, [1986] 1 CMLR 138; Case C-107/91 *ENU v Commission* [1993] ECR I-599 (a case under the corresponding provision of the Euratom Treaty). However, a complainant in competition matters (see para 238 below) is entitled to the adoption of an act by the Commission; see Case T-28/90 *Asia Motor France v Commission* [1992] ECR II 85, [1992] 5 CMLR 431; Case T-74/92 *Ladbroke Racing (Deutschland) GmbH v Commission*, judgment of 24 January 1995, not yet reported.
6 EC Treaty, art 176, 1st para.
7 Ibid, art 179; Decision 88/591 (para 84 above), art 3(1).
8 Hence including challenges by would-be recruits to the Community institutions; see Case T-72/89 *Viciano v Commission* [1990] ECR II-57.
9 See Appendix II.
10 The scope of this action is only beginning to be explored. For a full discussion of the numerous unresolved problems see Schermers et al (eds) *Non-Contractual Liability of the European Communities* (Nijhoff 1988). As to damages against national authorities see para 141 below.

under articles 178 and 215(2) of the Treaty is essentially an action in tort or action of reparation, the ground of action being that the Community or its servants have in the performance of their duties[1] unlawfully caused loss or damage. Fault (*culpa*), injury and causation must be proved. Where the allegedly injurious act is a negligent act or omission of an administrative nature, liability is relatively easy to prove[2]. Where the act is legislative, the injured party must show a clear breach on the part of the Community institution(s) of a superior rule of law for the protection of the individual[3] – in effect, a breach of one of the general principles of Community law[4]. The action of damages or indemnity is an independent form of action and unrelated to the action of annulment[5], although in practice the two are often raised together or the latter precedes the former. The action of damages must be raised within five years of the occurrence of the injury or of the time when the injured party ought reasonably to have known of it[6]. Serious difficulties arise in attributing wrongful conduct where national authorities are responsible for administering an allegedly unlawful Community act[7].

106. References for a preliminary ruling (article 177). The jurisdiction which now accounts for the largest number of cases before the Court of Justice consists in requests for preliminary rulings under article 177 of the Treaty. Modelled upon German and Italian constitutional procedures, this form of process is known in French as the *renvoi préjudiciel* – reference before judgment, which more accurately describes what it involves. The purpose is to enable a national court, faced with a problem of Community law in a case pending before it, to obtain an authoritative ruling from the Court of Justice on the law to be applied. A national court or tribunal[8] which, in the course of proceedings before it, encounters a question involving the interpretation of

1 Damages for injury caused by the Community or its servants *not* in the performance of their duties are a matter for the law (and the courts) of the place where the injury occurred.
2 See eg Case 145/83 *Adams v Commission* [1985] ECR 3539, [1986] 1 CMLR 506.
3 Case 5/71 *Schöppenstedt v Council* [1971] ECR 975; Case 83 & 94/76, 4, 15 & 40/77 *Bayerische HNL v Council and Commission* [1978] ECR 1209, [1978] 3 CMLR 566. For an instance in which these tests have been satisfied see Case C-104/89 *Mulder v Council and Commission* [1992] ECR I-3061.
4 See paras 152ff below.
5 Case 175/84 *Krohn v Commission* [1986] ECR 753, [1987] 1 CMLR 745.
6 Statute of the Court of Justice, art 43; Case 145/83 *Adams v Commission* [1985] ECR 3539, [1986] 1 CMLR 506.
7 See eg Case 175/84 *Krohn v Commission* [1986] ECR 753, [1987] 1 CMLR 745; Cases 106-20/87 *Asteris AE v Ministry of the Economy* [1988] ECR 5515; Case C-104/89 *Mulder v Council and Commission* [1992] ECR I-3061; Cases C-106 & 317/90 & 129/91 *Emerald Meats v Commission* [1993] ECR I-209, [1994] 1 CMLR 505.
8 As to what constitutes a court or tribunal (both English terms being required to encompass *juridiction, Gericht, rechterlijke instantie*) for these purposes see Case 61/65 *Vaasen-Goebbels v Bestuur van het Beambtenfonds voor het Mijnbedrijf* [1966] ECR 261; Case 246/80 *Broekmeulen v Huisarts Registratie Commissie* [1981] ECR 2311, [1982] 1 CMLR 91; Case 14/86 *Pretore di Salò v Persons Unknown* [1987] ECR 2545.

Community law or the validity of an act of a Community institution[1], can stay (sist) those proceedings and refer that question to the Court of Justice[2]. The ruling of the Court of Justice is transmitted back to, and is binding upon, the national court, which must apply it in disposing of the case[3].

107. The decision to refer. Any national court or tribunal may request a preliminary ruling when it considers that a decision on a question of Community law 'is necessary to enable it to give judgment'[4]. The discretion to do so rests with the national court alone; it may do so of its own motion, and is under no obligation to do so at the request of one or even all of the parties. The Court of Justice may not question the decision to refer[5] and must deal with the reference save in the most exceptional circumstances[6]. In England the Court of Appeal has set aside an order of the Divisional Court making a reference because, there being no reasonable doubt as to the correct application of Community law (which could be determined 'with complete confidence'), it was unnecessary to seek a ruling from the Court of Justice[7]. In Scotland, the decision of a sheriff to refer is subject to appeal only if his exercise of discretion was plainly wrong[8]. The discretion to refer is otherwise subject to two exceptions only. First, where a question of interpretation or validity is at issue before a national court or tribunal from which there is no

---

1 The Treaty refers to the validity and interpretation of acts of 'the institutions of the Community and of the ECB' (art 177, 1st para). Technically there are five Community institutions (see para 44 above). However, if the criteria for annulment of a Community act under art 173 were applied, an act of any Community authority capable of producing legal effects would be susceptible to examination and invalidation under art 177.

2 EC Treaty, art 177, 1st para.

3 Case 52/76 *Benedetti v Munari* [1977] ECR 163.

4 EC Treaty, art 177, 2nd para.

5 See eg Case 26/62 *van Gend en Loos v Nederlandse Tariefcommissie* [1962] ECR 1, [1963] CMLR 105.

6 In a very few cases the Court of Justice has declined jurisdiction on the grounds that the questions referred were too vague or the reference amounted to an abuse of process (see Case 104/79 *Foglia v Novello* (No 1) [1980] ECR 745, [1981] 1 CMLR 45; Case 244/80 *Foglia v Novello* (No 2) [1981] ECR 3045, [1982] 1 CMLR 585; Case C-83/91 *Meilicke v ORGA Meyer* [1992] ECR I-4871; Case C-428/93 *Monin Automobiles* (No 2) [1994] ECR I-1707) or where the referring court had failed to provide sufficient information as to the factual and legal background to the case to enable the Court adequately to identify the issues (see Case C-320/90 *Telemarsicabruzzo v Circostel* [1993] ECR I-393; Case C-157/92 *Pretore di Genova v Banchero* [1993] ECR I-1085; Case C-386/92 *Monin Automobiles* (No 1) [1993] ECR I-2049; Case C-378/93 *La Pyramide* [1994] ECR I-3999).

7 *R v International Stock Exchange of the United Kingdom and the Republic of Ireland, ex parte Else* [1993] 1 All ER 420, [1993] 2 CMLR 677. See also the earlier judgment of *Bulmer v Bollinger* [1974] Ch 401, [1974] 2 CMLR 91 (CA).

8 *Procurator Fiscal, Elgin v Cowie and Wood* 1991 SLT 401, [1990] 3 CMLR 445 (J). By comparison, the Irish Supreme Court held that the discretion to refer is so unfettered that a decision to refer cannot be reviewed in any circumstances; see *Campus Oil Ltd v Minister for Industry and Energy* [1984] 1 CMLR 479.

appeal, that court or tribunal *must* refer the question to the Court of Justice[1], unless the matter in question has already been decided by the Court of Justice or the correct application of Community law is so obvious as to leave no scope for any reasonable doubt (*acte clair*)[2]. Second, where the 'question' concerns the validity of a Community act[3], the Court of Justice alone has jurisdiction definitively to declare that act invalid[4]. Consequently, the national court must refer such a question unless it is satisfied that the Community act is valid, as it is in any event presumed to be[5]. Having referred a question on validity of a Community act, the national court may *ad interim* suspend application of national implementing measures based upon it, provided that certain conditions are met[6]. Having declared an act to be invalid, the Court may declare all or some of its provisions to be operative[7]. Procedure and forms for use of article 177 have been adopted into British rules of court[8].

108. Temporal limitation of preliminary rulings. The Court of Justice may, in the judgment making the ruling, limit its retrospective effect[9]. Such

---

1 EC Treaty, art 177, 3rd para. There is debate as to the courts or tribunals to which this obligation applies, ie whether it applies only to courts against whose decision there is never a right of recourse, or also to courts against whose decision there is no (or there is unlikely to be) right of recourse in the instant case. Lord Denning MR (and British courts generally) clearly favours the former approach (*Bulmer v Bollinger* [1974] Ch 401 at 420, [1974] 2 All ER 1226 at 1233 (CA)), the Court of Justice implicitly the latter (Case 6/64 *Costa v ENEL* [1964] ECR 585, [1964] CMLR 425). The dangers inherent in the former approach are well illustrated by the English case of *Magnavision v General Optical Council* [1987] 2 CMLR 262 (QBD).

2 Case 283/81 *CILFIT v Ministero della Sanità* [1982] ECR 3415, [1983] 1 CMLR 472. On the House of Lords' view of when a question is so clear from doubt as to absolve it from the duty to refer see *Henn and Darby v DPP* [1981] AC 850, [1980] 2 All ER 166; *Garland v British Rail Engineering Ltd* [1983] 2 AC 751, [1982] 2 All ER 402. However, in *R v London Borough Transport Committee, ex parte Freight Transport Association* [1992] 1 CMLR 5, the House of Lords was strongly urged to refer but refused to do so. Owing to the urgency of the proceedings a court of last instance is not required to have recourse to the Court of Justice in interlocutory proceedings for an interim order; Case 107/76 *Hoffmann-La Roche v Centrafarm* [1977] ECR 957, [1977] 2 CMLR 334.

3 Questions addressing the validity of a Community act, as opposed to interpretation of a Community act or the Treaty, comprise the subject matter of roughly one in six preliminary references.

4 Case 314/85 *Foto-Frost v Hauptzollamt Lübeck-Ost* [1987] ECR 4199, [1988] 3 CMLR 57.

5 See para 102 above.

6 Cases 143/88 and C-92/89 *Zuckerfabriken Süderdithmarschen und Soest v Hauptzollämter Itzehoe und Paderborn* [1991] ECR I-415, [1993] 3 CMLR 1. Far more detailed guidance is expected from the Court in Case C-465/93 *Atlanta Fruit v Germany* (pending).

7 Case 112/83 *Société des Producteurs de Maïs v Administration des Douanes* [1985] ECR 719; Case C-228/92 *Roquette Frères v Hauptzollamt Geldern* [1994] ECR I-1445, applying art 174 by analogy; see para 102 above.

8 See eg in England and Wales, RSC, Ord 114, rr 1–6; County Court Rules, Ord 19, r 11; Crown Court Rules 1982 (SI 1982/1109), r 29; in Scotland, RC 65.2-65.5; Act of Adjournal (Consolidation) 1988, rr 63–67 and 113–118; and the Sheriff Courts (Scotland) Act 1907, c 51, Sch I, r 134.

9 See eg Case 43/75 *Defrenne v SABENA* (No 2) [1976] ECR 455, [1976] 2 CMLR 98; Case 292/88 *Barber v Guardian Royal Exchange* [1990] ECR I-1889, [1990] 2 CMLR 513; Case C-163/90 *Administration des Douanes et Droits Indirects v Legros* [1992] ECR I-4625.

temporal limitation will be applied only in exceptional circumstances[1] and cannot be applied retrospectively after the judgment making the ruling[2].

109. Preliminary rulings and international conventions. The Court of Justice may have jurisdiction similar to article 177 conferred upon it by international conventions to which the member states are parties. So, for example, Protocols to both the Brussels Judgments Convention[3] and the Rome Contracts Convention[4] provide that national courts may refer questions of interpretation of those conventions to the Court of Justice. In contradistinction to the EC Treaty, the power to refer is reserved in both cases to the higher appellate courts. Under both Conventions a member state or a Procurator General of a court of a member state may request from the Court of Justice a ruling on a point of law where a judgment of a national court of last instance is inconsistent with a judgment of a court of last instance in another member state or with a judgment of the Court itself. The ruling does not affect the judgment in question[5].

110. Indirect challenge of Community acts and the plea of illegality (article 184). It is very difficult for a natural or legal person (other than the addressee of an administrative act) to establish the title and interest necessary to raise an action of annulment of an act of a Community institution[6]. In particular, non-privileged applicants cannot challenge directly the lawfulness of legislative, or 'general' acts of the Community institutions. They can, however, challenge the application of such acts to them, where this involves an administrative act on the part of a Community authority or of a national authority. The administrative act is challenged, not on the ground that it is unlawful *per se*, but that it is based upon an unlawful parent act. Where the parent act has been applied by a subsequent national measure, the challenge must be mounted in the appropriate national court which can then ask the Court of Justice, under article 177, to rule upon the validity of the parent (Community) act. The Court of Justice has ruled that a declaration of invalidity in a preliminary ruling under article 177 has effect *erga omnes*[7]. The practical difference between annulment (article 173) and invalidity (article 177) therefore lies in the means by which the issue is raised rather than in the

---

1 Case C-163/90 *Legros* [1992] ECR 1-4625 at 4670.
2 See eg Case 309/85 *Barra v Belgium* [1988] ECR 355; Case C-163/90 *Legros*, above; Case C-57/93 *Vroege v NCIV Instituut voor Volkshuisvesting* [1994] ECR I-4541.
3 Protocol to the Brussels Convention (see para 124 below) of 3 June 1971, consolidated text in OJ C97, 11.4.83, p 12.
4 First Protocol to the Rome Convention (see para 124 below) of 19 December 1988, L48, 20.2.89, p 1. At the time of writing this protocol has yet to enter into force. A protocol to the Convention on Mutual Recognition of Companies (see para 219 below) makes similar provision, but the Convention itself has yet to enter into force.
5 Protocol to the Brussels Convention, art 4; Protocol to the Rome Convention, art 3.
6 See para 101 above.
7 Case 66/80 *International Chemical Corporation v Amministrazione delle Finanze dello Stato* [1981] ECR 1191, [1983] 2 CMLR 593. Great care should be taken with this judgment, as the English text (in both ECR and CMLR) is misleading on this point.

legal outcome. Where the parent act has been applied by a Community authority, the act applying it must be challenged by a direct action before the Court of First Instance, normally under article 173. In the context of such proceedings the lawfulness of the parent act can be challenged, without time limit, by the so-called 'plea of illegality' (*exception d'illégalité*) under article 184. If the plea is successful, the administrative act, deprived of its legal foundation, is annulled, rendering the general, parent act 'inapplicable' to the person concerned. Article 184 does *not* constitute an independent form of action; the plea of illegality may be raised only within the context of other proceedings properly before the Court[1].

111. Appeal from the Court of First Instance. An appeal against a judgment of the Court of First Instance lies to the Court of Justice on points of law only[2]. The appeal must be lodged within two months of the notification of the Court of First Instance judgment to the parties[3]. Where a judgment of the Court of First Instance has annulled a regulation the judgment takes effect only when an appeal becomes time-barred or is dismissed[4]. An appeal may be raised by one of the parties to proceedings before the Court of First Instance; by a member state or a Community institution, even where they were not parties to, and did not intervene in, proceedings at first instance; and by third parties if (apparently) they had intervened at first instance and if the judgment directly affects their interests[5]. An appeal against an interlocutory order of the Court of First Instance, for example a refusal to permit a third party to intervene or to grant interim measures, may be taken directly to the Court of Justice by way of summary procedure[6]. If an appeal is successful, the Court of Justice sets aside the judgment of the Court of First Instance, and may either remit it back for rehearing or, where the state of proceedings so permits, decide the case itself[7]. Where a case is remitted back, the Court of First Instance is bound by the judgment of the Court of Justice on points of law[8].

112. Opinions. The Court of Justice may be called upon by a member state or by a Community institution to give an opinion on the compatibility with the

---

1 Cases 31 & 33/62 *Wöhrmann v EEC Commission* [1962] ECR 501, [1963] CMLR 152.
2 EC Treaty, art 168a(1) and Statute of the Court of Justice, arts 49-54.
3 Statute of the Court of Justice, art 49. A case taken on appeal to the Court of Justice is given a new 'C' number and is distinguished by an additional letter 'P', for *pourvoi* (appeal).
4 Ibid, art 53. In other cases a judgment of the Court of First Instance can be suspended only by interim order of the Court of Justice; see para 113 below.
5 Ibid, art 49.
6 Ibid, art 50. On intervention and interim measures see para 96 above and 113 below.
7 Ibid, art 54. See eg Case C-137/92P *Commission v BASF* (PVC) [1994] ECR I-2555; Case C-360/92P *Publishers Association v Commission*, judgment of 17 January 1995, not yet reported. However, where the successful appeal has been raised by other than a party to proceedings before the Court of First Instance, the Court of Justice may, if it considers it necessary, declare some or all of the legal effects of the original judgment to be definitive for the parties; Statute of the Court of Justice, art 54, 3rd para.
8 Statute of the Court of Justice, art 54, 2nd para.

EC Treaty of a proposed agreement between the Community and a third state, group of states or international organisation[1]. If the Court finds the agreement to be inconsistent with the Treaty, the Community may proceed only if the agreement is altered in accordance with the Court's opinion or the Treaty is amended[2]. This jurisdiction may be invoked to determine whether the Community has exclusive or shared competence to enter into such an agreement[3]. The Court may also be asked to give an opinion as to whether certain proposed amendments to the ECSC Treaty are compatible with that Treaty[4].

113. Interim measures. An action raised before the Court of Justice has no suspensory effect[5]. However, the Court may, upon an application from a party to a case before it, order that the application of a contested Community act be suspended 'if it considers that the circumstances so require'[5] or in any action order any 'necessary' interim or interlocutory measures[6]. An application for interim order is by way of summary procedure[7]. The order may be, and usually is, made by the President sitting alone[7]. The Court is competent to suspend the application of any Community act (including a judgment of the Court of First Instance) or of any national measure which is in issue in the main action, and it will do so where there is a *prima facie* case, urgency and a likelihood of serious and irreparable injury by the continuing application of that measure[8]. An order of the Court of First Instance granting or refusing interim measures may be appealed directly to the Court of Justice by way of summary procedure[9].

114. The Court of Justice and EMU. The Treaty on European Union created a number of 'financial organs' with responsibility to administer economic and monetary union (EMU). There are special procedures by which these

---

1 EC Treaty, art 228(6).
2 Ibid. For an example of an opinion which held up Community ratification of an international agreement see Opinion 1/91 *re the EEA Agreement* [1991] ECR I-6079, [1992] 1 CMLR 245.
3 See eg Opinion 1/94 *re the World Trade Organisation*, opinion of 15 November 1994, not yet reported.
4 ECSC Treaty, art 95. For an example see Opinion 1/61 [1961] ECR 243. See further para 299 below.
5 EC Treaty, art 185.
6 Ibid, art 186. Interim measures cannot be sought without raising a 'main action' to which the application for interim measures is ancillary; Rules of Procedure of the Court of Justice, art 83(1), Rules of Procedure of the Court of First Instance, art 104(1). An application for interim measures is given the same number as the main action but may be distinguished by an additional letter 'R', for *référé*.
7 Statute of the Court of Justice, art 36.
8 Rules of Procedure of the Court of Justice, art 83(2), Rules of Procedure of the Court of First Instance, art 104(2); for examples see Case C-246/89R *Commission v United Kingdom* [1989] ECR 3125; Case C-120/94R *Commission v Greece* [1994] ECR I-3037.
9 See para 111 above.

institutions may raise matters within their province before the Court. They are indicated below[1].

115. The Court of Justice and the EEA Treaty. The Treaty establishing the European Economic Area (EEA) provides that the contracting parties may agree to confer upon the Court of Justice limited jurisdiction to provide 'advisory rulings' upon the interpretation of the EEA Treaty. They have not done so[2].

(4) THE COURT OF AUDITORS

116. The Court of Auditors. An independent Court of Auditors was first created in 1975 by the Treaty amending Certain Financial Provisions[3]. By virtue of the Treaty on European Union it was elevated to the status of a full Community institution[4]. It consists of fifteen – in practice one from each member state – 'especially qualified' members with experience of external audit bodies appointed by the Council, after consulting the Parliament, for a six-year term[5]. Its task is to carry out the audit[6]. To this end it is to 'examine the accounts of all revenue and expenditure of the Community'[7] and, in particular, 'examine whether all revenue has been received and all expenditure incurred in a lawful and regular manner and whether the financial management has been sound'[8]. The audit is carried out in liaison with national audit bodies or government departments[9]. The Court of Auditors is required to publish an annual report[10]. Its prominence has increased with allegations of financial mismanagement of Community expenditure, and it has delivered a number of stinging rebukes to the responsible authorities. The Court of Auditors is based in Luxembourg.

(5) OTHER ORGANS

117. The Economic and Social Committee. The EC Treaty provides for the appointment of an Economic and Social Committee with advisory

---

1 See paras 121-122 below.
2 See further Appendix I below.
3 See EEC Treaty, art 206(1), now repealed. The French name is *Cour des Comptes*; the nearest United Kingdom equivalent is the National Audit Office.
4 EC Treaty, art 4.
5 Ibid, art 188b(1-3).
6 Ibid, art 188a.
7 Ibid, art 188c(1).
8 Ibid, art 188c(2).
9 Ibid, art 188c(3).
10 Ibid, art 188c(4).

status[1]. In terms of the Treaty it is to consist of 'representatives of the various categories of economic and social activity, in particular, representatives of producers, farmers, carriers, workers, dealers, craftsmen, professional occupations and representatives of the general public'[2]. The Committee must be consulted by the Council before certain legislative acts are adopted. It has adopted its own Rules of Procedure[3] and has its own secretariat, chamber and offices in Brussels. The Treaty provides that 'the composition of the Committee shall take account of the need to ensure adequate representation of the various categories of economic and social activity'[4]. It consists now of 222 members drawn from the member states by fixed allocation[5]. In practice, they are appointed and work in three groups: Group I representing employers, Group II employees and Group III others (eg, consumers, representatives of the liberal professions, farmers).

118. The Committee of the Regions. The entry into force of the Treaty on European Union created a Committee of the Regions with advisory status[6], which came into being in January 1994[7]. It consists of 222 members drawn by fixed allocation from 'representatives of regional or local bodies'[8]. It is required to be consulted by the Council before certain legislative acts are adopted, principally those which have an impact upon regional constitutional competences in various of the federal or devolved member states or upon local government[9]. It must also be informed each time an opinion is sought from the Economic and Social Committee and may issue an opinion if it considers that the proposal has regional implications[10]. It has adopted its own Rules of Procedure[11] and its seat is in Brussels, sharing the same infrastructure as the Economic and Social Committee[12]. The creation of the Committee was a (modest) step towards bringing regional influence to bear upon the Community legislative machinery.

119. The European Investment Bank (EIB). The EC Treaty established a European Investment Bank (EIB) with legal personality[13]. Its task is 'to

---

1 EC Treaty, arts 4(2) and 193, 1st para. See generally arts 193-198. The Committee also acts under the Euratom Treaty (see arts 165-170) but not under the ECSC Treaty, for which there is an analogous body called the Consultative Committee (ECSC Treaty, arts 7, 18).
2 EC Treaty, art 193, 2nd para.
3 See OJ L257, 5.10.94, p 32.
4 EC Treaty, art 195(1), 2nd para.
5 EC Treaty, art 194.
6 EC Treaty, arts 4(2) and 198a, 1st para. The Committee acts only under the EC Treaty.
7 Decision 94/65, OJ L31, 4.2.94, p 29.
8 EC Treaty, art 198a.
9 For example, proposals in the fields of education (art 126(4)), culture (art 128(5)), public health (art 129), trans-European networks (art 129d) and economic and social cohesion (arts 130b, 130d, 130e). On all of these see paras 281-283 below.
10 EC Treaty, art 198c(3).
11 See OJ L132, 27.5.94, p 49.
12 See Protocol on the Economic and Social Committee and the Committee of the Regions.
13 EC Treaty, arts 4b and 198d.

contribute by having recourse to the capital market and utilizing its own resources, to the balanced and steady development of the common market in the interest of the Community'. For this purpose the Bank 'shall, operating on a non-profit making basis, grant loans and give guarantees which facilitate the financing of . . . : (a) projects for developing less-developed regions; (b) projects for modernizing or converting undertakings or for developing fresh activities; (c) projects of common interest to several Member States'[1]. Projects in the latter two categories must be 'of such size or nature that they cannot be entirely financed by the various means available in the individual Member States'[1]. The Statute of the Bank establishes the system of direction and management and lays down more detailed rules as to the ways in which loan and guarantee operations may be carried out[2]. The Board of Directors of the Bank is competent to raise enforcement proceedings before the Court of Justice, analogous to article 169 proceedings, where member states fail in their obligations under the EIB Statute[3]. The seat of the EIB is Luxembourg.

120. The European Investment Fund. In 1994 a European Investment Fund was created by the Board of Governors of the EIB[4]. The Fund has legal personality and financial autonomy. The founder members of the Fund are the European Community (represented by the Commission), the EIB and a number of financial institutions. Its task is to support financially the development of trans-European networks and small and medium-sized enterprises. The seat of the Fund is Luxembourg.

121. The European Monetary Institute (EMI). In January 1994 – the beginning of the second stage of economic and monetary union[5] – the European Monetary Institute (EMI) was created[6]. Its membership comprises the central banks of each member state, and it is directed and managed by a Council composed of a President appointed by the common accord of the member states and the governors of each of the central banks. The EMI has legal personality, is competent to adopt opinions and recommendations and guidelines and decisions addressed to the national central banks, the latter two subject to judicial review by the Court of Justice. Its primary task is to assist in progress towards the third stage of economic and monetary union, which is discussed more fully below[7]. During the second stage it enjoys the power to raise actions before the Court of Justice which is to be conferred upon the European Central Bank when it comes into existence. The EMI will then be liquidated.

---

1 EC Treaty, art 198e.
2 EC Treaty, Protocol on the Statute of the European Investment Bank.
3 EC Treaty, art 180.
4 Statute of the European Investment Fund, OJ L173, 7.7.94, p 1.
5 See para 264 below.
6 See EC Treaty, art 109f and Protocol on the European Monetary Institute.
7 See paras 262-267 below.

122. The European System of Central Banks (ESCB) and the European Central Bank (ECB). The EC Treaty provides for the creation of a European System of Central Banks (ESCB) and the European Central Bank (ECB) at the beginning of the third stage of EMU[1]. Both are to have legal personality and are to be completely independent in the performance of their tasks[2]. The ESCB is to be composed of the ECB and the national central banks and governed by the decision-making bodies of the ECB[3]. The ECB is to be governed by an Executive Board, comprising six members appointed by the common accord of the governments of the member states participating in EMU[4] for an eight year non-renewable term[5], and a Governing Council, comprising the Executive Board and the governors of each of the participating national central banks[6]. The ECB may adopt legislative measures except directives and impose fines and periodic penalty payments upon undertakings[7] subject to the judicial control of the Court of First Instance[8], and the Governing Council may raise enforcement proceedings before the Court of Justice where a member state or a national bank has failed in its obligations under the Treaty or under the Statute[9]. It is to be assisted by an Economic and Financial Committee[10], which is to replace the Monetary Committee established at the entry into force of the TEU[11], and a General Council[12]. The primary function of the ESCB and the ECB is to oversee economic and monetary union, which is discussed below[13]. The seat of the ECB is to be Frankfurt.

123. Other bodies. Between 1990 and 1993 a number of Community acts proposed the creation of other bodies for the administration of Community affairs. With agreement reached in 1993 on their seats[14], the following bodies were established: the European Environment Agency (based in Copenhagen); the European Training Foundation (Turin); Office for Veterinary and Plant Health Inspection (Dublin); European Monitoring Centre for Drugs and Drug Addiction (Lisbon); European Agency for Evaluation of Medicinal Products (London); European Centre for the Development of Vocational Training (moved from Berlin to Thessaloniki);

---

1 EC Treaty, arts 4a and 105-106 and Protocol on the European System of Central Banks and of the European Central Bank (hereinafter ESCB/ECB Statute).
2 EC Treaty, arts 106(2) and 107, ESCB/ECB Statute, arts 7 and 9.
3 EC Treaty, arts 106(1) and 106(3).
4 See paras 266-267 below.
5 EC Treaty, art 109a and ESCB/ECB Statute, art 11. The term of appointment is intended to promote the independence from political interference of the members of the Board.
6 EC Treaty, art 109a and ESCB/ECB Statute, art 10.
7 EC Treaty, arts 108a(1) and 108a(3) and ESCB/ECB Statute, art 34.
8 EC Treaty, art 173 and ESCB/ECB Statute, art 35.1.
9 EC Treaty, art 180 and ESCB/ECB Statute, arts 35.5 and 35.6.
10 EC Treaty, art 109c(2).
11 Ibid, art 109c(1).
12 ESCB/ECB Statute, arts 45-47.
13 See paras 262-267 below.
14 Decision of the Representatives of the Governments of the Member States on the Location of the Seats of Certain Bodies and Departments, OJ C323, 30.11.93, p 1.

Agency for Health and Safety at Work (Bilbao); Office for Harmonisation in the Internal Market (Trade Marks and Designs) (Alicante); and the Europol Drugs Unit (the Hague). The Euratom Treaty also attached to the Commission a consultative Scientific and Technical Committee[1] and established an Agency with right of option on, and important administrative powers in, the supply of ores, source materials and special fissile materials[2].

1 Euratom Treaty, art 134.
2 Ibid, arts 52ff.

3. THE SOURCES AND METHODS OF COMMUNITY LAW

124. Sources. The sources of European Community law can be categorised as follows:

(1) (a) the treaties:
- (i) the 'founding Treaties' establishing the three Communities;
- (ii) treaties amplifying, modifying or amending the founding Treaties, notably and principally the Single European Act and the Treaty on European Union, the latter also comprising the constitutional basis of the European Union;
- (iii) the Treaties of Accession providing for the accession of new member states[1];
- (iv) protocols, conventions, and acts ancillary to the founding Treaties and the Treaties of Accession;

(b) conventions between the member states distinct from, but concluded within the context of, the founding Treaties, notably the Brussels Judgments Convention[2] and the Rome Contracts Convention[3];

(c) agreements with third countries, concluded either by the Community and the member states together or by the Community alone, notably
- (i) the Treaty establishing the European Economic Area (EEA);
- (ii) the Lomé Convention with the ACP countries;
- (iii) the 'Europe Agreements' with some of the countries of Eastern Europe;
- (iv) other 'association agreements';
- (v) other agreements[4];

(2) legislative acts and lawfully binding decisions of the Community institutions acting under the powers conferred upon them by the treaties, including judgments of the Court of Justice in so far as they are binding on the parties and upon the courts and tribunals of the member states;

(3) legislative acts and lawfully binding decisions of the governments of the member states meeting in the Council and acting under the powers conferred upon them by the treaties[5];

---

1 See para 300 below.
2 (Brussels) Convention of 27 September 1968 on Jurisdiction and Enforcement of Judgments in Civil and Commercial Matters, OJ C97, 11.4.83, p 2; Cmnd 7395. The United Kingdom (and Denmark and Ireland) acceded to the Convention by virtue of an Accession Convention of 9 October 1978, OJ L304, 30.10.78, p 1; it is incorporated in the United Kingdom by the Civil Jurisdiction and Judgments Act 1982, c 27, in force from 1 January 1987.
3 (Rome) Convention of 19 June 1980 on the Law Applicable to Contractual Obligations, OJ L266, 9.10.80, p 1; incorporated in the United Kingdom by the Contracts (Applicable Law) Act 1990, c 36, and in force from 1 April 1991 for contracts signed after 1 July 1991.
4 See para 269 below.
5 See para 57 above.

(4) the jurisprudence (case law) of the Court of Justice in so far as it states or applies principles of Community law or provides an interpretation of the treaties or of legislative provisions in cases involving different parties;
(5) 'general principles of law' derived from the constitutions and laws of the member states or from international agreements, such as the European Convention on Human Rights, to which the member states, but not the Community, are party[1].

125. Ancillary sources. Although they are not strictly speaking 'sources' of law, the following may be invoked as offering guidance to the interpretation and application of Community law:
(1) declarations, communiqués and resolutions of the Community institutions;
(2) notices and other statements of policy issued by the Commission;
(3) answers to parliamentary questions in the European Parliament;
(4) learned opinion, such as academic writing (*la doctrine* being a respected guide to law in continental member states) and other respected reports such as those of the House of Lords Select Committee on the European Communities.

126. Languages. The ECSC Treaty was drawn up in French and French is its sole authentic language text. Otherwise the basic Treaty texts, conventions and international agreements exist in twelve language versions – Spanish, Danish, German, Greek, English, French, Irish[2], Italian, Dutch, Portuguese, Finnish and Swedish – all equally authentic. All these languages except Irish are 'official languages' of the Community[3]. All legislative acts are adopted in all official languages, each text equally authentic. Where a discrepancy emerges as amongst the various language versions, the Court will have recourse to all of them in order to determine the legislative intent and purpose[4]. Decisions and other administrative acts addressed to particular member state(s) or person(s) are adopted in the language(s) of the addressee(s).

127. Methods of interpretation. It is sometimes suggested that the approach of the Court of Justice to the interpretation of the sources of Community law is in some sense 'continental' and unlike that of the common law. This is true to the extent that the Court of Justice does not adopt the literal method of interpretation customarily adopted by United Kingdom courts in construing statutes, and that judgments of the Court of Justice do not constitute binding precedent the effect of which can be altered only by legislation[5]. In other

---

1 See paras 152ff below.
2 Not all international agreements exist in an Irish version.
3 Regulation 1, JO 17, 6.10.58, p 385 (S Edn 1952-58, p 59), as amended. However, Irish is a language of the Court of Justice; see para 91 above.
4 Case 29/69 *Stauder v Ulm* [1969] ECR 419, [1970] CMLR 112; Case 19/83 *Wendelboe v LJ Music* [1985] ECR 457; Case C-327/91 *France v Commission* [1994] ECR I-3641, [1994] 5 CMLR 517; see also paras 129, 130 below.
5 See para 132 below.

respects the suggestion is based upon a misconception as to the nature of the sources of Community law.

128. Contractual nature of the Treaties. The Treaties themselves are not legislative acts but international agreements. They state the purposes for which they have been concluded and create reciprocal rights and obligations for the signatory states and their nationals. The courts of the United Kingdom are accustomed to interpret contracts in such a way as to give them business efficacy and, where the parties have expressly stated the purpose of the contract, in such a way as to give effect to that purpose. The approach of the Court of Justice to the interpretation of the Treaties is not materially different, and is consistent with the rule of international law that 'a treaty shall be interpreted in good faith in accordance with the ordinary meaning to be given to the terms of the treaty [including its preamble and annexes] in their context and in the light of its object and purpose'[1].

129. Context of interpretation. The approach of the Court of Justice to the interpretation of legislative and other binding acts of the Community institutions is equally understandable in its context. In the first place, the powers of the institutions are derived from the Treaties and can be exercised only in a manner compatible with the Treaties. In the second place, the Treaties provide that legislative and other binding acts of the institutions must 'state the reasons on which they are based and ... refer to any proposals or opinions which were required to be obtained'[2]. That being so, it would be inappropriate to construe the dispositive provisions of such acts as if they were sections of a United Kingdom statute.

130. The autonomy of Community law. Community law is an autonomous legal system drawing inspiration from, but independent of, the legal systems of the member states[3]. The consequences for the interpretation of Community law were summarised by the Court of Justice as follows:

'To begin with, it must be borne in mind that Community legislation is drafted in several languages and that the different language versions are all equally authentic. An interpretation of a provision of Community law thus involves a comparison of the different language versions.

It must also be borne in mind, even when the different language versions are entirely in accord with one another, that Community law uses terminology which is peculiar to it. Furthermore, it must be emphasized that legal concepts do not necessarily have the same meaning in Community law and in the law of the various member states.

Finally, every provision of Community law must be placed in its context and

---

1 Vienna Convention on the Law of Treaties (TS 58 (1980); Cmnd 7964), art 31.
2 EC Treaty, art 190; see para 144 below.
3 See eg Case 28/67 *Mölkerei-Zentrale Westfalen/Lippe GmbH v Hauptzollamt Paderborn* [1968] ECR 143, [1968] CMLR 187.

interpreted in the light of the provisions of Community law as a whole, regard being had to the objectives thereof and to its state of evolution at the date on which the provision in question is to be applied'[1].

131. The *'acquis communautaire'*. Community law is an evolving legal order. Its substantive rules, rights, obligations and remedies develop over time, and the Court of Justice makes frequent reference to 'the present state of Community law'. However, there is a presumption that evolution, or 'progression', is in one direction, that at any point in time there can be identified a state of the development of the law which embodies essential rights, obligations and remedies and which cannot be reversed[2]. This state of the law is referred to as the *acquis communautaire* and is fundamental to the continuous development of the Community legal order.

132. Precedent. In the United Kingdom the courts are directed by statute to take notice of judgments of the Court of Justice on the meaning or effect of the Treaty and of Community legislation[3]. It is important to understand precisely what this means. A declaratory judgment under article 169 has the force of *res judicata* and is binding for the defaulting member state. A preliminary ruling under article 177 binds the referring court in relation to the case in which the reference has been made. In cases where a successful appeal to the Court of Justice is remitted back to the Court of First Instance, the latter is bound by the former's judgment on points of law. These are the only circumstances in which a judgment of the Court of Justice is formally 'binding' in the sense that another court must comply with it. But the Court has also said that a declaration of invalidity in article 177 proceedings may be relied upon by other national courts[4] and that there is no obligation for a national court of last resort to refer to the Court of Justice a question of Community law where 'the Community provision in question has already been interpreted by the Court'[5]. These *dicta* imply that a previous decision on the interpretation of a specific legislative provision can, for practical purposes, be treated as binding. Further, the Court frequently makes reference to the consistent or well-established case law (*jurisprudence constante*) of the Court, implying that a series of decisions in the same sense upon an issue of principle can be treated as binding authority. Nevertheless, as in any case law-based system, the Court may depart from, or modify, its previous case law, and has on two occasions expressly 'reversed' previous judgments[6]. So, it is always open to a national court to invite the Court of Justice to 'reconsider' a previous decision or line of case law.

---

1 Case 283/81 *CILFIT v Ministero della Sanità* [1982] ECR 3415 at 3430, [1983] 1 CMLR 472 at 491.
2 See eg Cases 80 & 81/77 *Société les Commissionnaires Réunis v Receveur des Douanes* [1978] ECR 927.
3 European Communities Act 1972, s 3.
4 Case 66/80 *International Chemical Corporation v Amministrazione delle Finanze dello Stato* [1981] ECR 1191, [1983] 2 CMLR 593; see para 110 above.
5 Case 283/81 *CILFIT v Ministero della Sanità* [1982] ECR 3415, [1983] 1 CMLR 472; see para 107.
6 Case C-10/89 *SA CNL-Sucal NV v HAG GF AG* (Hag II) [1990] ECR I-3711, [1990] 3 CMLR 571; Cases C-267-8/91 *Criminal Proceedings against Keck and Mithouard* [1993] ECR I-6097.

(1) THE NATURE AND ENFORCEMENT OF COMMUNITY LAW

133. Direct effect. In the early case of *Van Gend en Loos*[1] it was argued that, whilst the EEC Treaty conferred rights and obligations upon the signatory states, it did not confer rights upon individuals which they could enforce directly in their national courts. The Court of Justice disagreed; it said that:

> 'the Community constitutes a new legal order of international law, for the bene-
> fit of which the states have limited their sovereign rights, albeit within limited
> fields, and the subjects of which comprise not only the Member States but also
> their nationals[2]. Independently of the legislation of Member States, Community
> law therefore not only imposes obligations on individuals but is also intended to
> confer upon them rights which become part of their legal heritage'[3].

Hence the doctrine of 'direct effect', which holds that Community law is of itself capable of creating rights and obligations enforceable before national courts. As developed and refined by the Court of Justice[4], the doctrine applies where a Treaty or legislative provision:

* is clear and concise;
* is unconditional and unqualified and is not subject to the taking of any further measures on the part of a Community or national authority; and
* leaves no substantial discretion in its implementation to a Community or national authority.

In such circumstances, where the provision in question creates rights or obligations, it is said to have direct effect and may be enforced before the appropriate national court or tribunal. The Court of Justice has held that a number of articles of the Treaty have direct effect. It has also held directly effective a great mass of Community legislation which implements those Treaty rights and obligations which are not themselves directly effective. In terms of the European Communities Act 1972, rights created by directly effective Community law are 'enforceable Community rights' in the United Kingdom[5].

134. Primacy. In another early case, *Costa v ENEL*[6], it was argued that the Italian courts were bound to apply Italian legislation subsequent in date to the entry into force of the EEC Treaty. Again the Court of Justice disagreed:

> 'The integration into the laws of each Member State of provisions which derive
> from the Community, and more generally the terms and spirit of the Treaty,

---

1 Case 26/62 *Van Gend en Loos v Nederlandse Tariefcommissie* [1963] ECR 1, [1963] CMLR 105.
2 This formula was reiterated by the Court in a 1991 opinion verbatim, except that it substituted 'in ever wider fields' for 'albeit within limited fields'; see Opinion 1/91 *re the Draft EEA Treaty* [1991] ECR I-6079 at 6102, [1992] 1 CMLR 245 at 269.
3 [1963] ECR 1 at 12; [1963] CMLR 105 at 129. 'Heritage' is an inadequate translation of *patri-moine*; 'patrimonial rights' or 'assets' would be a more meaningful translation.
4 See eg Case 148/78 *Pubblico Ministero v Ratti* [1979] ECR 1629 at 1651, [1980] 1 CMLR 96 at 102 per Advocate General Reischl.
5 See para 136 below.
6 Case 6/64, [1964] ECR 585, [1964] CMLR 425.

make it impossible for the states, as a corollary, to accord precedence to a unilateral and subsequent measure over a legal system accepted by them on a basis of reciprocity. . . . The obligations undertaken under the Treaty establishing the Community would not be unconditional, but merely contingent, if they could be called in question by subsequent legislative acts of the signatories'[1].

This application of the doctrine of international law that *pacta sunt servanda* is known as the doctrine of the primacy (or supremacy) of Community law. It is a doctrine which is well known in federal systems where, in the event of conflict, the law of the federal authority will usually have precedence over the law of the regional authorities.

135. The status of Community law generally. The doctrine of direct effect seeks to ensure that rights accruing from Community law are available to the individual, whilst the doctrine of primacy ensures that such rights will take precedence over any conflicting national rule or practice. So far as Community law is concerned, the obligations imposed upon national courts and tribunals are clear, and are best stated in the *Simmenthal* judgment in 1978:

'[I]n accordance with the principle of the precedence of Community law, the relationship between provisions of the Treaty and directly applicable measures of the institutions on the one hand and the national law of the Member States on the other is such that those provisions and measures . . . render automatically inapplicable and conflicting provisions of current national law . . . [and] preclude the valid adoption of new national legislative measures to the extent to which they would be incompatible with Community provisions. . . . [E]very national court must, in a case within its jurisdiction, apply Community law in its entirety and protect rights which the latter confers on individuals and must accordingly set aside any provision of national law which may conflict with it, whether prior or subsequent to the Community rule'[2].

136. The status of Community law in the United Kingdom. Community law is incorporated into United Kingdom law by the European Communities Act 1972, which provides, in effect, that rights arising from the Treaty are 'enforceable Community rights' to be applied and enforced as part of the law of the United Kingdom[3]. There are, at least in theory, constitutional difficulties in applying the doctrine of primacy in a number of member states. In the United Kingdom the difficulty stems from the doctrine of parliamentary supremacy, according to which there are no entrenched laws and the provisions of an Act of Parliament will impliedly repeal any prior rule of law (which might include Community rules) with which they are inconsistent. The most authoritative judicial consideration of the meaning and breadth of the 1972 Act is now provided in the speech of Lord Bridge in *Factortame*:

---

1 [1964] ECR 585 at 593 and 594, [1964] CMLR 425 at 455.
2 Case 106/77 *Amministrazione delle Finanze dello Stato v Simmenthal* [1978] ECR 629 at 643, [1978] 3 CMLR 263 at 383.
3 European Communities Act 1972, s 2(1).

'If the supremacy within the European Community of Community law over national law was not always inherent in the EEC Treaty, it was certainly well established in the jurisprudence of the European Court of Justice long before the United Kingdom joined the Community. Thus, whatever limitations of its sovereignty Parliament accepted when it enacted the European Communities Act 1972 was entirely voluntary. Under the terms of the Act of 1972 it has always been clear that it is the duty of a United Kingdom court, when delivering final judgment, to override any rule of national law found to be in conflict with any directly enforceable rule of Community law'[1].

So, constitutional difficulties which, according to Lord Bridge, were in any event 'based on a misconception'[2], appear to be resolved. This is so where the Community right is embodied in terms which can be construed as having direct effect (an 'enforceable Community right'). Different problems arise with the enforcement of rights granted by provisions which are not directly effective[3].

137. Enforcement of Community rights before the Court of Justice. The EC Treaty provides for judicial review of acts of the Community institutions, through direct actions or references by the procedure of article 177, and an action for damages for loss caused by the Community and its institutions. In all these actions the Court of Justice has (or shares with the Court of First Instance) exclusive jurisdiction. They are discussed above[4].

138. Enforcement of Community rights before national courts. Since the day-to-day administration of most substantive aspects of Community law lies with national authorities, and since in accordance with the doctrine of direct effect Community law gives rise to rights and obligations enforceable by national courts, the availability of appropriate and satisfactory national remedies is an essential element in the proper application and enforcement of Community law.

139. Methods of enforcement. Where a person wishes to enforce a Community right against a public authority before a national court, the basic principle is that, in the absence of relevant Community rules, national

---

1 *R v Secretary of State for Transport, ex parte Factortame* [1991] 1 AC 603 at 658-659, [1990] 3 CMLR 375 at 379-380 (HL). For earlier *dicta* in the English courts see *Macarthys Ltd v Smith* [1979] 3 All ER 325 at 329, [1979] 3 CMLR 44 (CA) at 47 per Lord Denning; *Garland v British Rail Engineering* [1983] 2 AC 751 at 771, [1982] 2 CMLR 174 (HL) at 178-179 per Lord Diplock; *Stoke-on-Trent City Council v B & Q plc* [1990] 3 CMLR 31 (Ch D) at 34 per Hoffmann J. For a judgment subsequent to, and implicitly approving, *Factortame* see *R v Secretary of State for Employment, ex parte Equal Opportunities Commission* [1995] 1 AC 1 (HL). The constitutional issues have yet to be fully addressed by the courts in Scotland (*pace Gibson v Lord Advocate* 1975 SC 136, [1975] 1 CMLR 563 (OH)) and in Northern Ireland.
2 *R v Secretary of State for Transport*, above.
3 See para 140 below.
4 See paras 100–110.

remedies and procedures should be used[1], provided that the conditions for the enforcement of the Community right are

● no less favourable than those relating to similar domestic actions and
● not such as to render virtually impossible the exercise of the Community right[2].

In the United Kingdom therefore a person would normally seek judicial review[3] (including injunction or interdict[4]) or damages[5] as appropriate. A rule of national law – for example, the rule against granting an injunction against the Crown[6] – cannot be invoked to prevent the national court granting a remedy to ensure the effective protection of a Community right[7]. Where a national substantive or procedural rule would have the effect of limiting that protection – for example, a fixed (and insufficient) statutory limit on the quantum of damages[8] or an irrebuttable legal presumption of national law[9] – that rule must be set aside. A time limit for bringing a claim is not in principle contrary to Community law, but may be so if it makes it impossible to assert a Community right[10]. In criminal proceedings a defence may be raised that the national measure creating the offence is contrary to Community law[11]; if the

---

1 Case 33/76 _Rewe-Zentralfinanz and Rewe-Zentral v Landwirtschaftskammer für das Saarland_ [1976] ECR 1989, [1977] 1 CMLR 533.

2 See eg Case 199/82 _San Giorgio v Amministrazione delle Finanze dello Stato_ [1983] ECR 3595; Case C-410/92 _Johnson v Chief Adjudication Officer_, judgment of 6 December 1994, not yet reported. So a domestic rule imposing a time limit upon applications for judicial review could not be invoked where the national authorities had made it impossible for the claimant to apply for review within the time limit; Case C-208/90 _Emmott v Minister for Social Welfare and Attorney General_ [1991] ECR I-4269 (but see note 10 below).

3 For recent examples see _Kincardine and Deeside District Council v Forestry Commissioners_ 1992 SLT 1180, [1994] 2 CMLR 869 (OH); _R v Secretary of State for the National Heritage, ex parte Continental Television_ [1993] 2 CMLR 333 (QBD); _National Union of Public Employees v Grampian Regional Council_, judgment of 11 March 1993 (OH), not yet reported; _R v Secretary of State for Employment, ex parte Equal Opportunities Commission_ [1995] 1 AC 1 (in which the House of Lords confirmed the availability of declaratory relief in judicial review proceedings).

4 See eg _R v Secretary of State for Transport, ex parte Factortame_ [1990] 2 AC 55, [1989] 3 CMLR 1; and [1991] 1 AC 603, [1990] 3 CMLR 375 (HL).

5 See para 141 below.

6 _R v Secretary of State for Transport, ex parte Factortame_ [1990] 2 AC 55, [1989] 3 CMLR 1 (HL); since reversed in English law in _M v Home Office_ [1993] 3 All ER 537 (HL), but not in Scots law owing to the terms of the Crown Proceedings Act 1947; see _McDonald v Secretary of State for Scotland_ 1994 SLT 692 (2nd Div).

7 Case C-213/89 _R v Secretary of State for Transport, ex parte Factortame_ [1990] ECR I-2433, [1990] 3 CMLR 1.

8 Case C-271/91 _Marshall v Southampton and South West Hampshire Area Health Authority (No 2)_ [1993] ECR I-4367, [1993] 3 CMLR 293.

9 Case 222/84 _Johnston v Chief Constable of the RUC_ [1986] ECR 1651, [1986] 3 CMLR 240.

10 The very broad statement in Case C-208/90 _Emmott v Minister for Social Welfare and Attorney General_ [1991] ECR I-4269 to the effect that time does not start to run until the provisions of a directive have been fully and clearly transposed into national law should be treated with caution; see Case C-335/91 _Steenhorst-Neerings v Bedrijfsvereniging voor Detailhandel, Ambachten en Huisvrouwen_ [1993] ECR I-5475 and Case C-410/92 _Johnson v Chief Adjudication Officer_, judgment of 6 December 1994, not yet reported.

11 Use of this 'Euro-defence' arose most famously in the recent clutch of cases involving Sunday trading legislation in England and Wales; see para 187 below.

national measure is found to be so, a conviction is incompatible with Community law[1]. Where a person can establish an enforceable Community right against another person or persons, which arises most frequently under Community employment rules[2] and the rules on competition[3], the national court must enforce that right[4]. It is not yet clear whether judicial review must precede a private law action[5] or whether the existence of a private law remedy pre-empts judicial review[6], nor whether such rules are compatible with the effective protection of Community rights.

140. Article 5 remedies. Where a Community right is articulated in a manner which is not directly effective, the right is not, as such, enforceable in the national courts. However, the Court of Justice has drawn from article 5 of the Treaty[7] two principles which enable the indirect enforcement of such rights: the 'uniform interpretation' of national law, which is discussed below[8], and a remedy in damages against public authorities, as follows.

141. Damages against public authorities: *Francovich* liability. There is a wide disparity in national law of public tort liability and so a risk that the right to damages as a means of protecting a Community right will vary from member state to member state. Very generally, the civilian systems have tended to provide easy access to damages against public authorities[9], whilst the common law jurisdictions have not[10]. However, in *Francovich*[11] the Court of Justice held that where a member state has failed timeously to implement into national law the requirements of a directive[12], so giving rise to economic loss on the part of an individual who would have acquired rights had the directive been properly implemented, a remedy in damages lies against the state. In the United Kingdom an action in damages will therefore lie against the appropriate Minister of the Crown or the Attorney-General[13], and the

1 See Case 269/80 *R v Tymen* [1981] ECR 3079, [1982] 2 CMLR 111.
2 See para 278 below.
3 See para 239 below.
4 See eg *Argyll v Distillers* 1987 SLT 514, [1986] 1 CMLR 764 (OH); *Hopkins v National Power* [1994] 1 CMLR 147 (QBD), referred to the Court of Justice as Case C-18/94 (pending).
5 Eg *R v Secretary of State for Employment, ex parte Equal Opportunities Commission* [1995] 1 AC 1 (HL).
6 *National Union of Public Employees v Grampian Regional Council*, judgment of 11 March 1993 (OH), not yet reported; *R v Secretary of State for Employment, ex parte Equal Opportunities Commission* [1994] 1 All ER 910 (HL).
7 See para 167 below.
8 See para 148.
9 See eg *Ministre des Affaires Economiques v Fromagerie Franco-Suisse 'Le Ski'* [1972] CMLR 330 (Belgian *Cour de Cassation*); *Ministre du commerce extérieur v Société Alivar* [1984] Rec Dalloz 128 (French *Conseil d'Etat*); *Rothmans v Ministère des Finances* [1993] 1 CMLR 253 (French *Conseil d'Etat*).
10 See the English case of *Bourgoin v Minister for Agriculture, Fisheries and Food* [1985] 3 All ER 585, [1986] 1 CMLR 267 (CA). This judgment can no longer be considered safe.
11 Cases C-6 & 9/90 *Francovich and Bonifaci v Italy* [1991] ECR I-5357, [1993] 2 CMLR 66.
12 As to directives see paras 147-148 below.
13 See *R v Secretary of State for Employment, ex parte Equal Opportunities Commission* [1995] 1 AC 1 (HL) at 32 per Lord Keith; see also *Kirklees Municipal Borough Council v Wickes Building Supplies Ltd* [1993] AC 227 (HL) at 282 per Lord Goff.

Crown Proceedings Act 1947 must now be read and applied in the light of *Francovich*. *Francovich* has been considered by the Court of Justice in only two subsequent cases[1]. Its full implications will become clearer with judgment in two cases pending before the Court[2].

(2) COMMUNITY LEGISLATION

142. Forms of Community legislation. Article 189 of the EC Treaty provides:

'In order to carry out their tasks and in accordance with the provisions of this Treaty, the European Parliament acting jointly with the Council, the Council and the Commission shall make regulations and issue directives, take decisions, make recommendations or deliver opinions.

A regulation shall have general application. It shall be binding in its entirety and directly applicable in all Member States.

A directive shall be binding, as to the result to be achieved, upon each Member State to which it is addressed, but shall leave to the national authorities the choice of form and methods.

A decision shall be binding in its entirety upon those to whom it is addressed.

Recommendations and opinions shall have no binding force.'

The ECSC and Euratom Treaties have similar but not identical provisions[3].

143. Form and substance. The difference between the various forms of act lies not in any hierarchical ordering but in their scope and effect. Regulations and decisions have immediate legal effect; directives require further implementing measures. Regulations are of the nature of general legislation; decisions are more particular in their application. The simplicity of these distinctions has become blurred, and the Court of Justice will always consider the substance of an act rather than its form in order to determine its legal effects.

144. Substantive requirements of Community legislation. The Community legislative process is subject to procedural requirements, discussed above[4]. It

---

1 Case C-334/92 *Wagner Miret v Fondo de Garantía Salarial* [1993] ECR I-6911; Case C-91/92 *Faccini Dori v Recreb* [1994] ECR I-3325, in which the Court simply confirmed that where national implementation of a directive provides insufficient protection for a right provided in the directive, an injured party has a remedy in damages against the state.
2 Case C-46/93 *Brasserie de Pêcheur v Germany* and Case C-48/93 *R v Secretary of State for Transport, ex parte Factortame (No 3)*.
3 Article 161 of the Euratom Treaty is in identical terms but omitting the words 'the European Parliament acting jointly with the Council'. Under art 14 of the ECSC Treaty 'decisions' and 'recommendations' correspond respectively to regulations and directives adopted under the EC and Euratom Treaties.
4 See paras 76–81.

is also subject to substantive requirements. All Community institutions are required to act within the limits of the powers conferred upon them by the Treaty[1]; they may legislate (or adopt other binding acts with legislative effect) only when acting pursuant to express authority in the Treaty, which normally prescribes the form of legislative act to be adopted. Further, all Community acts are required to state the reasoning upon which they are based[2]. The Court of Justice has found that it is necessary not only to state reasons but also to state sufficient and correct reasons. Thus an act which is insufficiently reasoned[3] or which cites as its legal base the wrong article of the Treaty[4], is an infringment of the Treaty within the meaning of article 173 and so liable to annulment or invalidation[5]. This has acquired especial significance with the variety of legislative procedures introduced by the Single European Act and the Treaty on European Union, as the Treaty basis of an act determines the procedures required to be followed.

145. Regulations. A regulation is analogous to statute law, and is 'binding in its entirety and directly applicable in all Member States'. 'Direct applicability' – to be carefully distinguished from direct effect – means that a regulation requires no implementation or further action in the member states. Indeed, a member state may not even attempt to pass implementing measures which might have the consequence of limiting or altering the effects of a regulation which must be enforced as it stands[6]. A provision of a regulation may or may not have direct effect, depending upon whether it fulfils the necessary criteria[7].

146. Decisions. Decisions, generally more limited and specific application than regulations, are 'binding . . . upon those to whom [they] are addressed'. The Treaty requires notification of a decision to its addressee and provides

1 EC Treaty, art 4(1).
2 Ibid, art 190.
3 See eg Case 158/80 *Rewe Handelsgesellschaft Nord v Hauptzollamt Kiel* [1981] ECR 1805, [1982] 1 CMLR 449; Case T-38/92 *All Weather Sports Benelux v Commission* [1994] ECR II-211; Case C-41/93 *France v Commission* [1994] ECR I-1829.
4 The appropriate legal base is determined by an objective analysis (the 'objective and content') of the act in question; see Case C-300/89 *Commission v Council* (Titanium Dioxide) [1991] ECR I-2867, [1993] 3 CMLR 359; Case C-155/91 *Commission v Council* (Waste Disposal) [1993] ECR I-939; Case C-187/93 *European Parliament v Council* (Waste Removal) [1994] ECR I-2857.
5 For examples see the cases cited in the previous note; also Case 45/86 *Commission v Council* (Generalised Tariff Preferences) [1987] ECR 1493, [1988] 2 CMLR 131; Case 131/86 *United Kingdom v Council* (Battery Hens) [1988] ECR 905, [1988] 2 CMLR 364; Case C-295/90 *European Parliament v Council* (Students) [1992] ECR I-4193, [1992] 3 CMLR 281; Case C-316/91 *European Parliament v Council* (European Development Fund) [1994] ECR I-625, [1994] 3 CMLR 149. If the choice of Treaty basis is an attempt intentionally to evade a particular legislative procedure it is a misuse of powers within the meaning of art 173; Case 331/88 *R v Minister for Agriculture, Fisheries and Food, ex parte FEDESA* [1990] ECR I-4023, [1991] 1 CMLR 507.
6 See eg Case 40/69 *Hauptzollamt Hamburg v Bollmann* [1970] ECR 69, [1970] CMLR 141; Case 93/71 *Leonesio v Ministry of Agriculture and Forestry* [1972] ECR 287, [1973] CMLR 343.
7 See para 133 above.

that it will take effect upon notification[1]. A decision therefore has immediate legal effect for its addressee (either a member state or a natural or legal person). A decision may also create rights for third parties. Where, for example, a decision is addressed to a member state and the decision fulfils the criteria of direct effect[2], it may be relied upon by third parties as against the state[3].

147. Directives. A directive is always addressed to member states. In principle, it prescribes a particular result to be achieved by a particular date, leaving it to the member states, in accordance with their own constitutional rules, to determine how and by whom it should be implemented or 'transposed' into national law. So far as Community law is concerned, the obligation to implement fully and timeously rests with the member state as such, and the member state cannot excuse its failure to do so upon the ground of internal difficulties[4]. So far as the individual is concerned, rights and obligations are brought into being in principle by the national implementing measures, not by the directive.

148. Uniform interpretation and direct effect of directives. Whilst the individual is normally concerned only with national measures implementing a directive, there are important exceptions.
- First, where there is a divergence between the national measures and the directive the national measures must, so far as it is possible for the national court to do so, be interpreted and applied so as to give effect to the directive[5]. This interpretative duty, called uniform interpretation (*interprétation conforme*), is derived from article 5 of the Treaty[6] and applies even where the directive remains unimplemented and even where the national rule in question existed prior in time to the adoption of the directive[7]. Hitherto the House of Lords has been prepared to comply with it only partially[8].

---

1 EC Treaty, art 191(3).
2 See para 133 above.
3 Case 9/70 *Grad v Finanzamt Traunstein* [1970] ECR 825, [1971] CMLR 1.
4 See eg Cases C-1 & 176/90 *Aragonesa de Publicidad Exterior v Departmento de Sanidad y Securidad Social de la Generalitat de Cataluña* [1991] ECR I-4151, [1994] 1 CMLR 887.
5 Case 14/83 *Von Colson and Kamann v Land Nordrhein-Westfalen* [1984] ECR 1891, [1986] 2 CMLR 430.
6 See para 167 below.
7 Case 106/89 *Marleasing v La Comercial Internacional de Alimentación* [1990] ECR I-435, [1992] 1 CMLR 305; Case C-334/92 *Wagner Miret v Fondo de Garantía Salarial* [1993] ECR I-6911; Case C-421/92 *Habermann-Beltermann v Arbeiterwohlfahrt Bezirksverband* [1994] ECR I-1657, [1994] 2 CMLR 681; Case C-91/92 *Faccini Dori v Recreb* [1994] ECR I-3325.
8 The House of Lords has held that where Parliament or the government has acted to implement a directive, it is proper for the courts to give a 'purposive' interpretation to the implementing national law in order that it accords with the provisions of the directive (*Pickstone v Freemans* [1989] AC 66, [1988] 3 CMLR 221; *Litster v Forth Dry Dock Ltd* 1989 SC 96, [1989] 2 CMLR 194). But where Parliament or the government has not so acted, the House of Lords has refused to construe (or 'distort') British legislation so as to conform with the provisions of a directive (*Duke v GEC Reliance Ltd* [1988] AC 618, [1988] 1 CMLR 719; *Finnegan v Clowney Youth Training Programme* [1990] 2 AC 407, [1990] 2 CMLR 859). Implicit in the House of Lords' view is that there is a limit beyond which British courts cannot go in seeking to ensure UK compliance with a directive; beyond that limit responsibility lies with Parliament and/or the government.

- Second, where the directive imposes upon the member state a clear, precise and unconditional obligation intended to create rights for individuals, then even if the member state has failed to implement, those individuals can rely upon the 'vertical direct effect' of the directive as against the state[1] or an 'emanation of the state'[2].
- Third, a directive cannot of itself have 'horizontal direct effect', creating rights as between private (non-state) parties[3]. But where an individual has suffered loss in consequence of a member state failure to implement, which is not, or cannot be, remedied by uniform interpretation of national law, the individual may, by application of *Francovich* principles[4], be able to claim damages from the state[5].

The full implications of these rules are still to be worked out. The practitioner must in any event develop antennae to detect the Community 'inspiration' of national legislation[6], and also be aware of directives which, although not properly implemented, may nevertheless give rise to rights against the state and may, or must, be used as a guide to the construction of national statutes.

149. Recommendations and opinions. According to the Treaty, recommendations and opinions have no binding force. This means that a *true* recommendation or opinion cannot create an enforceable right. However, the Court of Justice will consider whether an act in the form of a recommendation or opinion is in substance a different type of act which is intended to create and capable of creating such rights[7]. Even if it is not, a national court is bound to take them into consideration, in particular where they cast light upon the interpretation of other provisions of national or Community law[7].

150. Other binding acts. The list of measures prescribed in article 189 of the Treaty is not exhaustive. The Community institutions may create legally

---

1 Case 41/74 *van Duyn v Home Office* [1974] ECR 1337, [1975] 1 CMLR 1; Case 148/78 *Pubblico Ministero v Ratti* [1979] ECR 1629, [1980] 1 CMLR 96. 'The state' includes here any public authority.
2 As to what constitutes an emanation of the state see Case C-188/89 *Foster v British Gas* [1990] ECR I-3313, [1990] 2 CMLR 833. Cf the English cases of *Doughty v Rolls Royce* [1992] 1 CMLR 1045 (CA) and *Griffin v South West Water* [1995] IRLR 15 (Ch D).
3 Case 152/84 *Marshall v Southampton and South West Hampshire Area Health Authority (No 1)* [1986] ECR 723, [1986] 1 CMLR 768; Case C-91/92 *Faccini Dori v Recreb* [1994] ECR I-3325. A national authority may not however rely, as against an individual, on a provision of a directive which has not been implemented as it should have been; see Case 80/86 *Officier van Justitie v Kolpinghuis Nijmegen* [1987] ECR 3969, [1989] 2 CMLR 18.
4 See para 141 above.
5 See eg Case C-91/92 *Faccini Dori v Recreb* [1994] ECR I-3325.
6 Directives are sometimes given effect in the United Kingdom by amendment of relevant statutes, but also by Order in Council or regulation by authority of s 2(2) of the European Communities Act 1972. Their Community origin is therefore not always obvious. The notes in *Current Law Statutes* will normally identify British enactments which have been 'inspired' by Community directives. The Explanatory Memorandum annexed to statutory instruments will identify any Community measure upon which subordinate legislation is based.
7 Case 322/88 *Grimaldi v Fonds des Maladies Professionnelles* [1989] ECR 4407, [1991] 2 CMLR 265.

binding acts – and therefore acts capable of creating enforceable rights – by means other than those mentioned in article 189, for example through a resolution[1], through administrative memoranda[2] or by entering into a treaty with third states[3].

151. Judicial review. The means by which these legislative and administrative acts of the Community institutions may be challenged before the Court of Justice is discussed above[4]. It will be observed that a natural or legal person has no standing to challenge either a true regulation or a true directive under article 173, as the former will be of no individual concern, and the latter of no direct concern, to him[5]. He will have access to the Court only indirectly under article 184 or article 177[6]. True recommendations and opinions are expressly barred from review by the Court of Justice under article 173[7], but they may properly be the subject of a preliminary reference under article 177[8].

(3) THE GENERAL PRINCIPLES OF COMMUNITY LAW

152. The general principles of Community law. As in other legal systems, it has been necessary for the Court of Justice to develop legal principles of general application to assist in applying the law and to temper its rigidities. Article 164 of the Treaty requires the Court to 'ensure that . . . the law is observed'. 'The law' in this context means more than the written law of the Treaties. The principles developed by the Court are 'general principles common to the law of the member states', the shared tradition of the member states being seen as a source of law prior to the written law of the Treaty. However, the Court has not limited itself to principles found in the law of every member state and has adopted those which seemed best adapted to the Community system. Since much of Community law is administrative law, some of the most important principles have been taken from the highly developed administrative law of France and Germany. But the Court has also adopted some of the principles of natural justice as developed in the

1 See Case 22/70 *Commission v Council* (ERTA) [1971] ECR 263, [1971] CMLR 335; Case 230/81 *Luxembourg v European Parliament* [1983] ECR 255, [1983] 2 CMLR 726; Cases 213/88 & C-39/89 *Luxembourg v European Parliament* [1991] ECR I-5643, [1994] 1 CMLR 351.
2 Case 366/88 *France v Commission* [1990] ECR I-3571, [1992] 1 CMLR 205.
3 See para 284 below.
4 See paras 100-110.
5 But he may challenge a regulation the legal effect of which, properly construed, is that of a decision or a series of decisions (see Cases 16-17/62 *Confédération Nationale des Producteurs des Fruits et Légumes v EEC Council* [1962] ECR 471, [1963] CMLR 160; Case C-309/89 *Codorniu v Council* [1994] ECR I-1853) or even a directive which can be deemed to produce similar effects (Case C-298/89 *Government of Gibraltar v Council* [1993] ECR I-3605, [1994] 3 CMLR 425).
6 See para 110 above.
7 See para 100 above.
8 Case 322/88 *Grimaldi v Fonds des Maladies Professionnelles* [1989] ECR 4407, [1991] 2 CMLR 265.

United Kingdom. The most important principles referred to by the Court fall into five groups: fundamental rights; legal certainty; proportionality; equal treatment or non-discrimination; and subsidiarity.

153. The principle of fundamental human rights. From the early 1970s the Court of Justice has held that 'respect for fundamental human rights forms an integral part of the general principles of law protected by the Court of Justice'[1]. Such rights find their sources in 'the constitutional traditions common to the Member States' and 'international treaties for the protection of human rights on which the Member States have collaborated or of which they are signatories'[2]. The most important of the international treaties is of course the European Convention on Human Rights[3]. The Court's case law was codified in the Common Provisions of the Treaty on European Union (and so within the constitutional order of the Union), which provides that

> '[T]he Union shall respect fundamental rights, as guaranteed by the European Convention for the Protection of Human Rights and Fundamental Freedoms . . . and as they result from the constitutional traditions common to the Member States, as general principles of Community law'[4].

Respect for fundamental rights constitutes a constraint not only upon the legislative and executive action of the Community institutions but also upon that of the authorities of the member states when acting within the scope of Community law – when they are applying, obliged to apply, or seeking to justify derogation from, Community rules[5]. This means, *inter alia*, that there must be an effective means of judicial review of all national measures adopted in the Community sphere[6]. So, even though the ECHR has never been incorporated into United Kingdom law, British courts must apply it as appropriate when dealing with matters which fall within the sphere of Community law.

Principles related to fundamental rights, and aligned with British concepts of natural justice, include:

1 Case 11/70 *Internationale Handelsgesellschaft mbH v Einfuhr- und Vorratsstelle für Getreide und Futtermittel* [1970] ECR 1125 at 1134, [1972] CMLR 255 at 283.
2 Case 11/70, above; Case 4/73 *Nold v Commission* [1974] ECR 491 at 507, [1974] 2 CMLR 338 at 354; Case 29/69 *Stauder v Ulm* [1969] ECR 419, [1970] 1 CMLR 112; Case 44/79 *Hauer v Land Rheinland-Pfalz* [1979] ECR 3727, [1980] 3 CMLR 42.
3 The Community itself is not a party to the ECHR, but both the Parliament and the Commission have urged that it ought to be; see EP Resolution of 9 July 1991, OJ C240, 16.9.91, p 45; Bull EC 10-1990, p 74. In 1994 the Council requested from the Court of Justice an Opinion as to whether accession to the ECHR would be consistent with the EC Treaty; see Opinion 2/94 *re Accession to the European Convention on Human Rights* (pending).
4 TEU, art F(2).
5 See Case 5/88 *Wachauf v Germany* [1989] ECR 2609, [1991] 1 CMLR 328; Case 260/89 *Elliniki Radiophonia Tiléorasi v Dimotiki Etairia Pliroforissis* [1991] ECR I-2925, [1994] 4 CMLR 540; Case C-159/90 *Society for the Protection of Unborn Children v Grogan* [1991] ECR I-4685, [1991] 3 CMLR 849; Case C-168/91 *Konstantinidis v Stadt Altensteig* [1993] ECR I-1191, [1993] 3 CMLR 401 per Advocate General Jacobs.
6 Case 222/84 *Johnston v Chief Constable of the RUC* [1986] ECR 1651, [1986] 3 CMLR 240; Case 222/86 *UNECTEF v Heylens* [1987] ECR 4097, [1989] 1 CMLR 901; Case C-97/91 *Borelli v Commission* [1992] ECR I-6313.

(1) *Audi alteram partem*: a person is entitled to be heard in his own defence before a penalty is imposed or a measure taken which will prejudice his interests[1]. It is a necessary precondition that he should be informed of the case against him before being required to state his defence. However, an infringement of the right to be heard can result in annulment only if it can be established that, but for the irregularity, the outcome of the procedure might have been different[2].

(2) *Nulla poena sine lege*: a penalty, even of a non-criminal nature, cannot be imposed unless it rests upon a clear and unambiguous legal basis[3].

(3) *Non-retroactivity*: a law cannot be applied to a person who could not have known of its existence. In particular, criminal offences cannot be declared retrospectively[4].

(4) *Non bis in idem*: no one should be tried twice for the same offence; and no one should be subjected to two penalties for the same offence[5].

(5) *The right to legal assistance*: a person is entitled to the help and presence of a lawyer, and to be represented by a lawyer when his legal rights are in issue[6]. This principle leads in turn to two further principles: (a) that the lawyer is entitled to see all relevant documents, and (b) that communications between lawyer and client are confidential[7].

(6) *Protection from self-incrimination*: whilst a person may be required to supply information to a Community authority, even if the information supplied would incriminate him, he cannot be compelled to answer leading questions the answers to which would constitute an admission of unlawful activity, that being for the Community authority to establish[8].

(7) *Respect for private life and inviolability of premises*: a person cannot be compelled to undergo medical examination in order to reveal the state of his health prior to appointment to a Community post, although refusal to consent to a test objectively necessary for fulfilling the tasks of the post will justify a refusal to employ him[9]. The inviolability of the home is a

---

1 See eg Case 17/74 *Transocean Marine Paint Association v Commission* [1974] ECR 1063, [1974] 2 CMLR 459; Case 85/76 *Hoffmann-La Roche v Commission* [1979] ECR 461, [1979] 3 CMLR 211; Case 322/81 *Michelin v Commission* [1983] ECR 3461, [1985] 1 CMLR 282; Case 49/88 *Al-Jubail Fertiliser Company v Council* [1991] ECR I-3187, [1991] 3 CMLR 377; Case C-135/92 *Fiskano v Commission* [1994] ECR I-2885.
2 Case 142/87 *Belgium v Commission* [1990] ECR I-959.
3 Case C-172/89 *Vandemoortele v Commission* [1990] ECR I-4677.
4 Case 63/83 *R v Kirk* [1984] ECR 2689, [1984] 3 CMLR 522. However, the principle is not applied vigorously outwith the sphere of criminal law; see Case 331/88 *R v Minister for Agriculture, Fisheries and Food, ex parte FEDESA* [1990] ECR I-4023, [1991] 1 CMLR 507.
5 See eg Cases 18 & 35/65 *Gutmann v Euratom Commission* [1966] ECR 103; Case 14/68 *Wilhelm v Bundeskartellamt* [1969] ECR 1, [1969] CMLR 100.
6 See eg Cases 46/87 & 227/88 *Hoechst v Commission* [1989] ECR 2859, [1991] 4 CMLR 410.
7 See eg Case 155/79 *A M & S Europe v Commission* [1982] ECR 1575, [1982] 2 CMLR 264.
8 See Case 374/87 *Orkem v Commission* [1989] ECR 3283, [1991] 4 CMLR 502. A subsequent judgment of the European Court of Human Rights in an unrelated case is thought to imply that parts of the *Orkem* judgment of the Court of Justice are inconsistent with the requirements of the Convention; see *Funke v France* [1993] 1 CMLR 897 (ECHR). But see also Case C-60/92 *Otto v Postbank* [1993] ECR I-5683.
9 Case C-404/92P *X v Commission*, [1994] ECR I-4737.

fundamental right; premises of legal persons enjoy lesser protection but cannot be subjected to arbitrary and disproportionate intervention by public authorities[1].

154. The principle of legal certainty. The principle is that application of the law to a specific situation must be predictable[2]. The Court of Justice applies this principle when it declares the provisions of a measure it has annulled to be operative[3] and when it limits the temporal effects of an interpretative judgment which is new, genuinely unforeseen and likely to give rise to significant difficulty[4]. From the general principle spring other principles:

(1) *Respect for acquired rights*: a legal right, once acquired, should not be withdrawn. Further, a case must be judged in the light of the law as it stood at the time of the events in question, not as it may have been changed or developed subsequently[5].

(2) *Legitimate expectation*: a person is entitled to act (and conduct his business) in the reasonable expectation that the law as it exists will continue to apply[6]. This is especially so in the event of assurances, explicit or implicit, being given by a Community authority[7].

(3) *Identifiability of persons affected*: the addressee of a decision intended to create rights or obligations must be clearly identifiable[8].

(4) *Understandable language*: a decision must be communicated to a person affected by it in a language he understands[9].

(5) *Prescription*: an act cannot be declared unlawful, a penalty exacted or performance of an obligation required after an excessive lapse of time[10].

155. The principle of proportionality. The principle of proportionality requires that the means employed must be proportionate to the end to be achieved. It was written into the EC Treaty by the Treaty on European Union as a formal principle of Community law thus:

---

1 Cases 46/87 & 227/88 *Hoechst v Commission* [1989] ECR 2859, [1991] 4 CMLR 410.

2 On the application of the principle in Community law generally see Case C-338/91 *Steenhorst-Neerings v Bedrijfsvereniging voor Detailhandel, Ambachten en Huisvrouw* [1993] ECR I-5475 per Advocate-General Darmon.

3 See para 102 above.

4 Case 43/75 *Defrenne v SABENA* [1976] ECR 455, [1976] 2 CMLR 98; Case 24/86 *Blaizot v University of Liège* [1988] ECR 379, [1989] 1 CMLR 57; Case C-262/88 *Barber v Guardian Royal Exchange* [1990] ECR I-1889, [1990] 2 CMLR 513; Case C-163/90 *Administration des Douanes et Droits Indirects v Legros* [1992] ECR I-4625.

5 See eg Case 12/71 *Henck v Hauptzollamt Emmerich* [1971] ECR 743; see also Case 80/86 *Officier van Justitie v Kolpinghuis Nijmegen* [1987] ECR 3969, [1989] 2 CMLR 18.

6 See eg Case 112/77 *Töpfer v Commission* [1978] ECR 1019.

7 See Case 74/74 *CNTA v Commission* [1975] ECR 533, [1977] 1 CMLR 171; Case 120/86 *Mulder v Minister for Agriculture and Fisheries* [1988] ECR 2321, [1989] 2 CMLR 1; Case T-123/89 *Chomel v Commission* [1990] ECR II-131.

8 Case T-38/92 *All Weather Sports Benelux v Commission* [1994] ECR II-211.

9 See Case 66/74 *Farrauto v Bau-Berufsgenossenschaft Wuppertal* [1975] ECR 157, [1976] 2 CMLR 334.

10 See eg Case 48/69 *Imperial Chemical Industries Ltd v Commission* [1972] ECR 619 at 653, [1972] CMLR 557 at 621.

'Any action by the Community shall not go beyond what is necessary to achieve the objectives of this Treaty'[1].

So, limitation of lawful economic activities is justifiable only where the measures taken are appropriate and necessary in order to achieve public objectives legitimately pursued. If there is a choice between several appropriate measures, recourse must be had to the least burdensome[2]. Penalties must be proportionate to the gravity of the offence, and a heavy burden should not be imposed upon some people in order to achieve something that is of only small importance to others[3]. Derogations from general Community rules must be limited to those which are necessary to achieve the purpose of the derogation[4].

156. The principle of equality of treatment or non-discrimination. Equal situations must be treated equally, or, otherwise expressed, similar situations should not be treated differently unless there is objective justification for doing so[5]. Conversely, unequal situations can, and sometimes should be, treated differently. The principle finds expression in the Treaty in two specific areas: a general prohibition of discrimination based upon nationality[6] and a prohibition of discrimination between men and women in the area of employment[7]. Nevertheless, equal treatment is recognised as a fundamental principle of Community law equally applicable elsewhere[8].

157. Subsidiarity. What is now called the principle of subsidiarity appears in other guises throughout the founding Treaties[9]. It was incorporated as a formal principle into the EC Treaty by the Treaty on European Union as follows:

'In areas which do not fall within its exclusive competence, the Community shall take action, in accordance with the principle of subsidiarity, only if and in so far as the objectives of the proposed action cannot be sufficiently achieved by the Member States and can therefore, by reason of the scale or effects of the proposed action, be better achieved by the Community.'[10]

1 EC Treaty, art 3b, 3rd para.
2 See eg Case 331/88 *R v Minister for Agriculture, Fisheries and Food, ex parte FEDESA* [1990] ECR I-4023, [1991] 1 CMLR 507.
3 See eg Case 8/55 *Fédération Charbonnière de Belgique v High Authority* [1954-56] ECR 292; Case 9/73 *Schlüter v Hauptzollamt Lörrach* [1973] ECR 1135; Case 30/77 *R v Bouchereau* [1977] ECR 1999, [1977] 2 CMLR 800.
4 See paras 192, 217 below.
5 See eg Case C-280/93 *Germany v Council* (Bananas), [1994] ECR I-4973.
6 See para 168 below.
7 See paras 275ff below.
8 See eg Cases 117/76 and 16/77 *Ruckdeschel v Hauptzollamt Hamburg-St Annen* [1977] ECR 1753, [1979] 2 CMLR 445; Case C-37/89 *Weiser v Caisse Nationale des Barreaux Français* [1990] ECR I-2395.
9 Subsidiarity – put simply, that decisions be taken as closely as possible to the citizens affected by them – is also recognised in the constitutional law of some member states; see eg art 72(2) of the German Basic Law.
10 EC Treaty, art 3b, 2nd para.

There is thus a two-fold test: Community action is justified only if it serves an end which both (a) cannot be achieved satisfactorily at the national level *and* (b) can be achieved better at Community level. The European Council and the Commission have indicated their views on the meaning of subsidiarity[1], the three political institutions have agreed a procedure amongst them which takes account of its requirements[2], and the Parliament now scrutinises every legislative proposal in order to determine whether it complies with the principle[3]. How far the principle is, as such, justiciable remains to be tested. There are, however, numerous judgments of the Court of Justice which can be read as implicit application of the principle.

158. Applicability of the general principles. Although the Court of Justice has upheld all these principles in decided cases, it has quite often found that the principle invoked did not apply to the facts of the case before it. Even where they apply, the rights are not absolute and may, as permitted both by the European Convention and in national law, legitimately be restricted in the general interest[4]. In relation to the confidentiality of communications between lawyer and client, the Court limited itself, exceptionally, to adoption of the principle only in so far as it had been shown to be common to all the member states[5].

---

1 European Council in Edinburgh, Conclusions of the Presidency, Bull EC 12-1992, pp 12-18; Commission communiqué on Subsidiarity, Bull EC 10-1992, pp 116-126.
2 Bull EC 10-1993, p 119.
3 Rules of Procedure, rule 54.
4 See eg Case 44/79 *Hauer v Land Rheinland-Pfalz* [1979] ECR 3727, [1980] 3 CMLR 42; Case 4/73 *Nold v Commission* [1974] ECR 491, [1974] 2 CMLR 338; Case 5/88 *Wachauf v Germany* [1989] ECR 2609, [1991] 1 CMLR 328.
5 Case 155/79 *A M & S Europe v Commission* [1982] ECR 1575, [1982] 2 CMLR 264.

4. THE STRUCTURE AND MAIN PROVISIONS OF THE EC TREATY

(1) INTRODUCTION

159. The structure of the EC Treaty. The EC Treaty consists of a Preamble and six Parts, as follows:
(1) Principles
(2) Citizenship of the Union
(3) Community Policies
(4) Association of the Overseas Countries and Territories
(5) Institutions of the Community
(6) General and Final Provisions.
The scheme of the Treaty is to progress from the general to the specific. Part One (the 'Principles') sets out the basic aims and principles in the light of which the remainder of the Treaty is to be interpreted and applied. The German text uses the word *Grundsätze* (ground rules), which expresses more clearly what is implied. The substantive rules, some of which require to be implemented by legislation adopted in accordance with the appropriate procedures, follow in Part Three.

160. Annexes, Protocols and Declarations. Annexed to the EC Treaty are four Annexes which supplement particular Treaty articles, 29 Protocols and a large number of Declarations. The Protocols, some of which are spent, form an integral part of the Treaty[1]. The Declarations indicate a policy intent on the part of the governments of the member states but are not binding as part of the Treaty text.

161. The substantive law of the Treaty. The substantive Treaty law of which students and practitioners must be aware are almost all contained in articles 2-7c (Principles), 9-84 (formerly called the 'Foundations') and 85-102 (the 'common rules'), together with article 119 (equal pay). It is especially important to note that the Court of Justice will have recourse to the Treaty as a whole, including its Preamble, and especially the Principles, as an aid to interpretation of a particular provision of the Treaty[2].

(2) THE PRINCIPLES

162. The 'task' of the Community. Article 2 sets out in general terms the economic, social and political 'task' (*mission; Aufgabe*) which the Community has been set up to perform.

1 EC Treaty, art 239.
2 See paras 128–129 above.

163. The common market. The most immediate task of the Community was the establishment of a 'common market' for all forms of economic activity (excepting those governed by the ECSC and Euratom Treaties[1]). There is no definition of a common market in the Treaty, but the Court of Justice said:

> 'The concept of a common market . . . involves the elimination of all obstacles to intra-Community trade in order to merge the national markets into a single market bringing about conditions as close as possible to those of a genuine internal market'[2].

In order to achieve this common market it is necessary to remove not only such obvious barriers to trade as tariffs and quotas, but also hidden 'non-tariff' barriers. These may consist in obvious protectionist devices designed to protect domestic producers and suppliers against foreign competition, but they may simply be the result of the fact that independent states have pursued their own policies, and developed their own laws and administrative practices in a different way from each other. Thus differences in the law of trade marks and patents may be an obstacle to the free flow of manufactured goods between countries, and differences in professional organisation and rules of conduct may be an obstacle to the professional person practising his profession in another country. Individuals and companies too may erect their own barriers to the free flow of goods or services where, for example, they agree not to compete with each other in the same market. The Treaty seeks to dismantle all these forms of barrier.

164. Economic and monetary union; financial discipline. Article 2 of the Treaty now also includes as part of the Community's task the establishment of 'an economic and monetary union', the details of which are considered below[3]. As it will require a high degree of economic convergence, article 3a imposes an obligation for both the Community and the member states to comply with 'guiding principles' of stable prices, sound public finance and monetary conditions and a sustainable balance of payments, all conducted in accordance with the principle of an open market economy with free competition.

165. The activities of the Community. Article 3 sets out, under twenty heads, the 'activities' of the Community. The list of activities is, in essence, the programme for Part Three ('Community Policies'). They include *inter alia*:

a)   the elimination of customs duties, quantitative restrictions and all measures having equivalent effect;

---

1 EC Treaty, art 232. Aspects of these sectors not expressly governed by the ECSC and Euratom Treaties fall within the domain of the EC Treaty; see eg Opinion 1/94 *re the World Trade Organisation*, opinion of 15 November 1994, not yet reported.
2 Case 15/81 *Gaston Schul v Inspecteur der Invoerrechten en Accijnzen* [1982] ECR 1409 at 1431-2, [1982] 3 CMLR 229 at 251. Cf the definition of the 'internal market' considered at para 170 below.
3 See paras 262-267.

b) a common commercial policy;
c) an internal market;
d) measures concerning the entry and movement of persons in the internal market;
e) a common policy in the sphere of agriculture and fisheries;
f) a common policy in the sphere of transport;
g) a system ensuring that competition is not distorted;
h) the approximation of national laws to the extent necessary for the common market to function.

166. General obligations of the Community. Article 3b lays down ground rules setting the parameters of the activities of the Community and its institutions. The Community is to act within the limits of powers conferred upon it and the objectives assigned to it by the Treaty. Its activities are subject to the principle of subsidiarity[1]; and they must be proportionate[2].

167. General obligations of the member states. Article 5 of the EC Treaty imposes upon the member states two general obligations, one positive, the other negative. There is a positive obligation for the member states to:

'take all appropriate measures, whether general or particular, to ensure fulfilment of the obligations arising out of this Treaty or resulting from action taken by the institutions of the Community. They shall facilitate the achievement of the Community's tasks'.

There is, correspondingly, a negative obligation to:

'abstain from any measure which could jeopardize the attainment of the objectives of this Treaty'.

These fundamental legal obligations require good faith, 'loyal co-operation and assistance' and are frequently referred to by the Court of Justice when assessing the lawfulness of the conduct of member states[3]. However, they apply only in so far as the situation in question is regulated by a specific subsequent provision of the Treaty[4]. It is of fundamental importance, here and elsewhere, to note that the obligation is imposed upon the member state. The internal allocation of tasks to regional or local authorities[5] and the constitutional allocation of power or jurisdiction amongst the various branches of

---

1 See para 157 above.
2 See para 155 above.
3 See eg Case 230/81 *Luxembourg v European Parliament* [1983] ECR 255, [1983] 2 CMLR 726; Case 44/84 *Hurd v Jones* [1986] ECR 29, [1986] 2 CMLR 1; Case C-374/89 *Commission v Belgium* [1991] ECR I-367.
4 Cases C-78-83/90 *Compagnie Commerciale de l'Ouest v Administration des Douanes* [1992] ECR I-1847; Case C-18/93 *Corsica Ferries Italia v Corpo dei Piloti del Porto di Genova* [1994] ECR I-1783; Case C-323/93 *Société civile agricole du Centre d'insémination de la Crespelle v Co-opérative d'élevage et d'insémination artificielle de département de la Mayenne*, judgment of 5 October 1994, not yet reported.
5 See eg Case 96/81 *Commission v Netherlands* [1982] ECR 1791; Cases C-1 & 176/90 *Aragonesa de Publicidad Exterior v Departmento de Sanidad y Securidad Social de la Generalitat de Cataluña* [1991] ECR I-4151, [1994] 1 CMLR 887.

government is not for the Community to determine and so, correspondingly, does not affect the obligations of the member state. This is why a national court, charged with applying Community law, may be required to set aside national rules which limit the effective protection of a Community right[1] or to interpret national law in accordance with the relevant provisions of Community law. This latter duty applies primarily in the context of directives[2], but extends to a duty to interpret national legislation in the light of the objectives of Treaty provisions so as to ensure that the exercise of Community rights does not produce less favourable treatment under national law[3].

168. Non-discrimination upon grounds of nationality. Article 6 of the EC Treaty states one of the most important principles affecting the rights of individuals:

'Within the scope of application of this Treaty, and without prejudice to any special provisions contained therein, any discrimination on grounds of nationality shall be prohibited'.

The effect, for practical purposes, is to require the member states to be 'nationality blind' and to ensure equality of treatment for the citizens of all Community countries in any sphere falling within Community activities. More specific rules of non-discrimination are provided in subsequent Treaty provisions, but article 6 applies autonomously in their absence[4]. On the other hand, Community law does not in general require member states not to practise 'reverse discrimination' by treating its own nationals less favourably than it is required to treat the nationals of other member states[5].

169. The transitional period. Article 7 (formerly article 8) of the EC Treaty laid down the timetable for the implementation of the Treaty within a 'transitional period' of twelve years ending on 31 December 1969. The timetable was not adhered to, but article 7(7) was important for the interpretation of some later Treaty articles. It provides that:

'Save for the exceptions or derogations provided for in this Treaty, the expiry of the transitional period shall constitute the latest date by which all the rules laid down must enter into force and all measures required for establishing the common market must be implemented'.

This enabled the Court of Justice to hold that, where a rule in the Treaty establishes a result to be achieved by the end of the transitional period, that

---

1 See para 139 above.
2 See para 148 above.
3 Case C-165/91 *Van Munster v Rijksdienst voor Pensioenen*, judgment of 5 October 1994, not yet reported.
4 Eg Case C-179/90 *Merci Convenzionali Porto di Genova v Siderurgica Gabrielli* [1991] ECR I-5889, [1994] 4 CMLR 422; Case C-213/90 *Association de Soutien aux Travailleurs Immigrés v Chambre des Employés Privés* [1991] ECR I-3507, [1993] 3 CMLR 621; Case C-18/93 *Corsica Ferries Italia v Corpo dei Piloti del Porto di Genova* [1994] ECR I-1783.
5 See paras 194, 209 below.

rule must, once that period has expired, have direct effect and be enforceable in the courts[1].

170. The internal market. The common market was not fully achieved by the end of the transitional period. In 1985 Lord Cockfield, then Commissioner with responsibility for the internal market, produced his White Paper[2], which identified the remaining barriers to trade within the Community, grouping them within three principal categories: physical barriers, technical barriers, and fiscal barriers. The White Paper then set out some three hundred items of legislation which, it argued, would be both necessary and sufficient to eliminate those barriers. As a means of implementing the Cockfield proposals the Single European Act amended the EEC Treaty to include a new definition of 'the internal market' as

'an area without internal frontiers in which the free movement of goods, persons, services and capital is ensured in accordance with the provisions of this Treaty'[3],

a new timetable for its completion by 31 December 1992[4] and specific legislative procedures to assist in achieving it[5]. Between 1985 and 1993 some 500 internal market measures were adopted, and much of the programme was in fact completed by the end of 1992. Some work however still remains; in particular the free movement of persons is not fully achieved[6]. The Court of Justice has not yet been called upon to determine whether these Treaty provisions on the internal market are directly effective[7]. Some measures which would assist in achieving the free movement of persons are now pursued outside Community machinery under Title VI of the Treaty on European Union on co-operation in the fields of justice and home affairs[8].

(3) CITIZENSHIP OF THE UNION

171. Citizenship of the Union. Articles 8 to 8e of the EC Treaty, added by the Treaty on European Union, create 'citizenship of the Union'. They do *not* confer upon the Community any competences as to citizenship or

---

1 See eg Case 2/74 *Reyners v Belgium* [1974] ECR 63, [1974] 2 CMLR 305; Case 41/76 *Donckerwolcke v Procureur de la République* [1976] ECR 1921, [1977] 2 CMLR 535.
2 See para 26 above.
3 EC Treaty, art 7a, 2nd para.
4 Ibid, art 7a, 1st para.
5 Ibid, arts 100a and 100b.
6 This was formally recognised by the European Council at the Edinburgh Summit in December 1992; see European Council in Edinburgh, Conclusions of the Presidency, Bull EC 12-1992, p 11.
7 A declaration annexed to the Single European Act provides: 'Setting the date of 31 December 1992 does not create an automatic legal effect'.
8 See paras 295–298 below.

naturalisation, which remain firmly within the sphere of national sovereignty[1]. Rather they provide simply that any citizen of a member state, as defined by the nationality law of each state[2], is also a citizen of the Union[3]. Citizens of the Union enjoy:

(1) the right to move and reside freely within the territory of the Community subject to the limitations and conditions laid down in the Treaty[4];

(2) the right to vote and stand as a candidate in municipal and European elections (but not for election to national or regional parliaments) in a member state in which he resides[5];

(3) the right to diplomatic representation by the diplomatic or consular authorities of another member state in the territory of a third country where the state of which he is a national is not represented[6]; and

(4) the right to petition the European Parliament on a matter which comes within the Community's fields of activity[7].

A most important provision of this Part of the Treaty may come to be that which provides:

'Citizens of the Union shall enjoy the rights conferred by this Treaty and shall be subject to the duties imposed thereby'[8].

This is the first express recognition *in the Treaty* of the individual as a person deriving rights and obligations directly from it[9].

(4) COMMUNITY POLICIES

172. General. Part Three of the Treaty, comprising articles 9 to 130y and arranged under seventeen Titles, is entitled 'Community Policies'. The most

---

1 So, a Declaration on Nationality of a Member State attached to the Treaty provides that 'the question whether an individual possesses the nationality of a Member State shall be settled solely by reference to the national law of the Member State concerned'.

2 Eg for the United Kingdom as defined by the British Nationality Act 1981, c 61; see also the Declaration by the United Kingdom replacing the Declaration on the Definition of the term 'Nationals', OJ C23, 28.1.83, p 1; Cmnd 9062. By virtue of these measures British citizens, British subjects with right of abode in the UK and British Dependent Territories and citizens of Gibraltar are citizens of the Union. Channel Islanders, Manxmen and nationals of British overseas territories are not, and such rights as they have in the United Kingdom continue to be governed by United Kingdom law.

3 EC Treaty, art 8(1).

4 Ibid, art 8a(1). As to specific Treaty rules see paras 205–206 and 209–210 below.

5 Ibid, art 8b; now implemented for the European Parliament by Directive 93/109, OJ L329, 30.12.93, p 34.

6 EC Treaty, art 8c.

7 Ibid, art 8d.

8 Ibid, art 8(2).

9 In Case 26/62 *Van Gend en Loos v Nederlandse Tariefcommissie* [1963] ECR 1, [1963] CMLR 105 (see para 133 above) the Court of Justice held that in its original form the Treaty by necessary implication directly created rights and obligations for natural and legal persons. The citizenship provisions of arts 8-8e apply only to natural persons.

important of these are the free movement of goods (of which agricultural products are a special category), persons, services (of which transport is a special category) and capital. Under the EEC Treaty these were called 'the Foundations of the Community' (the basic infrastructure of the Community system) and are frequently referred to as 'the Four Freedoms'.

(a) The Four Freedoms

173. The Four Freedoms: goods, persons, services, capital. As noted above, the immediate aim of the EC Treaty was to establish a free and open common market for all forms of economic activity. These are dealt with in Titles I to IV of Part Three of the Treaty under four general headings – goods, persons, services and capital. These four categories are intended to comprehend all possible forms of economic activity, but the lines of demarcation between them are not always clear-cut. Persons and services are dealt with under three headings ('chapters'): 'workers', 'right of establishment' and 'services'. The rules on movement of money, although it falls within the general chapter on 'capital', depends upon whether the movement is a self-standing investment or one connected with the movement of goods, persons or services.

174. 'Effects'. The Treaty frequently speaks of 'effects'. Thus, in dealing with the free movement of goods, the Treaty envisages the prohibition of 'customs duties . . . and of all charges having equivalent effect'[1]. The significance of this is that the Treaty considers the substance of what is done – what actually happens and what is its practical effect – rather than the form or method by which it is done.

175. 'Results'. The way in which a particular result is achieved may vary from state to state. Thus, one state may require action by the legislature or the judiciary where another can achieve the result through administrative action. The Treaty is not concerned with the method adopted, provided the required result is achieved. An important consequence is that action by the courts – for example the enforcement of a contract or the granting of an injunction or interdict for the protection of a property right – may, in Treaty terms, be action by the member state and involve a breach of the Treaty. Similarly, action by a regional or district authority, or by any public body, may constitute a breach of the Treaty by the member state.

(A) FREE MOVEMENT OF GOODS: THE CUSTOMS UNION

176. Goods. The EC Treaty provides that 'the Community shall be based upon a customs union which shall cover all trade in goods. . .'[1]. 'Goods' are

---

1 EC Treaty, art 9(1).

not defined in the Treaty[1], but the Court of Justice has established that 'by goods ... there must be understood products which can be valued in money and which are capable as such of forming the subject of commercial transactions'[2]. The category is therefore of very broad application. It is not restricted to consumer goods, articles of general use or ordinary merchandise, and may extend, to cite only two examples, to coinage which is no longer legal tender[3] and to non-recyclable waste which has negative economic value[4]. It does not however extend to physical objects which fall properly within other of the Four Freedoms. Thus banknotes which are legal tender[5] and lottery tickets[6] are not 'goods', but fall within the chapters on capital and services respectively. Sound records, film apparatus and other products used for the diffusion of television signals, in so far as they consist of tangible objects, are goods, but television broadcasting itself is a service[7].

177. Territory of the customs union. The territory of the customs union is set out in the Treaty[8] and in legislation[9]. Generally, the customs union incorporates the territory, the territorial sea and the air space of all the member states, including those European territories for whose external relations a member state is responsible. There are however significant anomalies. The customs territory does not include the Færoe Islands or the sovereign base areas in Cyprus, all of which are outside the territorial scope of the Treaty[10]. It does include the Canary Islands (but not Ceuta and Melilla), the Åland islands (with some derogations)[11] and the French overseas *départements*[12], which are fully part of the Community, but not the French overseas territories[13]. San Marino and Monaco, both independent states, are also part of the customs territory[14]. The Channel Islands and the Isle of Man are not part of the Community but are part of its customs territory[15], whilst Gibraltar is part of

---

1 Confusingly, the English text refers in some instances to 'goods' (art 9(1)) and in others to 'products' (arts 9(2), 10(1)). A similar distinction may be found in the other language texts except German, Danish and Swedish, which adopt the same word (*Waren, varer* and *varor*) throughout.
2 Case 7/68 *Commission v Italy* (First Art Treasures Case) [1968] ECR 423 at 428, [1969] CMLR 1 at 8.
3 Case 7/78 *R v Thompson* [1978] ECR 2247, [1979] 1 CMLR 47.
4 Case C-2/90 *Commission v Belgium* [1992] ECR I-4431, [1993] 1 CMLR 365.
5 Case 7/78 *R v Thompson* [1978] ECR 2247, [1979] 1 CMLR 47; Cases C-358 & 416/93 *Ministerio Fiscal v Bordessa*, judgment of 23 February 1994, not yet reported.
6 Case C-275/92 *HM Customs and Excise v Schindler* [1994] ECR I-1039, [1995] 1 CMLR 4.
7 Case 155/73 *Giuseppe Sacchi* [1974] ECR 409, [1974] 2 CMLR 177; Case C-23/93 *TV10 v Commissariat voor de Media*, judgment of 5 October 1994, not yet reported.
8 EC Treaty, art 227 as amended.
9 Regulation 2913/92, OJ L302, 19.10.92, p 1 (the Community Customs Code), art 3 as amended.
10 EC Treaty, arts 227(5)(a) and (b).
11 Ibid, art 227(5)(d) and Protocol No 2 to the Corfu Accession Treaty on the Åland islands.
12 EC Treaty, art 227(2). The *départements d'outre mer* are Guadeloupe, Guyane, Martinique and Réunion.
13 Including Mayotte and St Pierre et Miquelon.
14 Regulation 2913/92, art 3(2).
15 EC Treaty, art 227(5)(c) and Protocol concerning the Channel Islands and the Isle of Man. On the application of the Treaty in the Isle of Man, and implicitly in the Channel Islands, see Case C-355/89 *Department of Health and Social Security v Barr and Montrose Holdings Ltd* [1991] ECR I-3479, [1991] 3 CMLR 325.

the Community but is treated as being outside the customs territory[1].

178. Free circulation. Article 9 of the Treaty applies the Treaty provisions relating to the elimination of customs duties and quantitative restrictions between member states[2] to

- products originating in member states and
- products coming from third countries which are in 'free circulation' in member states.

Article 10 provides in effect that goods coming from third countries are in free circulation as soon as they are subject to no further control by the customs authorities. Once in free circulation, they are to be accorded treatment identical to that of goods produced within the Community[3]. This is the essence of a customs union, as compared with a free trade area. The purpose of the Chapter on the Customs Union is therefore, first, to abolish all customs and other charges on the movement of goods across an internal Comunity frontier, and second, to establish a uniform customs tariff for goods from a third country entering the Community via any member state.

179. Tariff and non-tariff barriers. The Treaty goes on to deal with the market in goods under two chapters: the Customs Union (articles 12-29), and the Elimination of Quantitative Restrictions between Member States (articles 30-37). The Chapter on the Customs Union deals with restrictions on the movement of goods created by the requirement to pay money when goods cross a frontier. The Chapter on Quantitative Restrictions goes beyond the customs union and deals with 'non-tariff barriers' – restrictions upon the volume of goods which may cross a frontier. The most obvious of such restrictions are import and export quotas, but restrictions may also arise in relation to a single article or category of articles. For example, export may be prohibited on the ground that the article in question forms part of the national heritage; import or sale may be prohibited on the grounds that the article does not meet national safety standards or (to an extent[4]) that it bears a trade mark protected in the receiving country.

180. Customs duties and charges of equivalent effect. Articles 12 and 13 of the Treaty provide for the elimination of customs duties and charges having equivalent effect upon imports within the Community. This prohibition is rigorously applied, and has been directly effective since 1969 (the end of the

---

1 On these and other peculiarities of the territory of the customs union see Special Report No 2/93 of the Court of Auditors on the customs territory of the Community and related trading arrangements, OJ C347, 27.12.93, p 1.
2 See paras 180-192 below.
3 See eg Case 41/76 *Donckerwolcke v Procureur de la République* [1976] ECR 1921, [1977] 2 CMLR 535.
4 See para 196 below.

transitional period)[1]. A charge having equivalent effect to a customs duty has been defined by the Court of Justice as:

'any pecuniary charge, however small, and whatever its designation and mode of application, which is imposed unilaterally on domestic or foreign goods by reason of the fact that they cross a frontier, and which is not a customs duty in the strict sense, . . . even if it is not imposed for the benefit of the State, is not discriminatory or protective in effect and if the product on which the charge is imposed is not in competition with any domestic product'[2].

Article 16 provides a like prohibition of duties and equivalent charges upon exports.

181. Customs duties and internal taxation. A charge imposed by national law upon imported goods which appears to have an effect equivalent to a customs duty may in fact be a facet of a member state's system of internal taxation, if taxes are also imposed upon a like domestic product at a similar stage of production. If so, the charge does not fall under article 12[3] but must be considered under article 95, which deals with internal taxation and is discussed below[4]. The two categories are mutually exclusive: a charge levied upon a good crossing a frontier may fall under article 12 or article 95, but cannot fall under both[5].

182. The Common Customs Tariff. As a customs union requires the creation of a uniform tariff wall applied to goods from third countries, the Treaty provides for the progressive establishment of the Common Customs Tariff (CCT), which was fully implemented by 1969[6]. The CCT, which was reorganised in 1987[7], is amended from time to time by the Council and published annually in the Official Journal in updated and consolidated form[8]. Since its coming into force, member states are no longer competent to impose any autonomous duties upon goods from third countries[9]. Other Community legislation has been adopted in order to provide for common customs rules so that goods from third countries undergo uniform valuation and procedures upon entry into the Community. The legislation was consolidated in 1992 in the Community Customs Code[10].

---

1 See eg Case 33/70 *SACE v Ministero delle Finanze* [1970] ECR 1213, [1971] CMLR 123; as to the transitional period see para 169 above.
2 Case 24/68 *Commission v Italy* [1969] ECR 193 at 201, [1971] CMLR 611 at 623.
3 EC Treaty, art 17.
4 See paras 257-260.
5 See eg Case 94/74 *IGAV v ENCC* [1975] ECR 699.
6 EC Treaty, arts 18-29; Regulation 950/68, JO L172, 22.7.68, p 1 (S Edn 1968 (I) p 275).
7 Regulation 2658/87, OJ L256, 7.9.87, p 1. The CCT is classified now by means of the Integrated Community Tariff ('Taric'), which is based upon a Combined Nomenclature ('CN').
8 For the most recent version see OJ C141A, 24.5.94, p 1.
9 Cases 37-38/73 *Sociaal Fonds voor de Diamantarbeiders v Indiamex* [1973] ECR 1609, [1976] 2 CMLR 222.
10 Regulation 2913/92, OJ L302, 19.10.92, p 1.

183. The Common Commercial Policy. The Treaty also provides for the gradual adoption of a common policy in commercial relations with third countries. Unlike the Common Customs Tariff, the Common Commercial Policy has not yet been fully achieved. It is the subject of a separate, subsequent title and is discussed below[1].

(B) FREE MOVEMENT OF GOODS: NON-TARIFF BARRIERS

184. The internal market in goods. Having established a common tariff wall vis-à-vis goods coming from countries outside the Community, the Treaty goes on to deal with national measures which limit trade in goods within the Community. The aim is:

> 'the elimination of all obstacles to intra-Community trade in order to merge the national markets into a single market bringing about conditions as close as possible to those of a genuine internal market'[2].

185. Imports and exports: Prohibition of quantitative restrictions and measures of equivalent effect. The Treaty declares that quantitative restrictions upon imports (article 30) and exports (article 34) and all measures having equivalent effect are prohibited between member states. By 'quantitative restrictions' is meant quotas – measures which prescribe the number or quantity of goods of a particular type which may enter the domestic market. 'Measures of equivalent effect' include all forms of action which may be taken by, or with the authority of, the state. So legislation, bye-laws, the administrative practice of any public authority, injunctions or interdicts pronounced by courts, rules promulgated by professional regulatory bodies, are 'measures' struck at by articles 30 and 34. The prohibition has direct effect[3].

186. 'Distinctly' and 'indistinctly' applicable measures. Non-tariff barriers to trade take a variety of forms. Some are overtly protectionist, discriminating directly against imported products by prescribing rules which apply only to them. Others have no protectionist intent and apply without distinction to imported and domestic products, but nevertheless constitute barriers to the entry of imported goods to the domestic market. For example, differences in national rules on additives to foodstuffs may make it more difficult to market imported goods. A distinction is made between:

- 'distinctly applicable measures', measures which make an explicit distinction between imported and domestic products, and
- 'indistinctly applicable measures', measures which apply without distinction to imported and domestic products alike.

---

1 See paras 268-270.
2 Case 15/81 *Gaston Schul v Inspecteur der Invoerrechten en Accijnzen* [1982] ECR 1409 at 1431-1432, [1982] 3 CMLR 229 at 251.
3 Case 74/76 *Iannelli e Volpi v Meroni* [1977] ECR 557, [1977] 2 CMLR 688.

Distinctly applicable measures fall directly under articles 30 and 34 and are prohibited unless they can be justified under article 36[1]. Indistinctly applicable measures require to be analysed more closely to see whether they are struck at.

187. Restrictions upon imports: the *Dassonville* test. In 1974 the Court of Justice declared that:

> 'All trading rules enacted by Member States which are capable of hindering, directly or indirectly, actually or potentially, intra-Community trade are to be considered as measures having an effect equivalent to quantitative restrictions'[2].

The *Dassonville* test, which is cited frequently by the Court, is comprehensive and applies whether the national measures in question are distinctly or indistinctly applicable. There is no *de minimis* rule: it need not be shown that a national rule inhibits the importation of goods to an appreciable extent[3]. But there must be a genuine (albeit only potential or indirect) *hindrance to trade* in imported goods, in law or in fact[4].

188. *Cassis de Dijon*. In 1979 in *Cassis de Dijon*[5] the Court of Justice laid down the general principle that where a product has been lawfully produced and marketed in one member state, it must be allowed to be traded freely throughout the Community. The effect of this judgment, which lies at the heart of the 1992 programme, was summarised subsequently by the Court thus:

> 'It is established by the case-law beginning with *Cassis de Dijon* . . . that, in the absence of harmonization of legislation, obstacles to free movement of goods which are the consequence of applying, to goods coming from other Member States where they are lawfully manufactured[6] and marketed, rules that lay down requirements to be met by such goods (such as those relating to designation, form, size, weight, composition, presentation, labelling, packaging) constitute

---

1 See para 191 below.
2 Case 8/74 *Procureur du Roi v Dassonville* [1974] ECR 837 at 852, [1974] 2 CMLR 436 at 453-4.
3 Case 16/83 *Criminal Proceedings against Karl Prantl* [1984] ECR 1299, [1985] 2 CMLR 238.
4 Case C-267-268/91 *Criminal Proceedings against Keck and Mithouard* [1993] ECR I-6097, disapproving a line of case law, notably the earlier Sunday trading cases (Case C-145/88 *Torfaen Borough Council v B & Q* [1989] ECR 3851, [1990] 1 CMLR 337; Case C-312/89 *Union Déparmentale des Syndicats CGT de l'Aisne v Conforama* [1991] ECR I-997; Case C-332/89 *Marchandise* [1991] ECR I-1027; Case C-169/91 *Stoke-on-Trent City Council v B & Q* [1992] ECR I-6635, [1993] 1 CMLR 426), which appeared to imply that the *Dassonville* test struck at *any* rule the effect of which was to limit in any way the number or amount of imported goods sold on the national market. See subsequently Case C-292/92 *Hünermund v Landesapothekerskammer Baden-Württemberg* [1993] ECR I-6787 (German regulations prohibiting advertising in chemists' shops); Cases C-401-2/92 *Tankstation 't Heukske and Boermans* [1994] ECR I-2199 (Dutch legislation on the opening hours of petrol stations); and Cases C-69 & 258/93 *Punto Casa v Sindaco del Commune di Capena* [1994] ECR I-2355 (Italian Sunday trading legislation).
5 Case 120/78 *Rewe Zentrale v Bundesmonopolverwaltung für Branntwein* (Cassis de Dijon) [1979] ECR 649, [1979] 3 CMLR 494.
6 This is perhaps a misleading formulation, as goods need not be produced in a member state to fall within the field of art 30, they need only be in free circulation (see para 178 above).

measures of equivalent effect prohibited by Article 30. This is so even if those rules apply without distinction to all products unless their application can be justified by a public-interest objective taking precedence over the free movement of goods'[1].

189. The 'mandatory requirements' or 'rule of reason'. The Court expressly recognised in *Cassis de Dijon* that some disparities in national rules have to be accepted even if their effect constitutes a barrier to trade. This is so where the rules are necessary to satisfy 'mandatory requirements' (a clumsy translation of *'exigences impératives'* – imperative/overriding needs) such as the effectiveness of fiscal supervision, public health, the fairness of commercial dealings, consumer protection[2], promotion of national culture[3] or protection of the environment[4]. To escape the reach of article 30, such rules must be:
- indistinctly applicable[5];
- objectively justified; and
- proportionate.

190. Restrictions upon exports. Article 34 of the Treaty prohibits quantitative restrictions and all measures having equivalent effect on exports. However, in contradistinction to article 30, the Court of Justice has held that national measures which impede exports will fall foul of article 34 only if they are distinctly applicable[6].

191. Exceptions: article 36. Article 36 is the only basis upon which distinctly applicable restrictions upon imports and exports can be justified[7]. It applies only to a strictly defined category of measures dealing with:
- public morality, public policy or public security;
- the protection of health and life of humans, animals or plants;
- the protection of national treasures possessing artistic, historic or archaeological value; and
- the protection of industrial or commercial property (including intellectual property).

---

1 Cases C-267-68/91 *Criminal Proceedings against Keck and Mithouard* [1993] ECR I-6097 at 6131.
2 These four 'mandatory requirements' were expressly cited in *Cassis de Dijon*, but it was clear that the Court did not intend to provide an exhaustive list.
3 Cases 60-61/84 *Cinéthèque v Fédération National des Cinemas Français* [1985] ECR 2605, [1986] 1 CMLR 365.
4 Case 302/86 *Commission v Denmark* (Returnable Bottles) [1988] ECR 4607, [1989] 1 CMLR 619; Case C-2/90 *Commission v Belgium* [1992] ECR I-4431, [1993] 1 CMLR 365.
5 Case 113/80 *Commission v Ireland* (Irish Souvenirs) [1981] ECR 1625, [1982] 1 CMLR 706, reaffirmed in Case 434/85 *Allen and Hanburys v Generics (UK) Ltd* [1988] ECR 1245, [1988] 1 CMLR 701.
6 Case 15/79 *Groenveld v Produktschap voor Vee en Vlees* [1979] ECR 3409, [1981] 1 CMLR 207; Cases 141-43/81 *Holdijk* [1982] ECR 1299, [1983] 2 CMLR 635.
7 Case 113/80 *Commission v Ireland* (Irish Souvenirs) [1981] ECR 1625, [1982] 1 CMLR 706, reaffirmed in Case 434/85 *Allen and Hanburys v Generics (UK) Ltd* [1988] ECR 1245, [1988] 1 CMLR 701.

Further, article 36 saves national measures only so long as they:
● are not 'a means of arbitrary discrimination or a disguised restriction on trade between Member States'[1];
● are not pre-empted by Community legislation[2];
● are objectively justified; and
● are proportionate.

192. Arbitrary discrimination, objective justification and proportionality. Since article 36 constitutes an exception to a basic principle of the Treaty, the Court of Justice has said that it must be interpreted restrictively[3]. So, for example, a national rule constitutes arbitrary discrimination when it has the effect of excluding goods alleged to endanger public morality but the law does not at the same time provide rules which effectively inhibit domestic production of the goods in question[4]. It is not enough to escape the reach of article 30, or to bring a measure within the scope of article 36, that the national rule-making body thinks the rule is necessary[5]; it must be shown to be necessary for the purpose it purports to achieve. And it must be proportionate, ie, it will be justified only if there are no other means less disruptive to trade which will achieve the same legitimate ends of the measure in question[6].

193. Harmonisation of technical barriers to trade. Where national measures which impede trade can be justified by recourse to article 36 or to the mandatory requirements, the impediment to trade can be resolved only by harmonisation of the national rules and standards at issue. Article 100 of the Treaty therefore empowers the Council to adopt directives in order to 'harmonise' (or 'approximate') national rules so as to eliminate 'technical barriers' to trade which affect the establishment or functioning of the common market. However, harmonisation of national law under article 100 requires unanimity in the Council. The Single European Act amended the Treaty so as to enable the Council, by qualified majority vote, to adopt harmonisation measures necessary for the completion of the internal market[7]. It is frequently important to determine whether a given measure harmonises the law minimally, partially or exhaustively[8]. Where harmonisation is

---

1 Article 36, final sentence.
2 See para 193 below.
3 See eg Case 4/75 *Rewe Zentralfinanz v Landwirtschaftskammer* [1975] ECR 843, [1977] 1 CMLR 599.
4 Case 121/85 *Conegate v HM Customs and Excise* [1986] ECR 1007, [1986] 1 CMLR 739. For a less than rigorous English approach to this principle see *R v Bow Street Magistrates Court, ex parte Noncyp* [1988] 3 CMLR 84 (QBD).
5 Case 178/84 *Commission v Germany* (Reinheitsgebot) [1987] ECR 1227, [1988] 1 CMLR 780.
6 See eg Case 261/85 *Commission v United Kingdom* (Pasteurised Milk) [1988] ECR 547, [1988] 2 CMLR 11; Case 382/87 *Buet v Ministère Public* [1989] ECR 1235.
7 EC Treaty, art 100a; see para 170 above.
8 See eg Case 148/78 *Pubblico Ministero v Ratti* [1979] ECR 1629, [1980] 1 CMLR 96; Case 60/86 *Commission v United Kingdom* ('Dim-Dip Headlamps') [1988] ECR 3921, [1988] 3 CMLR 437; Case C-169/89 *Gourmetterie van den Burg* [1990] ECR I-2143; Case C-11/92 *R v Secretary of State for Health, ex parte Gallaher* [1993] ECR I-3545, [1994] 3 CMLR 179.

exhaustive, the directive occupies the field and pre-empts the adoption of any autonomous national rules, so excluding any possibility of invoking article 36 or mandatory requirements. Where a directive harmonises the law only partially, there is a strong presumption that it precludes recourse to article 36 or the mandatory requirements in order to justify restrictions to inter-state trade[1], but it leaves member states free to adopt rules which continue to govern domestic production[2]. The Treaty provides that notwithstanding harmonisation measures adopted under article 100a (but not article 100), member states retain a right to protect 'major needs' (*exigences importantes*) such as those of article 36 or protection of the environment or the working environment by maintaining higher standards and excluding goods which do not meet them[3], unless the measure harmonises national law exhaustively. New technical requirements are required to be notified to the Commission[4] and cannot be introduced for a certain period[5].

194. Reverse discrimination. Application of *Cassis de Dijon* may have the effect of discriminating against home producers. Thus, where national rules regulate the production of goods in a manner more stringent than the rules which obtain in other member states, *Cassis de Dijon* will normally require that goods produced in those other member states must have access to the home market but the home producer, bound by the domestic rules, will be operating at a cost or other comparative disadvantage. It was argued that this offends the general Community principle of non-discrimination[6], so that a home producer ought to be exempt from the national rules to the same extent as competitors who have access to the home market. The Court of Justice held that such reverse discrimination is not prohibited by the Treaty, as such a prohibition would result in reducing all national rules to their lowest common denominator. So national rules (where there has been no exhaustive harmonisation) remain applicable to domestic production[7].

195. Public procurement. The Cockfield White Paper identified the continued partitioning of national markets in public procurement, and the universal tendency to 'buy national', as one of the most evident barriers to the achievement of a genuine internal market[8]. Public procurement is therefore

---

1 See eg Case 5/77 *Tedeschi v Denkavit Commerciale* [1977] ECR 1555, [1978] 1 CMLR 1; Case 251/78 *Denkavit v Minister für Ernährung* [1979] ECR 3369, [1980] 3 CMLR 513; Case C-323/93 *Société civile agricole du Centre d'insémination de la Crespelle v Co-opérative d'élevage et d'insémination artificielle du département de la Mayenne*, judgment of 5 October 1994, not yet reported.
2 See para 194 below.
3 EC Treaty, art 100a(4); see also art 130t. On the one judicial consideration of art 100a(4) see Case C-41/93 *France v Commission* [1994] ECR I-1829. For an example of the Commission endorsing a national derogation by authority of art 100a(4) see Decision 94/783, OJ L316, 9.12.94, p 43.
4 Directive 83/189, OJ L109, 26.4.83, p 8.
5 Ibid; Case C-139/92 *Commission v Italy* [1993] ECR I-4707.
6 See para 168 above.
7 See eg Case 98/86 *Ministère Public v Methot* [1987] ECR 809, [1988] 1 CMLR 411.
8 *Completing the Internal Market*, COM(85) 310, para 81.

now governed by a series of directives regulating public works contracts[1], public supplies contracts[2] and utilities contracts[3], combined with other directives seeking to co-ordinate procedures for the award of contracts[4] and to ensure transparency[5] and compliance[6]. Very generally, they impose upon national, regional and local authorities, when acting as 'contracting authorities' in all but minor contracts for building or civil engineering work (public works) or the purchase, lease, rental or hire purchase of products from a supplier (public supplies), an obligation to give notice of a contract they intend to award[7] and then award the contract in accordance with the procedures provided in the directives. Reservation of a proportion of contracts to tenders from a particular geographic area of a member state is a breach of article 30[8], even if the implementation of such a policy only deters or might deter imports from other member states[9]. Technical specifications which favour or eliminate certain makes or sources of contract goods or services are in principle prohibited[10]. A contract awarded in a manner inconsistent with these rules is voidable. Alternatively, the Commission may raise an enforcement action under article 169[11], and the Court of Justice has not been slow to order the interim supension of a contract shown *prima facie* to contravene the directives owing to the irreparable loss to contractors unable to tender or supply[12].

196. Industrial property rights. Another area in which the application of national rules may fragment the Community market is the protection of industrial and intellectual property rights. National rules governing property ownership are safeguarded by article 222 of the Treaty, whilst article 36 specifically mentions the protection of industrial or commercial property as a permitted exception to articles 30 and 34. However, the Court of Justice has held that whilst the *existence* of such rights is not affected by the Treaty, their *exercise* may infringe the rules on free movement[13]. The question therefore is not whether it is compatible with the Treaty for national law to confer exclusive rights upon inventors or manufacturers, but whether the proprietors of such rights should be entitled to enforce them in such a way as to restrict the free movement of goods. As a general rule, the power conferred by national law to restrict the importation of goods protected by the right is said to be 'exhausted' once the

1 Directive 71/305, JO L185, 16.8.71, p 5 (as amended).
2 Directive 77/62, OJ L13, 15.1.77, p 1 (as amended).
3 Directive 90/531, OJ L297, 29.10.90, p 1.
4 Directives 93/36, 93/37 and 93/38, OJ L199, 9.8.93, pp 1, 54 and 84.
5 Directive 80/723, OJ L195, 29.7.80, p 35.
6 Directive 89/665, OJ L395, 30.12.89, p 33.
7 The notice is submitted to the Community's office for Official Publications and then published in a special series of the Official Journal.
8 Case 21/88 *Du Pont de Nemours v Unita Sanitaria di Carrera* [1990] ECR I-889.
9 Case 132/88 *Commission v Greece* [1990] ECR I-1567.
10 See eg Case 45/87 *Commission v Ireland* [1988] ECR 4929.
11 See eg Case C-243/89 *Commission v Denmark* (Storebælt) [1993] ECR I-3353; Case C-45/91 *Commission v Greece* [1992] ECR I-2525.
12 See eg Case 45/87R *Commission v Ireland* [1987] ECR 783; Case 194/88R *Commission v Italy* [1988] ECR 5647. On the power of the Court to order interim relief see para 113 above.
13 Case 78/70 *Deutsche Grammophon v Metro* [1971] ECR 487, [1971] CMLR 631.

good has been put into free circulation in a member state by the proprietor of the right or with his consent[1]. Enforcement of an industrial property right in pursuance of a restrictive practice or of market dominance may also infringe the Community rules on competition[2]. There has been some harmonisation in the field – for example, the creation of the Community trade mark in 1994[3] – but generally it has proved a difficult process.

197. State monopolies of a commercial character. Article 37 of the Treaty deals with the special situation of 'state monopolies of a commercial charac- ter', ie, those enjoying exclusive rights under national law in the procure- ment and distribution of goods. Such monopolies must be 'adjusted' to the extent necessary to conform with Treaty rules on the free movement of goods, which requires the abolition of any exclusive right of import[4]. Article 37 applies only to those activities connected intrinsically with the function- ing of the monopoly and not other severable national rules[5], and is directly effective[6]. It must be read with later provisions of the Treaty relating to the application of the competition rules to public undertakings, to state aids and to discriminatory taxation[7].

(C) AGRICULTURE

198. Agriculture. The Treaty provides special and very complex rules gov- erning trade in agricultural products. Agriculture is an important part of the economy of some, and enjoyed subsidies in all, member states. Further, in the aftermath of the 1939-45 war self-sufficiency in food was regarded as an important and praiseworthy objective. The Treaty therefore made special provisions for agriculture in Title II of Part Three (articles 38 to 47), in two ways: first, by making special rules for trade in agricultural products, and second, by providing for the development of a Common Agricultural Policy. The workings of the CAP are beyond the scope of this book. Three general points should be noted.

First, 'agricultural products' are defined as 'the products of the soil, of stock-farming and of fisheries and products of first-stage processing directly related to these products'[8]. The fisheries policy is therefore an aspect of the CAP.

---

1 Case 78/70 *Deutsche Grammophon v Metro* [1971] ECR 487, [1971] CMLR 631. The consent must however be freely given (Case 19/84 *Pharmon v Hoechst* [1985] ECR 2281, [1985] 3 CMLR 775); scission of a national trade mark does not imply consent (Case C-10/89 *SA CNL-Sucal NV v HAG GF AG* (Hag II) [1990] ECR I-3711, [1990] 3 CMLR 571; Case C-9/93 *IHT Internationale Heiztechnik v Ideal Standard* [1994] ECR I-2789).
2 See para 237 below.
3 Regulation 40/94, OJ L11, 14.1.94, p 1.
4 Case 59/75 *Pubblico Ministero v Manghera* [1976] ECR 91, [1976] 1 CMLR 557.
5 Case 86/78 *Grandes Distilleries Peureux v Directeur des Services Fisceaux* [1979] ECR 897, [1980] 3 CMLR 337.
6 Case 6/64 *Costa v ENEL* [1964] ECR 585, [1964] CMLR 425.
7 See paras 249-260 below.
8 EC Treaty, art 38(1). An exhaustive list of products subject to the rules of the CAP are con- tained in Annex II and in Regulation 7a, JO 1961 p 71 (S Edn 1959-62 p 68).

Second, the Treaty provides that 'save as otherwise provided ..., the rules laid down for the establishment of the common market shall apply to agricultural products'[1]. This means that agricultural goods are isolated from the application of general Treaty rules, but only in so far as required by special provisions of the CAP. In particular, the competition rules apply virtually unhindered[2].

Third, the Treaty provides for the organisation of agricultural markets in three possible ways, one of which is the creation of 'European market organisations'[3]. This is the method which was in fact adopted, and detailed systems have been developed for the organisation of the market, including intervention and price support, in virtually all agricultural goods. The rules vary depending upon the instrument regulating the particular sector. The Court of Justice has held that products not specified in Annex II[4] or products which have not been made subject to a market organisation[5] are subject to the application of the normal rules of the Treaty, and that the creation of a market organisation has the effect of depriving the member states of the power to take any measure which might undermine or create exceptions to it[6].

(D) FREE MOVEMENT OF PERSONS AND SERVICES

199. The distinction between persons and services. The Treaty deals with persons and services in the three Chapters of Title III of Part Three, which address: 'Workers' (articles 48-51) – the right of wage and salary earners to work in other member states; 'Right of Establishment' (articles 52-58) – the right of self-employed individuals and companies or firms to establish a permanent base in another member state and there pursue economic activities in their own names; and 'Services' (articles 59-66) – the right to cross frontiers in order to provide or receive services without establishing a permanent base in another member state. The distinction is confusing since 'free movement of persons' would normally be taken to imply the right of individuals to move from one country to another, whether temporarily or permanently, whilst 'free movement of services' would be taken to imply the more abstract concept of an unrestricted right to provide or receive services in any part of the Community. But that is not how the Treaty approaches the matter.

---

1 EC Treaty, art 38(2).
2 For agricultural products not specified in Annex II the competition rules apply normally; Case C-250/92 *Gøttrup-Klim v Dansk Landbrugs Grovvareselskab*, judgment of 15 December 1994, not yet reported. For agricultural products falling within Annex II they are applied by Regulation 26, JO 1962 p 993 (S Edn 1959-62 p 129).
3 EC Treaty, art 40(2).
4 Cases 2-3/62 *EEC Commission v Luxembourg and Belgium* (Gingerbread) [1962] ECR 425, [1963] CMLR 199.
5 Case 48/74 *Charmasson v Minister for Economic Affairs and Finance* [1974] ECR 1383, [1975] 2 CMLR 208; Case 68/76 *Commission v France* [1977] ECR 515, [1977] 2 CMLR 161. The only major market not yet the subject of a common market organisation is that of potatoes.
6 See eg Case 51/74 *Van der Hulst's Zonen v Produktschap voor Siergewassen* [1975] ECR 79, [1975] 1 CMLR 236; Case 111/76 *Officier van Justitie v van den Hazel* [1977] ECR 901, [1980] 3 CMLR 12.

200. Clarification of the distinction: Workers. The Chapter on workers is concerned with enabling individual wage or salary earners (*'travailleurs'*) to find employment within the context of the economic operations of actual or potential employers. It applies therefore only to individuals who are, or wish to be, in a contract of employment and is not concerned with the freedom of employers to conduct their operations. Although not defined in the Treaty or in Community legislation, the term 'worker' has a specific Community law meaning[1]. It covers anyone pursuing or wishing to pursue effective and genuine employment (ie, under the direction of and remunerated by an employer), even if part time, so long as the work is not so infinitesimal as to be disregarded as such, and even if reimbursement is at a rate lower than a minimum guaranteed wage[2]. A person seeking to exercise economic activity under the Treaty in any other capacity must rely upon the Chapters on establishment and services.

201. Clarification of the distinction: Establishment and services. The Chapters on establishment and services apply to independent economic operators, whether individuals or other legal persons (*'personnes non-salariées'*), pursuing economic activities in their own names beyond the frontiers of their home member state. The difference between establishment and services is not always clear-cut. Establishment entails 'the actual pursuit of an economic activity through a fixed establishment in another Member State for an indefinite period'[3] and suggests domiciliation[4] and permanent or at least durable integration into the economy of another member state. Services entails the provision or enjoyment of economic activity in another member state upon a temporary basis. Generally, the Chapter on Services will apply where the provider and the recipient of a service (in its colloquial sense) are established ('domiciled'), or deemed to be established, in two separate member states[5].

202. Scheme. Subject to this framework, the rules governing workers, establishment and services follow the same general pattern. The Court of Justice tends to treat them as particular aspects of a uniform system and, unless concerned with the specific rules of a particular chapter, to construe them in the same manner. Essentially, the Treaty deals with three types of obstacle to the free movement of persons and services: (1) restrictions on grounds of nationality; (2) other unjustifiable restrictions which can be abolished altogether; and (3) restrictions which cannot be abolished altogether but whose adverse effects upon free movement can be removed by harmonisation or

---

1 Case 75/63 *Unger v Bestuur der Bedrijfsvereniging voor Detailhandel en Ambachten* [1964] ECR 177, [1964] CMLR 319.
2 Case 53/81 *Levin v Staatssecretaris van Justitie* [1982] ECR 1035, [1982] 2 CMLR 454; Case 139/85 *Kempf v Staatssecretaris van Justitie* [1986] ECR 1741, [1987] 1 CMLR 764; in Case 196/87 *Steymann v Staatssecretaris van Justitie* [1988] ECR 6159, [1989] 1 CMLR 449 work in a religious community in exchange for pocket money was held to constitute 'work' for these purposes.
3 Case C-221/89 *R v Secretary of State for Transport, ex parte Factortame* [1991] ECR I-3905 at 3965, [1991] 3 CMLR 589 at 627.
4 This is strongly implied by the German term for establishment *Niederlassung*.
5 Case 205/84 *Commission v Germany* (Insurance and Co-Insurance) [1986] ECR 3755 at 3801, [1987] 2 CMLR 69 at 100.

co-ordinating legislation. Most of the basic rules have direct effect and can be enforced in national courts without further legislation.

203. Beneficiaries. The primary beneficiaries of the Treaty provisions on the free movement of persons and services are nationals of a member state as defined by the nationality laws of that state (or, now, citizens of the Union)[1] and companies or firms formed in accordance with the laws of a member state[2]. There is no concept of 'free circulation' of third country nationals equivalent to that required by the customs union for goods[3]. Thus, a national of a third country lawfully resident in one member state enjoys no right of free movement – indeed, virtually no rights at all[4] – under Community law. The lack of uniform rules in this area is the chief obstacle to completion of the internal market[5]. The Treaty does however provide an option (not yet exercised fully) to extend the Chapter on Services to nationals of third countries[6]. Nationals of third countries may also enjoy 'parasitic' rights by virtue of Treaty rights conferred upon their spouses and families[7] or by virtue of being employees of a Community firm providing services in another member state[8]. Certain aspects of the treatment of third country nationals are now pursued by the European Union under Title VI of the Treaty on European Union[9].

204. Families. Persons entitled to free movement within the Community would be less inclined to exercise that freedom if they were unable to bring their families with them. Community legislation[10] therefore provides that the rules on entry and residence for persons seeking to work, establish themselves or provide or receive a service apply, irrespective of nationality[11], also to:
(1) their spouses, and their own and their spouses' descendants who are either under 21 years of age or are dependants; and
(2) dependant relatives in the ascending (and descending[12]) line of both spouses.

---

1 See para 171 above.
2 EC Treaty, art 58.
3 See para 178 above.
4 A national of a third country resident in the Community may petition the European Parliament and the Parliament's Ombudsman; see para 54 above.
5 See para 170 above.
6 EC Treaty, art 59, 2nd para.
7 See para 204 below.
8 Case C-113/89 *Rush Portuguesa v Office National de l'Immigration* [1990] ECR I-1417; Case C-43/93 *Vander Elst v Office des Migrations Internationales* [1994] ECR I-3801.
9 See paras 295-298 below.
10 Directive 68/360, JO L257, 19.10.68, p 13 (S Edn 1968 (II) p 485), art 1 (workers); Directive 73/148, OJ L172, 28.6.73, p 14, art 1 (establishment and services).
11 Non-Community nationals may be required to obtain visas.
12 Directive 68/360 provides only for the ascending line; Directive 73/148 provides for both.

·A 'spouse' exists only by virtue of a lawfully contracted marriage[1]. Admission of family members who do not fall within heads (1) or (2) but who are dependent upon the holder of the primary right must be 'facilitated' (workers) or 'favoured' (establishment and services). The meaning of these terms has not yet been tested. Family members of a worker or of a person established in another member state have the right to work there[2] (an important advantage for family members who are not Community nationals), even in a regulated profession, provided they have the necessary qualifications[3]. They also have a right to education and to vocational training in the member state upon an equal footing with home nationals[4].

205. Right of entry. The Treaty gives migrant workers (the term used to describe a Community national exercising rights as a worker) the right to move freely throughout the territory of the member states in order to accept 'offers of employment actually made', to stay within a member state for the purpose of employment and to remain there after employment[5]. The provisions on the Chapters on establishment and services are less explicit but have been construed as involving the same rights *mutatis mutandis*. Detailed rules applying equally to migrant workers and natural persons exercising their rights in relation to establishment and services confer the right to be issued with an identity card or passport, to leave the national territory and enter the territory of another member state merely upon the production of the identity card or passport[6]. A migrant worker may enter a member state in order to look for employment[7], even if unemployed and without an offer of work, so long as the intention to look for work is genuine. The period for which he may do so, though not defined, is generally understood to be a minimum of three months. The United Kingdom, which allows six months[8], was held to be entitled to expel a Belgian migrant worker who had failed to find work during that six-month period, unless he could prove that he was continuing to look for work and had a genuine chance of being engaged[9].

206. Right of residence. The right of residence in another member state depends upon whether the individual is exercising an economic activity by

---

1 Case 59/85 *Netherlands v Reed* [1986] ECR 1283, [1987] 2 CMLR 448. But the status of 'spouse' continues so long as the marriage survives, even if the spouses are separated and divorce proceedings are in progress; see Case C-370/90 *R v Immigration Appeal Tribunal and Singh, ex parte Secretary of State for the Home Department* [1992] ECR I-4265, [1992] 3 CMLR 358; also Case 267/83 *Diatta v Land Berlin* [1985] ECR 567, [1986] 2 CMLR 164.

2 Regulation 1612/68, JO L257, 19.10.68, p 2 (S Edn 1868 (II) p 475), art 11.

3 Case 131/85 *Gül v Regierungspräsident Düsseldorf* [1986] ECR 1573, [1987] 1 CMLR 501.

4 Regulation 1612/68, art 12; see further para 218 below.

5 EC Treaty, art 48(1). These rules are directly effective; see Case 48/75 *Procureur du Roi v Royer* [1976] ECR 497, [1976] 2 CMLR 614.

6 Directive 68/360, JO L257, 19.10.68, p 13 (S Edn 1968 (II) p 485), arts 2-3 (workers); Directive 73/148, OJ L172, 28.6.73, p 14, arts 2-3 (establishment and services); Case C-68/89 *Commission v Netherlands* [1991] ECR I-2637, [1993] 2 CMLR 839.

7 See eg Case 53/81 *Levin v Staatssecretaris van Justitie* [1982] ECR 1035, [1982] 2 CMLR 454.

8 *Statement of Changes in the Immigration Rules* HC Papers (1982-83) No 169, paras 67, 143.

9 Case C-292/89 *R v Immigration Appeal Tribunal, ex parte Antonissen* [1991] ECR I-745, [1991] 2 CMLR 373.

virtue of a right conferred by the Treaty. Once a migrant worker is in work, or a Community national is established in another member state, he is entitled to reside in the territory of that state[1] and to have a residence permit valid for at least five years and automatically renewable[2]. An individual providing or receiving a service has a right of residence for as long as is necessary[3]; if the period is longer than three months he is entitled to a certificate of 'right of abode' as proof of his right of residence[3]. A migrant worker or a person established in another member state has the 'right to remain' in residence following completion of employment or activity[4], for example upon retirement. Until 1992 an 'economic nexus', or some economic activity, however generously defined, was necessary in order to give rise to a right of residence[5]. In 1990 the Council adopted three directives (required to be implemented by July 1992) which confer a right of residence upon all Community nationals and their families who do not enjoy the right by virtue of any other provision of Community law. The directives apply expressly to pensioners[6], students[7] and to all others[8] who can show they have adequate medical insurance and sufficient resources to avoid becoming a burden upon social assistance for the duration of their residence[9].

207. Equal treatment: Regulation 1612/68. The Treaty lays down a general prohibition against discrimination based upon nationality[10]. The purpose is to ensure 'equal treatment' of the nationals of all member states (including companies and firms) wherever they may be within the Community and whatever the nature of the economic activity they wish to pursue. So any rule which makes it more difficult for a Community national to find work, establish himself or provide a service in another member state is *prima facie* contrary to the Treaty. This includes rules created by legislation, but also administrative rules and practices and rules made by autonomous professional bodies. The Treaty is concerned with the practical effect of the rule, rather than its theoretical nature or source. Under Regulation 1612/68[11], migrant workers have, in principle, the same priority and employment law

---

1 Directive 68/360, arts 4-7; Directive 73/148, art 4(1).
2 Ibid. In order to obtain the permit workers and persons may be required to furnish proof of employment or of economic activity. The first residence permit may be restricted to one year.
3 Directive 73/148, art 4(2).
4 Regulation 1251/70, JO L142, 30.6.70, p 24 (S Edn 1970 (II) p 402) (workers); Directive 73/34, OJ L14, 20.1.75, p 10 (establishment).
5 See eg Case 13/76 *Dona v Mantero* [1976] ECR 133, [1976] 2 CMLR 578; Case 196/87 *Steymann v Staatssecretaris van Justitie* [1986] ECR 1741, [1987] 1 CMLR 764.
6 Directive 90/365, OJ L180, 13.7.90, p 28.
7 Directive 90/366, OJ L180, 13.7.90, p 30. This directive was annulled by the Court of Justice in Case C-295/90 *European Parliament v Council* (Students) [1992] ECR I-4193, [1992] 3 CMLR 281 for want of correct legal basis in the Treaty; its legal effects were declared to be operative by the Court (see para 102 above) and it is now replaced by Directive 93/96, OJ L317, 18.12.93, p 59. On students, see further para 218 below.
8 Directive 90/364 (the 'playboy' directive), OJ L180, 13.7.90, p 26.
9 The effect of art 8a(1), added by the TEU (see para 171 above), is raised in Case C-229/94 *R v Secretary of State for the Home Department, ex parte Adams* (pending).
10 EC Treaty, art 6 and, more specifically for workers, art 48(2).
11 Regulation 1612/68, JO L257, 19.10.68, p 2 (S Edn 1968 (II) p 475).

protection as home nationals, as the Regulation seeks to guarantee the right to take up employment with the same priority and protection as home nationals. Thus any form of limitation of employment to home nationals, recruitment procedures designed specifically for them, restrictive advertising and eligibility limited to conditions which other Community nationals cannot reasonably meet are prohibited[1]. The prohibition applies not only to direct discrimination but also to rules and practices which produce a similar effect (ie covert or indirect discrimination)[2]. The only exceptions are language requirements where, given the nature of the employment, there is objective justification for the requirement[3], and discriminatory tax rules for which there is objective justification[4]. Migrant workers have, on the same footing as home nationals, a right to vocational training[5], to trade union membership and activities[6], and to housing and social and tax advantages[7]. Equal treatment for those exercising rights under the chapters on establishment and services is secured upon a different basis[8].

208. Social security: article 51 and Regulation 1408/71. Persons entitled to free movement within the Community would also be disinclined to exercise that freedom if by so doing they jeopardised any accrued entitlements to social security benefits – the most obvious example being pension rights. Regulation 1408/71[9] coordinates existing national social security schemes so as to ensure fair entitlement to Community nationals exercising their rights under the Treaty. The regulation applies to anyone affiliated with a social security scheme[10], thus including those exercising a right of establishment and, where appropriate, those providing or receiving a service. Families, as defined by the applicable national legislation, also fall within the ambit of the regulation[11]. The general scheme of the regulation is that benefits accrued anywhere within the Community are 'aggregated', so that affiliation in

1 Regulation 1612/68, arts 3-4.
2 See eg Case 152/73 *Sotgiu v Deutsche Bundespost* [1974] ECR 153; Case C-272/92 *Spotti v Freistaat Bayern* [1993] ECR 1-5185, [1994] 3 CMLR 629.
3 Regulation 1612/68, art 3(1); see Case 379/87 *Groener v Minister for Education* [1989] ECR 3967, [1990] 1 CMLR 401.
4 In Case C-204/90 *Bachmann v Belgian State* [1992] ECR I-249 the Court of Justice held that national legislation which makes the deductibility of sickness and invalidity insurance contributions or pension and life assurance contributions conditional upon the contributions being paid in the state is contrary to arts 48 and 49 but could be justified by the need to safeguard the cohesion of the applicable tax system. But cf Case C-279/93 *Finanzamt Köln-Altstadt v Schumacker*, judgment of 14 February 1995, not yet reported.
5 See para 218 below.
6 See eg Case C-213/90 *Association de Soutien aux Travailleurs Immigrés v Chambre des Employés Privés* [1991] ECR I-3507, [1993] 3 CMLR 621.
7 Regulation 1612/68, arts 7-9. As to the breadth of 'social advantages' see Case 59/85 *Netherlands v Reed* [1986] ECR 1283, [1987] 2 CMLR 448.
8 See paras 212-217 below.
9 Regulation 1408/71, JO L149, 5.7.71, p 1 (S Edn 1971 (II) p 416), implemented by Regulation 574/72, JO L74, 27.3.72, p 1 (S Edn 1972 (I) p 159), both updated and consolidated in OJ C325, 10.12.92, p 3.
10 Regulation 1408/71, art 2.
11 Ibid, art 1(f).

another member state must be taken into account in the disbursement of benefits by the 'competent state'[1]. The regulation covers sickness and maternity benefits, invalidity benefits, old age benefits; survivors' benefits, accident or occupational disease benefits, death grants, unemployment benefits and family benefits. Both the regulation and national law are to be interpreted in such a way that claimants receive their full entitlement[2].

209. Matters purely internal to a member state. A person can claim rights under the Treaty only by seeking genuinely to exercise them. Where there is no 'appreciable Community element' the matter is purely internal to the member state and Community rules will not apply[3]. Thus a British citizen cannot argue that a judicial order restricting her movements within the United Kingdom infringes any Treaty right[4]. A non-Community national cannot claim right of residence with family members who are Community nationals but have never resided outside their own member state[5]. The fundamental rights recognised as part of Community law cannot, as such, be invoked in a British court in the absence of a Community law element[6]. And a firm cannot seek to avoid planning rules in its own member state on the ground that they infringe Community rules on right of establishment[7].

210. Restrictions. The Treaty recognises certain permissible restrictions to the free movement of persons. They are:
(1) restrictions on entry or movement justified upon grounds of public policy, public security or public health[8]; and
(2) restrictions on employment in the public service or the exercise of public authority[9].
Like the exceptions to the rules governing the free movement of goods[10], they must be interpreted restrictively and be 'objectively justified' and proportionate. So, member states may define their own public policy but they may invoke it to deny a Community national the exercise of his Treaty rights

1 As to the determination of the competent state (and therefore the applicable schemes and legislation) see ibid, arts 12–15.
2 See eg Case 7/75 *Mr and Mrs F v Belgium* [1975] ECR 679, [1975] 2 CMLR 442; Case 24/75 *Petroni v ONPTS* [1975] ECR 1149; Case C-165/91 *Van Munster v Rijksdienst voor Pensioenen*, judgment of 5 October 1994, not yet reported.
3 Case C-229/94 *R v Secretary of State for the Home Department, ex parte Adams* (pending) raises the question whether this rule has to be modified in light of art 8a(1), added by the TEU (see para 171 above).
4 Case 175/78 *R v Saunders* [1979] ECR 1129, [1979] 2 CMLR 216.
5 Cases 35–36/82 *Morson and Jhanjan v Netherlands* [1982] ECR 3723, [1983] 2 CMLR 221; for an English case see *R v Secretary of State for Home Affairs, ex parte Tombofa* [1988] 2 CMLR 609 (CA). But where the family has resided and worked for a time elsewhere in the Community the Treaty rules apply upon their return; *R v Immigration Appeal Tribunal and Singh, ex parte Secretary of State for the Home Department* [1992] ECR I-4265, [1992] 3 CMLR 358.
6 *Kaur v Lord Advocate* 1981 SLT 322, [1980] 3 CMLR 79 (OH); on fundamental rights see para 153 above.
7 Case 204/87 *Bekaert v Procureur de la République, Rennes* [1988] ECR 2036, [1988] 2 CMLR 655; Cases C-29 etc/94 *Criminal Proceedings against Aubertin*, judgment of 16 February 1995, not yet reported.
8 EC Treaty, arts 48(3), 56(1), 66.
9 Ibid, arts 48(4), 55, 1st para, 66.
10 See paras 191ff above.

only if his presence would constitute 'a genuine and sufficiently serious threat to public policy'[1] affecting one of the fundamental interests of the state[2]. A member state may not rely upon grounds of public policy where it has adopted no measures effectively to combat the activities in question amongst its own nationals[3]. Nor may it take a broad view of what constitutes 'public service' or 'public authority' so as to restrict employment in those fields to its own nationals. Such restriction is justified only in areas in which powers are conferred to safeguard the interests of the state[4]. If a post requires previous experience in the public service, experience acquired in the public service of another member state must be taken into account[5].

211. Directive 64/221. Directive 64/221[6] lays down procedural safeguards in relation to restriction of Treaty rights on grounds of public policy, public security and public health[7]. The directive is directly effective[8]. The permitted grounds may not be invoked to serve economic ends. The only diseases or disabilities which may justify refusal of entry (but not expulsion) on grounds of public health are listed. Member states may not add unilaterally to the list. Measures adopted upon grounds of public policy or public security must be based exclusively upon an individual's 'personal conduct'. A criminal record is not in itself sufficient justification for exclusion or expulsion. A person has the right to be informed of the reasons for refusal of entry or expulsion, the right of appeal to a court of law and the right, except in cases of urgency, to remain for at least fifteen days (entry) or a month (expulsion). In the United Kingdom the provisions of the directive are incorporated into the Immigration Rules, which must, of course, be read and applied in the light of the directive.

---

1 Case 36/75 *Rutili v Minister of the Interior* [1975] ECR 1219 at 1231, [1976] 1 CMLR 140 at 155. The original French (*une menace reelle et suffisamment grave pour l'ordre public*) is clearer. It also illustrates the linguistic and cultural difficulties inherent in Community law. 'Public policy' is a very unsatisfactory translation of *ordre public; offentliche Ordnung; openbare orde* and *ordine pubblico*, all of which have well-established and specific meanings in the national law of other member states which are neither rendered by 'public policy' nor necessarily equivalent to the meaning to be given to the term in Community law. In this context 'public order' would probably be better than 'public policy'.
2 Case 30/77 *R v Bouchereau* [1977] ECR 1999, [1977] 2 CMLR 800.
3 Cases 115 & 116/81 *Adoui and Cornuaille v Belgium* [1982] ECR 1665, [1982] 3 CMLR 631; on a similar principle applied to the free movement of goods see para 192 above.
4 See Case 2/74 *Reyners v Belgium* [1974] ECR 631, [1974] 2 CMLR 305; Case 149/79 *Commission v Belgium (No 1)* [1980] ECR 3881, [1981] 2 CMLR 413 and *(No 2)* [1982] ECR 1845, [1982] 3 CMLR 539; Case 66/85 *Lawrie-Blum v Land Baden-Württemberg* [1986] ECR 2121, [1987] 3 CMLR 389; Case C-42/92 *Thijssen v Controledienst voor Verzekering* [1993] ECR I-4047; Case C-37/93 *Commission v Belgium* [1993] ECR I-6295.
5 Case C-419/92 *Scholz v Opera Universitaria di Cagliari* [1994] ECR I-505, [1994] 1 CMLR 873.
6 Directive 64/221, JO 1964 p 850 (S Edn 1963-64 p 117).
7 Directive 64/221 applied originally only to workers and their families, but was extended by Directive 75/35, OJ L14, 20.1.75, p 14 to apply also to persons exercising rights of establishment and services and their families, and by the three general residence directives (see para 206 above) to persons exercising rights thereunder and their families.
8 Case 41/74 *Van Duyn v Home Office* [1974] ECR 1337, [1975] 1 CMLR 1.

212. Right of establishment. As mentioned above[1], the Chapter on Establishment applies to both natural and legal persons. Its scope therefore extends to 'the setting up of agencies, branches and subsidiaries'[2], although it does not (yet) extend to a right to transfer the central management and control of a company to a member state other than that of incorporation[3]. The Treaty recognises that obstacles may exist (other than those connected with public policy, public security, public health and the public service) which are justified, as in the case of goods, for protection of the consumer or of the public generally. Obvious examples are the rules regulating the medical and allied professions, banking and insurance. The Chapter on right of establishment therefore has four distinct elements or phases:

(1) the prohibition of any new restrictions on the right of establishment of nationals of other member states ('the standstill'; article 53);

(2) the abolition of any restriction on the ground of nationality by the end of the transitional period and the prohibition of any such restriction after that date (article 52)[4];

(3) the implementation of a 'General Programme for the abolition of existing restrictions on freedom of establishment within the Community '(article 54)[5]; and

(4) the adoption of directives 'in order to make it easier for persons to take up and pursue activities as self-employed persons' (article 57)[6].

Phases (1) and (2) relate solely to the removal of restrictions which amount, directly or indirectly, to restrictions on grounds of nationality. The relevant provisions are directly effective[7]. They impose a duty to recognise the qualifications held by nationals of other member states[8] and a prohibition of restrictions whose *effect* is to discriminate against them[9]. Generally the Treaty is concerned with 'activities' – what people actually do and the practical restrictions upon whether or how they may do it – rather than the way in which member states happen to organise the performance of those activities. This is particularly important when considering professional activities[10], since the lines of demarcation between different professions in the member states are not always the same[11].

Phases (3) and (4) require the Community institutions to act. Phase (3), as

1 See para 201.
2 EC Treaty, art 53.
3 Case 81/87 *R v HM Treasury and Commissioners of Inland Revenue, ex parte Daily Mail* [1988] ECR 5483, [1988] 3 CMLR 713.
4 As interpreted in Case 2/74 *Reyners v Belgian State* [1974] ECR 631, [1974] 2 CMLR 305.
5 Such a programme was adopted in 1961; see JO 1962 p 36 (S Edn (2nd series) XI, p 7).
6 'Self-employed persons' is a bad translation of *personnes non-salariées*, which includes, in this context, companies and firms as well as self-employed individuals.
7 Case 6/64 *Costa v ENEL* [1964] ECR 585, [1964] CMLR 425; Case 2/74 *Reyners v Belgian State* [1974] ECR 631, [1974] 2 CMLR 305.
8 See paras 214-215 below.
9 Case 107/83 *Ordre des avocats au barreau de Paris v Klopp* [1984] ECR 2971, [1985] 1 CMLR 99; Case 3/88 *Commission v Italy* [1989] ECR 4035.
10 See eg Case 2/74 *Reyners v Belgian State* [1974] ECR 631, [1974] 2 CMLR 305.
11 See eg Case C-61/89 *Bouchoucha* [1990] ECR I-3551, [1992] 1 CMLR 1033.

the language of article 54 makes clear, is concerned with the *abolition* of restrictions. As to Phase (4), the language of article 57 (*'making it easier* to take up and pursue activities') shows that it is concerned not so much with abolition of restrictions as with positive measures to secure mutual recognition and co-ordination of the national regulatory regimes. The Treaty does not call for or require the creation of a market for professional or other services which is 'free' in the sense of being unregulated. Nor is it a manifesto for deregulation. Some of the measures adopted may have that effect, but that is in part a matter of political choice, and in part a consequence of the developed rules on competition[1] which complement the rules on the common market.

213. Harmonisation of qualifications. A significant barrier to the right of establishment consists in national requirements that access to certain 'regulated' trades or professions depends upon qualifications, which nationals of other member states are unlikely to possess. The Council therefore adopted directives in a number of sectors harmonising national rules on educational or professional qualifications, so enabling a person duly qualified in one member state to establish himself or provide a service in any other member state. These 'co-ordination' and/or 'mutual recognition' directives cover, amongst others, wholesale trade[2], retail trade[3], commercial agents[4], doctors[5], veterinarians[6], dentists[7], nurses[8], midwives[9], pharmacists[10] and architects[11]. The 'Lawyers' Services Directive'[12] grants to lawyers qualified in one member state a limited right of audience in the courts of another, but not a right of establishment[13].

214. Equivalence. The process of sectoral harmonisation proved to be excessively time-consuming, and, in the more difficult sectors in which national traditions vary widely, impossible. The Court of Justice had in the meanwhile developed the principle of 'equivalence' of qualifications. This means that, whilst the member states may still regulate qualifications and professional or academic titles[14], a person seeking to establish himself in a 'regulated' trade or profession in another member state has the right to have his existing qualifications taken into account. The competent authorities of the

1 See paras 223–260 below.
2 Directive 64/223, JO 1964 p 863 (S Edn 1963–64 p 123).
3 Directive 68/363, JO L260, 22.10.68, p 1 (S Edn 1968 (III) p 496).
4 Directive 64/224, JO 1964 p 869 (S Edn 1963–64 p 126).
5 Now consolidated in Directive 93/16, OJ L165, 7.7.93, p 1.
6 Directive 78/1026, OJ L362, 23.12.78, pp 1, 7.
7 Directive 78/686, OJ L233, 24.8.78, pp 1, 10.
8 Directive 77/452, OJ L176, 15.7.77, p 1.
9 Directive 80/154, OJ L33, 11.2.80, p 1.
10 Directive 85/432, OJ L253, 24.9.85, p 34.
11 Directive 85/384, OJ L223, 21.8.85, p 15.
12 Directive 77/249, OJ L78, 26.3.77, p 17.
13 See Case C-55/94 *Gebhard v Consiglio dell' Ordine degli Avvocati e Procuratori di Milano* (pending). The Commission has now put forward a draft directive on establishment of lawyers, not yet published.
14 See eg Case C-19/92 *Kraus v Land Baden-Württemberg* [1993] ECR I-1663.

host member state must consider whether those qualifications, even if different, are 'equivalent' to those required of home nationals, and may refuse him authorisation only if they decide on reasonable grounds that they are insufficient. The refusal must be reasoned, and it must be subject to judicial review. Where the existing qualifications are equivalent in some aspects but not in others, the person is entitled to pursue further training to make up the difference, and can be required to do no more[1]. The broad effect is that a requirement of educational, technical or professional qualifications can inhibit the right of a Community national to establish himself or provide a service in another member state only where he has no qualifications from his own state or where they are demonstrably deficient or demonstrably different compared to those required of nationals of the host state.

215. Mutual recognition. The case law of the Court of Justice led a policy shift from harmonisation to equivalence as part of the single market programme. Directive 89/48 creates a *general* system for 'mutual recognition' of higher education diplomas[2]. Equivalence is presumed, and (very broadly) member states must give the fullest possible recognition to university and similar qualifications gained in other member states. Directive 92/51[3] implements the same scheme for post-secondary training or education of one to three years' duration. These directives apply in all areas not subject to harmonisation by specific sectoral directives; Directive 89/48 therefore applies to lawyers' qualifications[4].

(E) SERVICES

216. Scope of the free movement of services. The Chapter on Services applies where the provider and the recipient are established in different member states. It applies in the increasingly important area of inter-state broadcasting[5] and other services provided by electronic or similar means.

---

1 The principle of equivalence ('*Cassis de Dijon*' for establishment and services) was developed through Case 71/76 *Thieffry v Conseil de l'ordre des avocats à la Cour de Paris* [1977] ECR 765, [1977] 2 CMLR 373; Case 11/77 *Patrick v Ministre des Affaires Culturelles* [1977] ECR 1199, [1977] 2 CMLR 523; Case 222/86 *UNECTEF v Heylens* [1987] ECR 4097, [1989] 1 CMLR 901; Case C-340/89 *Vlassopoulou v Ministerium für Justiz, Bundes- und Europaangelegenheiten Baden-Württemberg* [1991] ECR I-2357, [1993] 2 CMLR 221; Case C-319/92 *Haim v Kassenzahnärtzliche Vereinigung Nordrhein* [1994] ECR I-428, [1994] 2 CMLR 169.
2 Directive 89/48, OJ L19, 24.1.89, p 16. A higher education diploma is, in principle, one which requires at least three years' tertiary education evidenced by a degree or comparable award; art 1(a).
3 Directive 92/51, OJ L209, 24.7.92, p 25.
4 Although Directive 89/48 has no bearing upon recognition of legal qualifications as amongst the three jurisdictions within the UK (this being 'wholly internal' to a member state; see para 209 above), it served as inspiration for Parliament to adopt a similar scheme for transferability of UK legal qualifications; see the Courts and Legal Services Act 1990, c 41, s 60 (for England and Wales); and the Law Reform (Miscellaneous Provisions) (Scotland) Act 1990, c 40, s 30. No equivalent legislation has been adopted for Northern Ireland.
5 Case 155/73 *Giuseppe Sacchi* [1974] ECR 409, [1974] 2 CMLR 177.

The concept of services (in its Treaty sense) includes the right to *receive* a service as well as the right to provide it, and the Court of Justice has taken a liberal view of what may constitute a 'service'. Thus the provisions of the Chapter apply, for example, to tourism and health care[1], to the procurement of abortions[2] and, indeed, virtually any lawful but temporary presence of a Community national in another member state[3]. They may also be relied upon as against the state by any person (natural or legal) resident or established there wishing to provide a service to a recipient established in another member state[4]. Any national legislation which, without objective justification[5], impedes or makes more difficult a provider of a service from exercising the right to do so infringes article 59[6].

217. Services and imperative reasons of public interest. As in the case of establishment, freedom to provide services raises the problem of qualifications. Further, the provider of 'services' is, *ex hypothesi*, domiciled outwith the jurisdiction of regulatory bodies of the host state. Legitimate barriers to the provision of services (other than those expressly permitted on grounds of public policy, public security, public health and work in the public service) may therefore arise in the interests of 'prudential supervision'. The Court of Justice has developed principles, analogous to the *Cassis de Dijon* mandatory requirements[7], which permit member states to inhibit the provision of services for 'imperative reasons of public interest'. These cannot in principle result in discrimination as between 'home' and 'foreign' providers of services[8] and apply where, and only where, (a) there is objective justification for the restrictive national rule, (b) due account is taken of the standards and rules to which the provider of the service is subject in his home state, and (c) the restriction is proportionate[9]. But a person may not, in order to evade the professional rules of conduct in one member state, establish himself in another and then rely upon the Treaty in order to provide 'services' in the

1 Cases 286/82 and 26/83 *Luisi and Carbone v Ministero del Tesoro* [1984] ECR 377, [1985] 3 CMLR 52.
2 Case C-159/90 *Society for the Protection of Unborn Children v Grogan* [1991] ECR I-4685, [1991] 3 CMLR 849.
3 See eg Case 186/87 *Cowan v Trésor Public* [1989] ECR 195, [1990] 2 CMLR 613.
4 Case C-18/93 *Corsica Ferries Italia v Corpo dei Piloti del Porto di Genova* [1994] ECR I-1783; Case C-381/93 *Commission v France* (Maritime Transport), judgment of 5 October 1994, not yet reported.
5 See para 217 below.
6 Case C-288/89 *Stichting Collectieve Antennevoorziening Gouda v Commissariat voor de Media* [1991] ECR I-4007; Case C-76/90 *Säger v Dennemeyer* [1991] ECR I-4221; Case C-381/93 *Commission v France* (Maritime Transport), judgment of 5 October 1994, not yet reported. This is analogous to the *Dassonville* test developed in the context of free movement of goods; see para 187.
7 See paras 189ff above.
8 See Case C-76/90 *Säger v Dennemeyer* [1991] ECR I-4221; Case C-18/93 *Corsica Ferries Italia v Corpo dei Piloti del Porto di Genova* [1994] ECR I-1783.
9 Case 205/84 *Commission v Germany* (Insurance and Co-Insurance) [1986] ECR 3755, [1987] 2 CMLR 69; Case C-154/89 *Commission v France* (Tourist Guides) [1991] ECR I-659; Case C-288/89 *Stichting Collectieve Antennevoorziening Gouda v Commissariat voor de Media* [1991] ECR I-4007; Case C-211/91 *Commission v Belgium* [1992] ECR I-6757; Case C-275/92 *HM Customs and Excise v Schindler* [1994] ECR I-1039, [1995] 1 CMLR 4.

former; in such cases he will be deemed to be established in the former state and subject to its supervisory rules[1].

218. Students. Except in so far as it is ancillary to other Treaty rights – for example, schooling for the families of workers[2] – education falls largely outwith the Treaty[3]. Publicly-funded education is not a 'service' within the meaning of the Treaty[4]. Nevertheless, higher (ie tertiary and technical) education is closely bound to vocational training, which *is* a concern of the Treaty[5]. So, a student in higher education has a right of residence for the duration of his studies[6] and article 6 of the Treaty[7] prevents a member state from imposing higher fees upon students from other member states[8]. The Treaty does not (yet) require that subsistence grants paid to home students be provided to students from another member state[9], unless the student concerned has been a migrant worker in the member state where he wishes to study and is thereafter unintentionally unemployed, or there is a link between his former work and the course of education he wishes to pursue, or the purpose of further study is to improve his prospects in the labour market[10].

219. Financial services; company law. Banks, insurance companies and other providers of financial services are 'persons' enjoying right of free movement under the Treaty. But the Court of Justice has recognised that special rules are necessary in this field for the protection of the consumer[11]. There are a number of directives designed to ease the process of mutual

---

1 Case 33/74 *Van Binsbergen v Bestuur van de Bedrijfsvereniging voor de Mataalnijverheid* [1974] ECR 1299, [1975] 1 CMLR 298; Case 292/86 *Gullung v Conseil de l'ordre des avocats du barreau de Colmar et de Saverne* [1988] ECR 111, [1988] 2 CMLR 57; Case C-148/91 *Vereniging Veronica Omroep Organisatie v Commissariat voor de Media* [1993] ECR I-487; Case C-23/93 *TV10 v Commissariat voor de Media*, judgment of 5 October 1994, not yet reported.
2 See para 204 above.
3 But see paras 281ff below.
4 Case 263/86 *Belgium v Humbel* [1988] ECR 5365, [1999] 1 CMLR 393; Case C-109/92 *Wirth v Landeshauptstadt Hannover* [1993] ECR I-6447. However, education provided for fees at the full market rate might constitute a service.
5 EC Treaty, art 127. Higher education pursued for the sole purpose of an improvement in general knowledge may be different; see Case 293/85 *Commission v Belgium* [1988] ECR 305, [1989] 2 CMLR 527 at 3355ff and 538ff per Advocate General Slynn.
6 Case C-357/89 *Raulin v Minister for Education and Science* [1992] ECR I-1027, [1994] 1 CMLR 227. This right derives directly from the Treaty; the directive which grants a right of residence to students (see para 206 above) therefore has utility only in that it also grants a right of residence to their families.
7 See para 168 above.
8 Case 298/83 *Gravier v Ville de Liège* [1986] ECR 610, [1985] 3 CMLR 1; Case 24/86 *Blaizot v University of Liège* [1988] ECR 379, [1989] 1 CMLR 57; Case C-47/93 *Commission v Belgium* [1994] ECR I-1593, [1994] 3 CMLR 685.
9 Case 197/86 *Brown v Secretary of State for Scotland* [1988] ECR 3205, [1988] 3 CMLR 403; Case 39/86 *Lair v Universität Hannover* [1988] ECR 3161, [1989] 3 CMLR 545.
10 Case 39/86 *Lair v Universität Hannover*, above; Case C-357/89 *Raulin v Minister for Education and Science* [1992] ECR I-1027, [1994] 1 CMLR 227.
11 Case 205/84 *Commission v Germany* (Insurance and Co-Insurance) [1986] ECR 3755, [1987] 2 CMLR 69; see para 217 above.

recognition[1], and others dealing with the structure, capitalisation and management of companies in order to ensure that companies incorporated in one member state can operate freely in another[2]. Regulation 2137/85 provides for the 'European Economic Interest Grouping' (EEIG), the first corporate structure created by Community law, which enables firms in various member states to undertake joint ancillary activities without need for capitalisation[3]. In 1968 the member states entered into a convention on the mutual recognition of companies[4], but it has not yet entered into force. In 1989 the Commission published a draft regulation on the formation of the 'European Company' (*Societas Europæa*)[5], but the Council has shown no enthusiasm to adopt it into law.

(F) FREE MOVEMENT OF CAPITAL

220. Capital. Unlike the provisions on the free movement of goods, persons and services, the original Chapter of the Treaty on Capital (articles 67-73) did not, for practical purposes, have any direct effect. Current payments connected specifically with the free movement of goods, persons or services fell under a later provision of the Treaty which was directly effective[6] and so could not be impeded by exchange controls[7]. Two directives adopted in 1988 and 1989[8] required the liberalisation of a wide range of capital movements, so giving broad effect to the free movement of capital[9]. However, this

---

1 See eg Directive 64/225, JO 1964 p 878 (S Edn 1963-64 p 131) (re-insurance); Directive 73/183, OJ L194, 16.7.73, p 1 (banks and other financial institutions); Directive 73/239, OJ L228, 16.8.73, p 3 (non-life direct insurance); Directive 77/780, OJ L322, 17.12.77, p 30 (credit institutions); Directive 78/473, OJ L151, 7.6.78, p 25 (co-insurance); Directive 88/357, OJ L172, 4.7.88, p 1 (second non-life insurance directive); Directive 92/49, OJ L228, 11.8.92, p 1 (third non-life insurance directive); Directive 92/121, OJ L29, 5.2.93, p 1 (monitoring of credit institutions).

2 Eg, the company law directives on safeguards for the protection of company members (68/151, JO L65, 14.3.68, p 8 (S Edn 1968 (I) p 41)); safeguards for members in the formation of public limited companies and their capital (77/91, OJ L26, 31.1.77, p 1); mergers (78/855, OJ L295, 20.10.78, p 36); annual accounts (78/660, OJ L222, 14.8.78, p 11); consolidated accounts (83/349, OJ L193, 18.7.83, p 1); scission or 'de-merger' (82/891, OJ L378, 31.12.82, p 47); accountancy laws (83/349, OJ L193, 18.7.83, p 1); audits (84/253, OJ L126, 12.5.84, p 20); disclosure requirements for branches (89/666, OJ L395, 30.12.89, p 36); single member private limited companies (89/667, OJ L395, 30.12.89, p 40); taxation of mergers (90/434, OJ L225, 20.8.90, p 1); taxation of parents and subsidiaries (90/435, OJ L225, 20.8.90, p 6). These directives have been implemented in the UK by amendment of the Companies Acts.

3 Regulation 2137/85, OJ L199, 31.7.85, p 1.

4 Convention of 29 February 1968 on the Mutual Recognition of Companies, Firms and Legal Persons.

5 COM(89)268 final; see also the Commission proposal for employee participation in the European Company, OJ C263, 16.10.89, p 69.

6 EEC Treaty, art 106; now subsumed within EC Treaty, art 73b(2).

7 Cases 286/82 and 26/83 *Luisi and Carbone v Ministero del Tesoro* [1984] ECR 377, [1985] 3 CMLR 52.

8 Directive 88/361, OJ L178, 8.7.88, p 5; Directive 89/646, OJ L386, 30.12.89, p 1.

9 See Cases C-358 & 416/93 *Ministerio Fiscal v Bordessa*, judgment of 23 February 1995, not yet reported.

Chapter of the Treaty was replaced completely by the Treaty on European Union[1]. The Treaty now provides that all restrictions upon the movement of capital and payments between member states are prohibited[2]. The language of the prohibition is such as to create direct effect. There is also a general prohibition of restrictions upon the movement of capital and payments between member states and third countries[3]. National restrictions continue in force for capital movement to and from third countries involving direct investment, financial services and admission of securities to capital markets[4]. The Council may introduce regulatory measures[5]. Member states remain entitled (a) to differentiate in tax law regarding place of residence or place of investment, to provide for prudential supervision of financial institutions and to take measures justified on grounds of public policy or public security, so long as these measures do not constitute arbitrary discrimination or a disguised restriction to the free movement of capital[6]; and (b) to adopt unilateral safeguard measures regarding capital movements or payments from a third country for serious political reasons and upon grounds of urgency[7]. Otherwise, control of capital movements and payments now falls within the exclusive competence of the Community, and is intimately bound up with the drive towards economic and monetary union[8].

(G) TRANSPORT

221. Transport. Transport is governed by Title IV of the Treaty, comprising articles 74 to 84. Like agriculture[9], the Treaty envisaged not a free market but a regulated market in transport, and it was to be implemented by a Common Transport Policy[10]. In 1985 the Court of Justice condemned the Council's failure to agree upon a common policy[11]. Notwithstanding the absence of rules, the Court has held that the Chapter on provision of services applies fully to transport services with an inter-state dimension[12] and that the treaty rules on competition apply to some transport sectors[13].

---

1 EC Treaty, arts 73a-g.
2 EC Treaty, art 73b(1) and (2). A right of temporary derogation is provided to some member states (not the United Kingdom) until 31 December 1995; Ibid, art 73e.
3 Ibid, art 73b(1) and (2).
4 Ibid, art 73c(1).
5 Ibid, arts 73c(2), 73f and 73g(1).
6 Ibid, art 73d.
7 Ibid, art 73g(2).
8 See paras 262-267 below.
9 See para 198 above.
10 EC Treaty, art 74.
11 Case 13/83 *European Parliament v Council* [1985] ECR 1513, [1986] 1 CMLR 138.
12 Case C-18/93 *Corsica Ferries Italia v Corpo dei Piloti del Porto di Genova* [1994] ECR I-1783; see paras 216-217 above.
13 Case 66/86 *Ahmed Saeed Flugreisen v Zentrale zur Bekämpfung Unlauteren Wettbewerbs* [1989] ECR 803, [1990] 4 CMLR 102.

Nevertheless, legislative process towards a true common policy remains patchy and slow. There is Community legislation dealing, *inter alia*, with the following aspects of transport: market access[1]; user tariffs[2]; cabotage[3]; structural harmonisation[4]; mutual recognition of qualifications[5]; driving licences[6]; social conditions[7]; and technical and safety standards[8].

(b) Common Rules on Competition, Taxation and Approximation of Laws

222. General. Title V of the Treaty is entitled 'Common Rules on Competition, Taxation and Approximation of Laws', and is divided into three Chapters:
(1) Rules on competition (articles 85–94);
(2) Tax provisions (articles 95–99); and
(3) Approximation of laws (articles 100–102).
The chapter on approximation (or harmonisation) of laws prescribes the procedure for legislation to eliminate differences in the laws of the member states which impede the functioning of the common market (article 100) and the internal market (article 100a)[9]. The Treaty on European Union added a provision which empowers the Community to adopt rules regarding visas for third country nationals entering the Community[10]. Otherwise, whilst the harmonisation procedures are clearly of great importance in achieving the internal market and 'fine tuning' the common market, and the directives

---

1 First Directive on road carriage, JO 1970/2005; Directive 86/216, OJ L152, 6.6.86, p 47 (air services).
2 Directive 93/89, OJ L279, 12.11.93, p 32 (road transport).
3 Regulation 4059/89, OJ L390, 30.12.89, p 3 (road cabotage).
4 Eg Directive 91/439, OJ L237, 24.8.91, p 25 (infrastructure development of railways).
5 Directive 74/561, OJ L308, 19.11.74, p 18 (road hauliers); Directive 74/562, OJ L308, 19.11.74, p 23 (road passenger transport operators); Directive 76/135, OJ L21, 29.1.76, p 10 (navigability licences for inland waterway vessels); Directive 87/540, OJ L322, 12.11.87, p 20 (carriers of goods by waterway); Directive 91/670, OJ L373, 31.12.91, p 21 (civil aviation personnel); Directive 91/672, OJ L373, 31.12.91, p 29 (inland boatmasters).
6 Directive 80/1263, OJ L375, 31.12.80, p 12; Directive 91/439, OJ L237, 24.8.91, p 1.
7 Eg Regulation 3820/85, OJ L370, 31.12.85, p 1 (working conditions); Regulation 3821/85, OJ L370, 31.12.85, p 8 (tachographs); Directive 91/671, OJ L373, 31.12.91, p 26 (safety belts).
8 Directive 79/116, OJ L33, 8.2.79, p 33 (maritime tankers); Directive 80/51, OJ L18, 24.1.80, p 26 (noise emissions from subsonic aircraft); Directive 82/714, OJ L301, 28.10.82, p 1 (inland waterway vessels); Directive 85/3, OJ L2, 3.1.85, p 14 (road vehicles); Directives 92/6, OJ L57, 2.3.92, p 27 and 92/24, OJ L129, 14.5.92, p 154 (governors); Directive 92/22, OJ L129, 14.5.92, p 11 (glazing); Directive 92/62, OJ L199, 18.7.92, p 33 (steering equipment); Directive 93/65, OJ L187, 29.7.93, p 52 (air traffic management equipment and systems).
9 See para 193 above. On the breadth of art 100a as a legal base see Case C-359/92 *Germany v Council* [1994] ECR I-3681.
10 EC Treaty, art 100c; see para 297 below.

adopted under it may have relevance for the interpretation of national legislation[1], Chapter 3 does not of itself enact any substantive rules of law.

(A) THE RULES ON COMPETITION

(i) *Introduction*

223. General. Article 3(g) (formerly article 3(f)) of the Treaty prescribes as one of the 'activities' of the Community 'a system ensuring that competition in the internal market is not distorted'. The concept of 'distortion of competition' is fundamental to Community competition law, implying that the norm should be a situation where the market is allowed to operate freely. The aim set out in article 3(g) is implemented by the 'rules on competition' which are divided into three sections:
(1) Rules applying to undertakings (articles 85–90);
(2) Dumping (article 91); and
(3) Aids granted by States (articles 92–94).
The section on dumping is concerned only with dumping as between member states, and with the end of the transitional period is now spent (except transitionally for Austria, Finland and Sweden). Measures taken by the Community against the dumping of products from third countries on the Community market are taken under the provisions implementing the Common Commercial Policy[2].

The rules applying to undertakings follow the pattern established by the Sherman Act 1890 in the United States which prohibits, first, 'every contract, combination or conspiracy in restraint of trade', and second, the 'monopolization of trade and commerce' – in other words, distortion of free competition which results, in the first case, from the collusive action or conduct of two or more economic operators and, in the second, from the predominant market power of one. This has become a standard approach to competition law and has been adopted in a number of countries[3]. But the Treaty is concerned not just to ensure a 'level playing field' amongst competitors, but also to ensure that the barriers which the earlier provisions of the Treaty have abolished are not replaced by barriers created by the economic operators themselves and to promote interpenetration of national markets.

The rules on state aids complement the rules applying to undertakings by preventing member states from distorting competition by subsidising the operation and activities of domestic producers or suppliers of services.

The rules on competition are then further complemented by the rules relating to taxation which prevent member states from adopting the other

---

1 See para 148 above.
2 See para 270 below.
3 For recent examples see the (Canadian) Competition Act, RSC 1985, c C-34 as amended by SC 1986, c 26; the (Irish) Competition Act of 1990; the (Italian) Anti-Trust Law, Legge 287/1990; the Swedish Competition Laws of 1 July 1993.

possible method of providing financial assistance – by taxing domestic products in a manner different from imported products.

224. Complementarity of Treaty rules. Just as the common rules of this Title complement one another, so, together, they reinforce and complement the provisions on the free movement of goods, persons, services and capital. Indeed, the Court of Justice has recognised that the competition rules of the Treaty are 'so essential that without [them] numerous provisions of the Treaty would be pointless'[1].

(ii) The Rules Relating to Undertakings

(1) The Operative Provisions: Articles 85 and 86

225. General. Articles 85 and 86 are the main operative provisions of this section of the Treaty. Article 85(1) prohibits:

> 'All agreements between undertakings, decisions by associations of undertakings and concerted practices which may affect trade between Member States and which have as their object or effect the prevention, restriction or distortion of competition within the common market'.

Article 86, unlike the Sherman Act, does not outlaw monopolies as such. Rather it prohibits:

> 'Any abuse by one or more undertakings of a dominant position',

or (using words which more faithfully reflect the original language texts of the Treaty) 'the abusive exploitation of a dominant position'. Articles 85 and 86 state principles[2] and should not be construed as if they were statutory provisions. They are not mutually exclusive and an agreement or business practice may be caught by both[3]. The rules of Community law and of national law are likewise not mutually exclusive and, again, an agreement or business practice may be caught by both[4]. Subsequent articles provide for Community legislation to give effect to the principles of articles 85 and 86 (article 87); pending the adoption of such legislation, for their enforcement by national and Community authorities (articles 88 and 89); and special provisions for applying the competition rules to public and 'privileged' undertakings (article 90).

226. Undertakings. Articles 85 and 86 are concerned with the conduct of 'undertakings'. The word 'undertaking' (*entreprise; Unternehmer*) is not

---

1 Case 6/72 *Europemballage and Continental Can v Commission* [1973] ECR 215 at 244, [1973] CMLR 199 at 223.
2 EC Treaty, arts 87(1) and 89(1).
3 See eg Case 66/86 *Ahmed Saeed Flugreisen v Zentrale zur Bekämpfung Unlauteren Wettbewerbs* [1989] ECR 803, [1990] 4 CMLR 102; Case T-51/89 *Tetrapak v Commission* [1990] ECR II-309, [1991] 4 CMLR 334; Cases T-68 & 77-78/89 *Società Italiana Vetro v Commission* (Flat Glass) [1992] ECR II-1403, [1992] 5 CMLR 302.
4 See para 232 below.

defined in the Treaty, but it is very wide, covering every type of entity, regardless of its legal status, from a single individual to a multinational corporation, provided he or it has legal capacity and is engaged in economic activity of some sort. So, an opera singer[1], a sports federation[2], a public agency[3] and anything in between are undertakings in so far as they carry on economic or commercial activities.

227. Obligations of the member states. The competition rules are concerned with the conduct of undertakings, not with national legislation. However, member states have an obligation under articles 85 and 86, in conjunction with article 5[4], not to introduce or maintain in force any national rules which might render their application ineffective[5].

228. The prohibitions (articles 85(1) and 86). Both article 85(1) and article 86 expressly prohibit certain specific types of restrictive practice:
(1) practices relating to the fixing of purchasing or selling prices or other trading conditions (for example conditions of sale);
(2) practices which limit or control production, markets (outlets) or technical development;
(3) the application of dissimilar conditions to equivalent transactions, thereby placing other trading parties at a comparative disadvantage; and
(4) making the conclusion of contracts subject to acceptance of supplementary or unconnected obligations[6].

Article 85 further prohibits agreements to share markets or sources of supply[7]. But these lists of prohibited practices are not exhaustive. The Treaty is concerned, as always, with the practical economic effect of what is done, and any conduct falling within the general prohibitions of articles 85(1) and 86 is illegal.

229. Nullity of contracts (article 85(2)). According to article 85(2), any agreement or decision which infringes article 85(1) is 'automatically void'. Unlike the scheme of national law in some countries, no previous decision to that effect is required[8]. Article 86 contains no equivalent provision, but illegal conduct cannot, in any event, give rise to enforceable rights for the defaulting undertaking. The prohibitions therefore have horizontal direct effect[9],

---

1 Decision 78/516 (*RAI/Unitel*), OJ L157, 15.6.78, p 39, [1978] 3 CMLR 306.
2 Decision 92/521 (*re World Cup 1990 Package Tours*), OJ L326, 12.11.92, p 31, [1994] 5 CMLR 253.
3 Case C-41/90 *Höfner v Macrotron* [1991] ECR I-1979, [1993] 4 CMLR 306.
4 See para 167 above.
5 Case 13/77 *Inno v ATAB* [1977] ECR 2115, [1978] 1 CMLR 283; Case 311/85 *Vereniging van Flaamse Reisbureaus v Sociale Dienst van de Plaatselijke en Gewestelijke Overheidsdiensten* [1987] ECR 3801, [1989] 4 CMLR 213, and more recently Case C-2/91 *Criminal Proceedings against Wolf Meng* [1993] ECR I-5751, Case C-185/91 *Bundesanstalt für den Güterfernverkehr v Gebrüder Reiff* [1993] ECR I-5801 and Case C-245/91 *Criminal Proceedings against Ohra Schadeverzekeringen* [1993] ECR I-5851.
6 EC Treaty, arts 85(1) (a), (b), (d), (e) and 86 (a)-(d).
7 Ibid, art 85(1)(c).
8 Regulation 17/62, JO 1962 p 24 (S Edn 1959-62 p 87), art 1.
9 Case 127/73 *Belgische Radio en Televisie v SABAM* [1974] ECR 313, [1974] 2 CMLR 238.

and their enforcement is a matter for the national courts. It is also a matter for the Commission. The enforcement powers of each are discussed below[1].

230. Exemption (article 85(3)). Because some agreements or practices which fall within the prohibition of article 85(1) may nonetheless produce beneficial effects, article 85(3) provides authority for exempting certain types of agreements from the prohibition of article 85(1) (but not article 86). Exemption is discussed below[2].

231. The relevant market. The compatibility of any agreement or business practice with articles 85 and 86 must be assessed in the context of 'the relevant market', which is a function essentially of two characteristics, the 'relevant product or service market' and the 'relevant geographic market'[3]:

(1) *The relevant product or service market* includes any products or services which are identical or equivalent to those in question. The products or services must be 'interchangeable' or 'substitutable'. Whether or not this is the case must be judged from the vantage point of the user or consumer, normally taking the characteristics, price and intended uses of the product or service together. In other words, can one product or service be replaced with another whilst satisfying the same technical or consumer demands ? If it can, they form part of a product or service market comprising all the products or services which are interchangeable with, or capable of substitution for, one another. If it cannot, the produce or service in question forms its own market. For example, bananas have been held to constitute a single product market because of special characteristics which distinguish them from fresh fruit generally[4], whilst port services for ferries on the Holyhead-Dun Laoghaire route were held to constitute a single service market owing to the inconvenience for a number of passengers of using the other British-Irish ferry routes[5]. The market need not be a large one[6]; it is sufficient that there be an identifiable market in which the substitution of one product or service for another is burdensome or less attractive to the customer.

(2) *The relevant geographic market* is defined by reference to a geographic territory throughout which the product or service in question moves freely.

---

1 See paras 238-239.
2 See paras 240ff.
3 A third characteristic may be a 'temporal' consideration since markets may change over time (eg with technological development) or there may be seasonal variations; see eg Case 27/76 *United Brands v Commission* [1978] ECR 207, [1978] 1 CMLR 429.
4 Case 27/76 *United Brands v Commission*, above.
5 Decision of 11 June 1992 (*B & I/Sealink Harbours and Sealink Stena*), [1992] 5 CMLR 255; Decision 94/19 (*Sea Containers/Stena Sealink*), OJ L15, 18.1.94, p 8. See also Case 66/86 *Ahmed Saeed Flugreisen v Zentrale zur Bekämpfung Unlauteren Wettbewerbs* [1989] ECR 803, [1990] 4 CMLR 102.
6 See eg Case 22/78 *Hugin Kassaregister v Commission* [1979] ECR 1869, [1979] 3 CMLR 345, in which the relevant product market was found to be that in spare parts for a particular make of cash register.

The market may be the global market where the relevant product (for example, a type of aeroplane[1]) is available without hindrance throughout the world. It may be the whole of Europe, or the whole of the Community, if those areas constitute a geographically homogeneous area for the availability of a particular product or service. It may be narrower where the product or service is not available, or is available in limited quantities or at irregular intervals, in parts of the Community, where the nature of the product or service restricts mobility[2], or where there are other barriers, physical or legal, to entry into particular national markets.

232. Scope of article 85(1). The terms of article 85(1) must be analysed very carefully in order to determine its scope and application. The following points should particularly be noted.

(1) Although article 85(1) seems to apply to any anticompetitive co-operation between any two or more undertakings, the Court of Justice has held that it does not apply where the undertakings form a single economic unit, such as a group in which subsidiaries have no real freedom to determine their course of action, or where the agreement or practices in question are concerned merely with the internal allocation of tasks as between members of the same corporate family (the 'economic entity doctrine')[3]. Whether this is the case is a matter of fact. In any event, article 86 may still apply.

(2) *Prima facie*, article 85(1) strikes at all agreements and practices falling within its terms, both 'horizontal' (agreements between competitors) and 'vertical' (agreements between a manufacturer and a distributor/retailer or between any of these and a customer)[4], however innocuous or even beneficial they may be from the point of view of competition[5]. The Court of Justice has recognised a '*de minimis* rule' which excludes from the scope of article 85(1) agreements and practices whose effect upon competition between member states is not 'appreciable'[6]. The Commission has issued a series of notices which seek to define the scope of this rule[7]. In practice, the rule has limited application. The Court has also indicated that an agreement may fall outwith the scope of article 85(1) where it constitutes no real threat to competition or to the functioning of the common market and where its anticompetitive effects are a

1 Decision 91/619 (*Aerospatiale-Alenia/de Havilland*), OJ L334, 5.12.91, p 42, [1992] 4 CMLR M2.
2 Eg, linguistic barriers; Case C-360/92P *Publishers Association v Commission*, judgment of 17 January 1995, not yet reported.
3 Case 15/74 *Centrafarm v Sterling Drug* [1974] ECR 1147, [1974] 2 CMLR 480; Case T-102/92 *Viho Europe BV v Commission*, judgment of 12 January 1995, not yet reported.
4 The application of art 85(1) to vertical agreements was first recognised in Cases 56 & 58/64 *Consten & Grundig v EEC Commission* [1966] ECR 299, [1966] CMLR 418, which repays careful reading as it lays a foundation for much of the Court's thinking on art 85.
5 The benefits of an otherwise illegal agreement are taken into account in considering whether an exemption from the prohibition ought to be granted it under art 85(3); see para 241 below.
6 Case 56/65 *Société Technique Minière v Maschinenbau Ulm* [1966] ECR 235, [1966] CMLR 357; Case 5/69 *Völk v Vervaecke* [1969] ECR 295, [1969] CMLR 273; Case 22/71 *Béguelin v GL Import Export* [1971] ECR 949, [1972] CMLR 81. 'Appreciable' is a rendering of the French *sensible* and the German *spürbar*, which indicate a lower threshold than the word 'appreciable' conveys.
7 Notice on agreements of minor importance which do not fall under art 85(1), OJ C231, 12.9.86, p 2. The notice is a second revision (the first being in 1977) of an original 1970 notice.

necessary incident of the proper functioning of an agreement which is not, in its essence, anticompetitive[1]. But the existence of any rule to that effect – sometimes called the 'rule of reason' – has been expressly recognised by the Court only once in a (dated) opinion of an Advocate General[2], has never been recognised by the Commission, is on any view of more limited scope than its United States progenitor, and will require further elaboration from the Court before it may be relied upon with any degree of certainty.

(3) The reference in article 85(1) to 'agreements between undertakings, decisions by associations of undertakings and concerted practices' does not mean that a restrictive practice must be fitted into one of three mutually exclusive categories in order to fall foul of the Treaty prohibition. The phrase ought rather to be taken as a comprehensive description of the ways in which independent undertakings can get together to prevent, restrict or distort competition – by making written, oral or gentlemen's agreements, through trade or professional associations, or simply by informal concerted conduct or practices, the latter defined by the Court of Justice as parallel behaviour not corresponding to normal market conditions by which undertakings 'knowingly substitute practical co-operation between them for the risks of competition'[3]. Latterly the Commission has not concerned itself with identifying the existence of a formal agreement, but has simply adduced evidence that an agreement *and/or* a concerted practice exists[4]. All are prohibited, no matter how the objectionable result has been achieved.

(4) Article 85(1) refers to 'object *or* effect'. Thus, a restrictive agreement is prohibited if its object is prohibited, even if it has not yet taken effect or has ceased to have effect. Equally, an agreement which has the effect, actual or potential, of preventing, restricting or distorting competition, is prohibited whatever its objects may be[5]. This is why article 85(3) is needed to exempt agreements designed to achieve economically desireable objectives[6].

(5) The references in article 85(1) to 'trade between Member States' and 'competition within the common market' are of significance more in relation to jurisdiction than to substance. An agreement or practice all of

1 See eg Case 56/65 *Société Technique Minière v Maschinenbau Ulm* [1966] ECR 235, [1966] CMLR 357; Case 26/76 *Metro-SB-Großmärkte v Commission* [1977] ECR 1875, [1978] 2 CMLR 1; Case 258/78 *Nungesser v Commission* (Maize Seeds) [1982] ECR 2015, [1983] 1 CMLR 278; Case 243/83 *Binon v Agence et Messageries de la Presse* [1985] ECR 2015, [1985] 3 CMLR 800; Case 161/84 *Pronuptia de Paris v Schillgalis* [1986] ECR 353, [1986] 1 CMLR 414.

2 Case 56/65 *Technique Minière*, above, at 257 (ECR) and 368 (CMLR) per Advocate General Roemer.

3 Case 48/69 *ICI v Commission* (Dyestuffs) [1972] ECR 619 at 655, [1972] CMLR 557 at 622. For further consideration of the nature of concerted practices see Case T-1/89 *Rhône-Poulenc v Commission* (Polypropylene) [1991] ECR II-867.

4 See eg Decision 86/398 (*Polypropylene*), OJ L230, 18.8.86, p 1, [1988] 4 CMLR 347; Decision 89/93 (*Flat Glass*), OJ L33, 4.2.89, p 44, [1990] 4 CMLR 535.

5 See Cases 56 & 58/64 *Consten & Grundig v EEC Commission* [1966] ECR 299 at 341, [1966] CMLR 418 at 472.

6 See paras 240ff below.

whose actual or potential effects are confined within a single member state falls within the exclusive jurisdiction of the competition authorities (if any) of that state. If its effects are wider, and appreciable, it will fall within the jurisdiction of the national *and* of the Community authorities[1]. An agreement or practice which is implemented within the Community and has the effect of preventing, restricting or distorting competition within the common market is prohibited even if it is made, and the parties to it are domiciled, outside the Community[2].

233. Abuse of a dominant position. Article 86 of the Treaty prohibits abuse of a dominant position. The concept is, however, difficult to define. It has two components: market dominance, which is not of itself prohibited by article 86[3], and abusive exploitation of that dominance, which is. The abuse need not occur in the market in which the undertaking is dominant: using market power in one market in order to protect or strengthen the undertaking's position in another, but related, market is enough[4].

234. Dominance. Dominance can exist both in the supply and in the purchase of goods or services. In order to determine whether an undertaking occupies a dominant position it is necessary first to identify the relevant markets – ie the relevant product or service market and the relevant geographic market[5]. Application of article 86 requires dominance within the common market 'or a substantial part of it'. A 'substantial part' of the common market may be the territory of a single member state[6] or even part of a member state[7]. Having identified the relevant markets, it must then be shown that an undertaking (or group of undertakings[8]) is dominant in those markets. A very high market share – more than 85 per cent – is determinative of itself of a dominant position[9]; a market share of 50 per cent constitutes a dominant position except in exceptional circumstances[10]. Whether dominance can exist

---

1 See Regulation 17, JO 1962 p 24 (S Edn 1959-62 p 87), art 9(3); Case 14/68 *Wilhelm v Bundeskartellamt* [1969] ECR 1, [1969] CMLR 100.
2 Cases 89 etc/85 *Åhlström v Commission* (Woodpulp) [1988] ECR 5193, [1988] 4 CMLR 901.
3 Case 322/81 *Michelin v Commission* [1983] ECR 3461 at 3511, [1985] 1 CMLR 282 at 327.
4 Case 62/86 *AKZO v Commission* [1991] ECR I-3359, [1993] 5 CMLR 215.
5 See para 231 above.
6 See eg Case 322/81 *Michelin v Commission* [1983] ECR 3461, [1985] 1 CMLR 282, in which the relevant geographic market was the Netherlands.
7 Eg Cases 40 etc/73 *Coöperatieve Vereniging 'Suiker Unie' v Commission* [1975] ECR 1663, [1976] 1 CMLR 295, in which a relevant geographic market was Bavaria, Baden-Württemberg and parts of Hesse. In Case C-179/90 *Merci Convenzionali Porto di Genova v Siderurgica Gabrielli* [1991] ECR I-5889, [1994] 4 CMLR 422 and Case C-18/93 *Corsica Ferries Italia v Corpo dei Piloti del Porto di Genova* [1994] ECR I-1783 an undertaking was dominant in the provision of services in the port of Genoa and was held subject to the discipline of art 86 owing to the volume of trade processed in the port which affected a significant part of the common market.
8 See para 236 below.
9 Case 85/75 *Hoffmann-La Roche v Commission* [1979] ECR 461, [1979] 3 CMLR 211.
10 Case 62/86 *AKZO v Commission* [1991] ECR I-3359, [1993] 5 CMLR 215.

with a lower market share depends upon the respective market shares of the undertaking and its competitors[1], their respective technical, financial or other resources (such as intellectual property rights) and the undertaking's conduct in the market. A statutory monopoly in the territory of a member state constitutes of itself a dominant position[2]. Essentially, the question is whether the undertaking is subject to the normal constraints of competition or can behave to an appreciable extent without regard to its competitors and its customers[3]. Two or more undertakings may, together, be dominant[4].

235. Abuse. Once the existence of a dominant position is established, the next question is whether the dominant undertaking has abused that dominance, and has done so in a manner which affects trade between member states. Apart from the list in article 86 itself[5], the most common examples of abusive conduct have included predatory pricing[6], refusing without objective justification to deal or supply[7] or dealing or supplying on less favourable[8] or discriminatory[9] terms, tying[10] and giving loyalty rebates[11]. But so wide is the application of the prohibition that the simplest, and perhaps the best, test is this: since the very presence of a dominant undertaking in the market weakens the structure of competition[12], such an undertaking has a special responsibility not to allow its conduct further to impair genuine undistorted competition[13] or hinder the growth of competition[14]. If it does so by any means, that constitutes an abuse of its dominant position.

1 See Case 27/76 *United Brands v Commission* [1978] ECR 207, [1978] 1 CMLR 429; Case 322/81 *Michelin v Commission* [1983] ECR 3461, [1985] 1 CMLR 282. So, where one undertaking has, say, 30 per cent of the market and none of its competitors has more than 10 per cent, the first undertaking may have a dominant position; but this would not be so where, for example, one undertaking had 30 per cent, two others 25 per cent and others 10 per cent and less.
2 Case C-260/89 *Elliniki Radiophonia Tiléorassi v Dimotiki Etairia Pliroforissis* [1991] ECR I-2925, [1994] 4 CMLR 540; Case C-41/90 *Höfner v Macrotron* [1991] ECR I-1979, [1993] 4 CMLR 306. This may apply also to a statutory monopoly in only part of a member state; see Case C-179/90 *Merci Convenzionali Porto di Genova v Siderurgica Gabrielli* [1991] ECR I-5889, [1994] 4 CMLR 422; Case C-18/93 *Corsica Ferries Italia v Corpo dei Piloti del Porto di Genova* [1994] ECR I-1783.
3 Case 27/76 *United Brands v Commission* [1978] ECR 207, [1978] 1 CMLR 429.
4 See para 236 below.
5 See para 228 above.
6 Eg Case 86/76 *Hoffmann-La Roche* v *Commission* [1979] ECR 461, [1979] 3 CMLR 211; Case 62/86 *AKZO v Commission* [1991] ECR I-3359, [1993] 5 CMLR 215, in which the Court held that prices set lower than average variable cost necessarily constitutes predatory pricing.
7 Eg Cases 6 & 7/73 *Commercial Solvents v Commission* [1974] ECR 223, [1974] 1 CMLR 309; Cases T-69, 70 & 76/89 *RTE, BBC and ITP v Commission* [1991] ECR II-485, 535 and 575, [1991] 4 CMLR 586, 669 and 745.
8 Eg Case C-260/89 *Elliniki Radiophonia Tiléorassi v Dimotiki Etairia Pliroforissis* [1991] ECR I-2925, [1994] 4 CMLR 540.
9 Case 311/84 *CBEM v CLT and IPB* (Telemarketing) [1985] ECR 3261.
10 Case T-30/89 *Hilti v Commission* [1991] ECR II-1439.
11 Eg Cases 40 etc/73 *Coöperatieve Vereniging 'Suiker Unie' v Commission* [1975] ECR 1663, [1976] 1 CMLR 295; Case 322/81 *Michelin v Commission* [1983] ECR 3461, [1985] 1 CMLR 282.
12 Case 85/76 *Hoffmann-La Roche v Commission* [1979] ECR 461, [1979] 3 CMLR 211.
13 Case 322/81 *Michelin v Commission* [1983] ECR 3461, [1985] 1 CMLR 282; Case 62/86 *AKZO v Commission* [1991] ECR I-3359, [1993] 5 CMLR 215.
14 Case 85/76 *Hoffmann-La Roche v Commission* [1979] ECR 461, [1979] 3 CMLR 211; Cases T-24 & 28/92R *Langnese-Iglo & Schöller v Commission* [1992] ECR II-1839.

236. Oligopolies. In order to infringe article 85(1) there must be conscious conduct which does not correspond to normal market conditions[1]. In the absence of a formal agreement, parallel behaviour, especially price parallelism, is normally strong evidence of the existence of a concerted practice. But oligopolistic markets are not normal market conditions since price parallelism is the natural state of such a market. So difficulties arise in the application of article 85(1) to such a market. Article 86 however refers to 'abuse by one *or more* undertakings of a dominant position'. The combined position of two or more undertakings in an oligopolistic market could constitute 'collective' or 'joint' dominance so that their conduct would be subject to the discipline of article 86. The Court of First Instance has suggested circumstances in which this might be so[2]. The Court of Justice found that a combination of local statutory monopolies covering the whole territory of a member state constitutes a dominant position[3], which might be termed 'shared' dominance.

237. Intellectual property. The exercise of intellectual property rights is curtailed significantly by the exhaustion of rights principle under article 30[4]. An attempt to exercise or protect such a right may also be an infringement of article 85(1) if it is the object, means or consequence of an agreement or concerted practice which partitions the market[5]. Further, whilst ownership of intellectual property rights does not of itself constitute dominance and the exercise of such a right does not of itself constitute abuse, the manner of its exercise by a dominant undertaking – for example, refusal to supply, limiting production, arbitrary prices or royalties, tying, acquisition of rights to competing technology – may constitute an infringement of article 86[6].

(2) Enforcement

238. Enforcement by the Commission: Regulation 17. Regulation 17[7], the principal regulation implementing articles 85 and 86, gives the Commission wide powers of investigation and enforcement.

---

1 See para 232 above.
2 Cases T-68 & 77-78/89 *Società Italiana Vetro v Commission* (Flat Glass) [1992] ECR II-1403 at 1548, [1992] 5 CMLR 302 at 404. However, the Court annulled the Decision of the Commission (Decision 89/93 (*Flat Glass*), OJ L33, 4.2.89, p 44, [1990] 4 CMLR 535), which found that there had been collective dominance in that case.
3 Case C-323/93 *Société civile agricole de Centre d'insémination de la Crespelle v Co-opérative d'élevage et d'insémination artificielle du département de la Mayenne*, judgment of 5 October 1994, not yet reported.
4 See para 196 above.
5 Cases 56 & 58/64 *Consten and Grundig v EEC Commission* [1966] ECR 299, [1966] CMLR 418; Case 40/70 *Sirena v Eda* [1971] ECR 69, [1971] ECR 260; Case 15/74 *Centrafarm v Sterling Drug* [1974] ECR 1147, [1976] 1 CMLR 1; Case 144/81 *Keurkoop v Nancy Kean Gifts* [1982] ECR 2853, [1983] 2 CMLR 47. However, certain licensing agreements fall within the ambit of a 'block exemption'; see para 245 below.
6 Case 238/87 *Volvo v Veng* [1988] ECR 6211, [1989] 4 CMLR 122; Case T-51/89 *Tetrapak v Commission* [1990] ECR II-309, [1991] 4 CMLR 344; Cases T-69, 70 & 76/89 *RTE, BBC & ITP v Commission* [1991] ECR II-485, 535 and 575, [1991] 4 CMLR 586, 669 and 745; on appeal as Case C-241/91P (pending).
7 Regulation 17/62, JO 1962 p 24 (S Edn 1959-62 p 87).

Investigation. Upon a complaint ('application') from a member state or an undertaking with legitimate interest or upon its own initiative[1], the Commission may commence an investigation. It may require undertakings to provide information[2]. Authorised Commission officials may enter the premises of any undertaking, examine books and business records, take copies therefrom, and ask for oral explanations on the spot[3]. The Commission may, in some circumstances must[4], and in all cases invariably does, seek assistance from and co-operate with the appropriate national authorities[5] – in the United Kingdom, the Office of Fair Trading. Failure to provide the information called for or refusal to submit to an investigation may result in a fine[6].

Termination and fines. Where the Commission finds that a breach of articles 85(1) or 86 has occurred it may issue an order requiring the breach to be brought to an end[7], including the power to order any positive action necessary to cure the breach[8]. It may, and frequently does, issue a decision declaring the existence of an infraction, even if it has been brought to an end, in order to clarify a point of law and so prevent future infractions. This practice has been endorsed by the Court of Justice[9]. If it finds that the breach has been intentional or negligent, the Commission may impose a fine of up to one million ECU or 10 per cent of an undertaking's annual turnover, whichever is the higher[10]. It may also impose a liquidate penalty (known as a 'periodic

1　Regulation 17, art 3. The Commission has no duty to pursue a complaint but it has a duty to consider the issues raised in order to determine whether there is conduct which infringes arts 85(1) or 86 and justify any decision not to proceed; see Case T-24/90 *Automec v Commission* [1992] ECR II-2223, [1992] 5 CMLR 431; Case T-28/90 *Asia Motor France v Commission* [1992] ECR II-2285, [1992] 5 CMLR 431; Case T-37/92 *Bureau Européen des Unions des Consommateurs v Commission* [1994] ECR II-285; Case T-74/92 *Ladbroke Racing (Deutschland) Gmbh v Commission*, judgment of 24 January 1995, not yet reported.

2　Regulation 17, art 11. However, owing to the general principle of privilege against self-incrimination, an undertaking is not obliged to provide answers which would of themselves constitute an admission of unlawful conduct; see Case 374/87 *Orkem v Commission* [1989] ECR 3283, [1991] 4 CMLR 502 and para 153 above.

3　Regulation 17, art 14; an undertaking is protected to an extent from abuse of this power of search by a general principle of the inviolability of its premises; see Cases 46/87 and 227/88 *Hoechst v Commission* [1989] ECR 2859, [1991] 4 CMLR 410 and para 153 above.

4　Cases 46/87 and 227/88 *Hoechst*, above.

5　Regulation 17, arts 11, 13, 14(4)-(6).

6　Ibid, art 15(1).

7　Ibid, art 3.

8　Cases 6 & 7/72 *Commercial Solvents v Commission* [1974] ECR 223, [1974] 1 CMLR 309. The power of positive compulsion, although not fully explored, is most appropriate where an undertaking has infringed art 86; the Commission has in principle no power to order a party to enter into contractual agreements in order to cure a breach of art 85(1); see Case T-24/90 *Automec v Commission* [1992] ECR II-2223, [1992] 5 CMLR 431.

9　Case 7/82 *GVL v Commission* [1983] ECR 483, [1983] 3 CMLR 645.

10　Regulation 17, art 15(2). To date, the highest fine imposed has been 248 million ECU (about £200 million), imposed upon eight associations and thirty-three companies wilfully engaged in a longstanding and serious cartel in the cement market; see Decision 94/815 (*Cement*), OJ L343, 30.12.94, p 1 (appeal pending). The highest fine imposed upon a single undertaking has been 75 million ECU (£60 million) for serious, persistent and deliberate breach of art 86; see Decision 92/163 (*Tetrapak II*), OJ L72, 18.3.92, p 1, [1992] 4 CMLR 551, upheld by the Court of First Instance in Case T-83/91 *Tetrapak v Commission*, judgment of 6 October 1994, not yet reported.

penalty payment') of up to 1,000 ECU per day for each day on which an undertaking, having been ordered to do so, fails to put an end to an infringement, fails to comply with a request for information, or refuses to submit to an investigation[1]. Such a fine is, in the view of Community law, an administrative, not criminal, penalty[2], but certain guarantees of the 'rights of defence' nevertheless apply[3]. In the United Kingdom, a Commission decision imposing a financial penalty is registered by the High Court or the Court of Session as a 'European Community judgment'[4] and enforced by civil process[5].

Interim measures. The Commission may also order interim measures in the course of an investigation where there is a *prima facie* breach of articles 85(1) or 86, urgency, and either a likelihood of serious and irreparable injury or a situation intolerable for the public interest[6]. Interim measures are most likely to be adopted in cases involving injury through abuse of a dominant position. The Commission may, and frequently does, accept an undertaking rather than pronounce a formal order.

Judicial control of the Commission. Any decision adopted by the Commission under Regulation 17, including a decision imposing financial penalties[7] or adopting interim measures[8] is a decision within the meaning of article 189 of the Treaty[9] and so subject to judicial review by the Court of First Instance or the Court of Justice[10].

239. Enforcement: National courts. As noted above, articles 85 and 86 are directly effective and so create rights which national courts must protect. The remedies by which these rights are to be protected vary with the substance of the issue. Article 85(2) declares that an agreement or decision which infringes article 85(1) is 'automatically void' and so, unless the offending

---

1 Regulation 17, art 16.
2 Ibid, art 15(4); confirmed by the Court of Justice is Case 45/69 *Boehringer Mannheim v Commission* [1970] ECR 769. Although the distinction between 'administrative' and 'criminal' penalties is obscure to the common lawyer, it is of great importance in some other jurisdictions where a criminal record may seriously affect the right to pursue economic activities.
3 See eg Case 155/79 *AM & S v Commission* [1982] ECR 1575, [1982] 2 CMLR 264; Case 374/87 *Orkem v Commission* [1989] ECR 3283, [1991] 4 CMLR 502; Case C-36/92P *Samenwerkende Elektriciteits-Produktiebedrijven v Commission* [1994] ECR I-1911.
4 European Communities (Enforcement of Community Judgments) Order 1972, SI 1972/1590.
5 EC Treaty, art 192 and RSC, Ord 71, rr 15-24 (England and Wales); RC 62.18-62.25 (Scotland).
6 Case 792/79R *Camera Care v Commission* [1980] ECR 119, [1980] 1 CMLR 334; Case T-44/90 *La Cinq v Commission* [1992] ECR II-1, [1992] 4 CMLR 449.
7 Regulation 17, art 17.
8 Cases 228-9/82 *Ford Werke v Commission* [1984] ECR 1129, [1984] 1 CMLR 649; Case T-23/90 *Automobiles Peugeot v Commission* [1991] ECR II-653, [1993] 5 CMLR 540.
9 See paras 142, 146 above.
10 As to what constitutes a reviewable decision in this particular context see Case 60/81 *IBM v Commission* [1981] ECR 2639, [1981] 3 CMLR 635; Case T-64/89 *Automec v Commission* [1990] ECR II-367, [1991] 4 CMLR 177; Case T-116/89 *Prodifarma v Commission* [1990] ECR II-843; Case T-138/89 *Nederlandse Bankvereniging v Commission* [1992] ECR II-2181, [1993] 5 CMLR 436; Case T-28/90 *Asia Motor France v Commission* [1992] ECR II-2285, [1992] 5 CMLR 431; Case T-37/92 *Bureau Européen des Consommateurs v Commission* [1994] ECR II-285.

provisions are severable (severance being permissible[1] and a matter for national, not Community, law[2]), they cannot be enforced by the courts. This would apply even if the proper law of the contract is that of a non-Community country since a court of the Community cannot give effect to such an agreement. Article 86 contains no equivalent provision, but conduct infringing it cannot give rise to enforceable rights for the defaulting undertaking. Third parties affected by an infringement of articles 85 or 86 may seek appropriate remedies from their national courts such as damages[3] or injunction/interdict[4]. But the lawfulness of a Commission decision, even where it is to be registered and enforced as a European Community judgment, is, in principle, subject to judicial review only before the Community courts. Where a competition case arising before a national court appears to raise a question of the application of articles 85 or 86, the Court of Justice is often asked to rule on the question in a reference under article 177[5].

240. Exemption (article 85(3)). There is an important difference between articles 85 and 86 in that conduct prohibited by article 86 is always illegal[6], whereas a restrictive agreement can, under article 85(3), be exempted from the prohibition provided it meets certain strict criteria. The procedure for obtaining exemption is laid down in Regulation 17. Exemption may be granted only by the Commission[7]. A national court which is called upon to consider an agreement which has not been formally exempted by the Commission cannot presume that it should or will be exempted simply because it appears to the national court to satisfy the criteria for exemption[8].

241. Conditions for exemption. The conditions for exemption set out in article 85(3) are both positive and negative. The agreement must both:

---

1 Cases 56 & 58/64 *Consten & Grundig v EEC Commission* [1966] ECR 299, [1966] CMLR 418; Case 56/65 *Société Technique Minière v Maschinenbau Ulm* [1966] ECR 235, [1966] CMLR 357.

2 Case 319/82 *Societé de Vente de Ciments et Bretons v Kerpen et Kerpen* [1983] ECR 4173, [1985] 1 CMLR 511.

3 *Garden Cottage Foods Ltd v Milk Marketing Board* [1984] AC 130, [1983] 3 CMLR 43 (HL).

4 See eg *Argyll v Distillers* 1987 SLT 514, [1986] 1 CMLR 764 (OH); *Holleran v Thwaites* [1989] 2 CMLR 917 (Ch D); *Leyland DAF v Automotive Products* [1994] 1 BCLC 245 (Ch D and CA).

5 See paras 106ff above.

6 See Case T-51/89 *Tetrapak v Commission* [1990] ECR II-309, [1991] 4 CMLR 344.

7 Regulation 17, art 9.

8 See para 241 below. The exception to this rule is an 'old' or 'accession' agreement which benefits from 'provisional validity' - that is, an agreement which pre-dates the entry into force of the competition rules (ie, March 1962 or the date of accession for new member states; as to Austrian, Finnish and Swedish accession agreements see Corfu Accession Treaty, Annex I, III) and was duly notified to the Commission is deemed to be exempted from the prohibition of article 85(1), and so is enforceable in national courts, until such time as the Commission adopts a formal decision; see Case 48/72 *Brasserie de Haecht v Wilkin-Janssen* (No 2) [1973] ECR 77, [1973] CMLR 287; Case 99/79 *Lancome v Etos* [1980] ECR 2511, [1981] 2 CMLR 264; Case C-39/92 *Petrogal v Correia Simoes* [1993] ECR I-5659. The exact renewal of a standard contract enjoying provisional validity keeps the provisional validity alive; see Case 1/70 *Marcel Rochas v Bitsch* [1970] ECR 515, [1971] CMLR 104.

(1) *positively*, contribute to 'improving the production or distribution of goods or to promoting technical or economic progress, while allowing consumers a fair share of the resulting benefit'; and

(2) *negatively*, neither 'impose on the undertakings concerned restrictions which are not indispensable to the attainment of these objectives' nor 'afford such undertakings the possiblity of eliminating competition in respect of a substantial part of the products in question'.

Both sets of conditions must be satisfied before exemption can be granted, and an assessment of whether they are satisfied depends upon economic as well as legal considerations.

242. Notification. Exemption from the prohibition of article 85(1) can be granted only if the agreement has been 'notified' to the Commission. The procedures and forms ('Form A/B') are laid down by the Council[1]. There is a right to be heard, and a procedure for exercising it[2], prior to a final decision being adopted by the Commission. Information provided in a notification enjoys a degree of privilege[3]; it cannot be used in national proceedings as proof of infringement of national competition rules[4]. Proper notification[5] provides immunity from the Commission's power to impose fines in respect of any act occurring after notification, the immunity being operative from the date of notification until the Commission adopts a formal decision refusing to grant exemption or, following a preliminary examination, issues a preliminary notice withdrawing immunity[6]. It does not affect the power and duty of a national court, under article 85(2), to strike down a prohibited agreement[7].

243. Negative clearance. Application may also be made, in a like manner and on the same forms, for 'negative clearance'[8]. Negative clearance is a declaration by the Commission that the agreement or conduct in question falls outwith the prohibitions of the competition rules altogether. Two points ought therefore to be observed. First, whilst there can be no exemption from conduct which infringes article 86, an undertaking which is, or may be, in a

---

1 Regulation 17, arts 4, 5; Regulation 27/62, JO 1962 p 1118 (S Edn 1959-62 p 132). Regulation 17, art 4(2) relaxes the requirement to notify certain types of agreement, which may but need not be notified. The exact status of art 4(2) agreements remains unclear; they are *not* immune from Commission fines under Regulation 17 (Case 240/82 *Stichting Sigarettenindustrie v Commission* [1985] ECR 3831), and except in the case of old or accession agreements (see previous note) art 4(2) ought to be treated with great caution. In the United Kingdom, SI 1973/950 provides that notification is required also to be made to the Registrar of Restrictive Trade Agreements.
2 Regulation 17, art 19; Regulation 99/63, JO 1963 p 2268 (S Edn 1959-62 p 47).
3 Regulation 17, art 20.
4 Case C-67/91 *Dirección General de Defensa de la Competencia v Asociación Española de Banca Privada* [1992] ECR I-4785; cf Case C-60/92 *Otto v Postbank* [1993] ECR I-5683; Case T-353/94 *Postbank v Commission* (pending).
5 It is very important that notification comply with all procedural requirements, otherwise it will not be recognised; see Case 30/78 *Distillers v Commission* [1980] ECR 2229, [1980] 3 CMLR 121.
6 Regulation 17, art 15(2), (6).
7 See para 239 above.
8 Regulation 17, art 2.

dominant position may ask the Commission to rule whether a certain course of conduct would constitute an abuse of its (possible) dominance. Negative clearance may therefore, unlike exemption, be applied for in the context of article 86. Second, negative clearance is a declaration by the Commission that, *in the light of the information available to it,* and *in the view of the Commission,* the agreement or conduct falls outwith the provisions of articles 85 and 86. The declaration does not in the same way as an exemption bind the national court, which may take a different view as to whether an agreement or conduct infringes articles 85 or 86, though it would be likely to accord great weight to the Commission view.

244. 'Comfort letters'. Formal exemption or negative clearance for a notified agreement can be granted only by a Commission decision. In practice, such decisions are rare, and response to a notification often results in a 'comfort letter' (or 'administrative letter'). Most cases are now resolved by 'closing the file' in this way, and Form A/B asks whether the applicant(s) would be satisfied with a comfort letter in lieu of a formal decision. A comfort letter will be issued where the Directorate General for competition (DG IV) is satisfied upon the information before it that the agreement does not infringe article 85(1) or, if it does, would qualify for an exemption. It will state that the Commission feels there is no reason to intervene in the matter or to proceed to a final decision. Before issuing a comfort letter the Commission frequently publishes a summary of the contents of a notified agreement in the Official Journal and invites interested parties to submit observations[1]. A comfort letter, which can be issued only in respect of a properly notified agreement or practice, does *not* constitute exemption or negative clearance[2]. The agreement is immune from Commission fines unless the Commission re-opens the file. But national courts are not precluded from holding that article 85(1) or 86 applies and that the agreement or conduct is illegal. The views expressed by the Commission may be taken into account in determining whether this is so[3]. However, the terms of a comfort letter issued in response to an application for an exemption (as opposed to an application for negative clearance) may be such as to imply that the agreement is *prima facie* inconsistent with article 85(1), and so afford little comfort in a national court.

245. 'Block exemptions'. The Commission is empowered by article 85(3) to grant exemptions not only to individual agreements but also to categories of agreements. Such 'block exemptions' constitute an important mechanism for the implementation of Commission policy in the competition field. The exemptions are set out in regulations which, like article 85(3) itself, lay down positive ('white list') and negative ('black list') criteria for exemption. An

---

1 See Reg 17, art 19(3). Care should be taken as third parties are frequently given very short notice to submit observations.
2 Cases 253/78 and 1-3/79 *Procureur de la République v Giry et Guerlain* (the Perfume cases) [1981] ECR 2327, [1981] 2 CMLR 99.
3 Case 31/80 *L'Oréal v De Nieuwe* [1980] ECR 3775, [1981] 2 CMLR 235.

agreement which satisfies all the criteria is, without need for notification, automatically exempt from article 85(1). Some block exemption regulations further provide that agreements which do not fall entirely within the stated criteria may be notified to the Commission and will be automatically exempt unless the Commission has started 'opposition procedure' within six months. Otherwise, agreements are exempt only if they fall wholly within the four corners of the relevant regulation. (Application can always be made for individual exemption of an agreement whose subject matter falls within the scope of a block exemption regulation, but whose terms do not or may not comply with the block exemption criteria.) As at 1 January 1995 the Commission has adopted block exemptions in the following fields: exclusive distribution agreements[1]; exclusive purchasing agreements (with special provisions on petrol and beer purchasing)[2]; motor vehicle distribution and servicing agreements[3]; patent licensing agreements[4]; specialisation agreements[5]; research and development agreements[6]; franchising[7]; know-how agreements[8]; agreements in the insurance sector[9]; and commercial air transport agreements[10]. The block exemptions allow for a high degree of legal certainty, but they are sometimes criticised for discouraging innovation in commercial dealing.

246. Problems of co-enforcement; *Delimitis*. It will be apparent that the present scheme for the enforcement of article 85 leaves open the question as to the proper course for a national court to take when seized of a question involving a new agreement which appears to be prohibited by article 85(1), which does not fall within one of the block exemptions, which has been notified to the Commission, and which might be, but has not yet been, granted an individual exemption. In *Delimitis*[11], the Court of Justice said that in such circumstances a national court ought first to determine, in the light of case law and previous Commission decisions, whether article 85(1) applies. If it does, the court ought then to determine, again in the light of previous case law and Commission decisions, whether the agreement is *unlikely* to be granted an exemption. If it so concludes, it should proceed to exercise its power under article 85(2). If it concludes that exemption of the agreement is

1 Regulation 1983/83, OJ L173, 30.6.83, p 1.
2 Regulation 1984/83, OJ L173, 30.6.83, p 5.
3 Regulation 123/85, OJ L15, 18.1.85, p 16.
4 Regulation 2349/84, OJ L219, 16.8.84, p 15.
5 Regulation 417/85, OJ L53, 22.2.85, p 1.
6 Regulation 418/85, OJ L53, 22.2.85, p 5.
7 Regulation 4087/88, OJ L359, 28.12.88, p 46.
8 Regulation 556/89, OJ L61, 4.3.89, p 1.
9 Regulation 3932/92, OJ L398, 31.12.92, p 7.
10 Regulation 1617/93, OJ L155, 26.6.93, p 18 (schedules, joint operation, tariff consultation and slot allocation at airports); Regulation 3652/93, OJ L333, 31.12.93, p 37 (computer reservation systems). Both regulations replace earlier block exemptions in the area.
11 Case C-234/89 *Delimitis v Henninger Bräu* [1991] ECR I-935, [1992] 5 CMLR 210; cf the earlier judgment in Case 48/72 *Brasserie de Haecht v Wilkin-Janssen (No 2)* [1973] ECR 77, [1973] CMLR 287.

a possibility, it ought to stay (sist) proceedings, supplying any appropriate national interim remedy, until such time as the Commission has reached a decision. In the meanwhile, the Commission has a duty to co-operate fully with the national court, for example, by letting the national court know of the state of play with the notification, giving priority to it and providing information on factual data. These considerations were subsequently set out, and essentially codified, in a 1993 Commission Notice[1]. More recently the Court reconfirmed that a national court is competent to rule upon the legality of a notified (but not yet exempted) agreement if it finds that the conditions for application of article 85(1) are clearly not joined[2].

(3) Mergers and Concentrations

247. Mergers and concentrations. Mergers and concentrations are not addressed specifically in the EC Treaty[3]. It was not at first clear which, if any, of the competition provisions of the Treaty applied to them. The Court of Justice held in 1973 that the acquisition of a competitor by an already dominant undertaking, thereby diminishing competition still further, could constitute an abuse of its dominant position[4]. So, article 86 applies to mergers, but only in a situation where an undertaking which is already dominant seeks further to reinforce that dominance. The view of the Commission[5] was that article 85 could not apply to mergers, since the end product of a merger is a single undertaking. However in 1987 the Court of Justice found that certain forms of concentration (*in casu* a company acquiring an equity interest in a competitor) can in some circumstances fall within the prohibition of article 85(1)[6]. The effect of that judgment has not yet been fully explored, but it gave new life to a Commission draft regulation on merger control, first proposed in 1973 and finally adopted by the Council in 1989[7].

248. The merger regulation. The merger regulation, which addresses 'concentrations', imposes a requirement of prior notification to and approval by the Commission before concentrations 'with a Community dimension'[8] may proceed. If a merger has no Community dimension – if it is, for example,

---

1 Notice on Co-operation between National Courts and the Commission in applying Articles 85 and 86 of the EEC Treaty, OJ C39, 13.2.93, p 5; [1993] 4 CMLR 12.
2 Case C-250/92 *Gøttrup-Klim v Dansk Landbrugs Grovvareselskab*, judgment of 15 December 1994, not yet reported.
3 They are addressed in the ECSC Treaty, arts 65-66.
4 Case 6/72 *Europembellage and Continental Can v Commission* [1973] ECR 215, [1973] CMLR 199. See more recently Case T-51/89 *Tetrapak v Commission* [1990] ECR II-309, [1991] 4 CMLR 334; Decision 93/352 (*Warner-Lambert/Gillette & Eemland*), OJ L116, 12.5.93, p 21, [1993] 5 CMLR 559.
5 See eg *Memorandum on the Problems of Concentration in the Common Market*, Competition Series, Study No 3 (Brussels, 1966) and *Fifteenth Report on Competition Policy* (1986) para 26.
6 Cases 142 & 156/84 *British American Tobacco Ltd v Commission* (Philip Morris) [1987] ECR 4487, [1988] 4 CMLR 24.
7 Regulation 4064/89, OJ L395, 30.12.89, p 1; revised text in OJ L257, 21.9.90, p 14; [1990] 4 CMLR 859.
8 Article 1(2).

below the (very high) threshold set by the regulation[1] – it is presumed to be solely of national concern[2]. Unlike article 86, the regulation applies not only to the strengthening but also to the creation of a dominant position through concentration[3], and the Commission has asserted the right to control even creation of joint dominance[4]. The regulation disapplies Regulation 17 to concentrations, provides specific means of enforcement more appropriate to the field, and seeks more clearly to define the division of jurisdiction between national and Community competition authorities. The rights and obligations of the Commission and of undertakings notifying proposed mergers are laid down in an implementing regulation[5]. There is a form for notification ('Form CO')[6] and there are two Commission notices offering guidelines[7]. Upon notification, the Commission is required to determine, first, whether it is a concentration within the meaning of the regulation and second, if so, whether it is 'compatible with the common market'. The criteria provided for determining compatibility with the common market are those of competition only[8]; the Commission may not, for example, take into account industrial or social policy considerations. The regulation provides very short time periods in which the Commission must act[9]; if it fails to act, the concentration may proceed[10]. The Commission may, and frequently does, allow a concentration to proceed only upon prescribed modifications to the original agreement. It has refused permission outright only once[11]. All decisions adopted under the merger regulation are subject to judicial review by the Court of First Instance or the Court of Justice.

(4) Public Undertakings and Monopolies

249. Public undertakings and monopolies (article 90). Article 90 applies the competition rules to two special categories of undertaking:

---

1 A concentration has a Community dimension only if the annual turnover of all participating undertakings exceeds 5 thousand million ECU (about £4 thousand million), the Community turnover is more than 250 million ECU, and more than a third of that turnover arises in more than one member state; see Regulation 4064/89, art 1(2). The threshold was to be revised in 1993 (art 1(3)) but the Council failed to act to do so.
2 Although a concentration with no Community dimension may be referred to the Commission at the instance of a member state in which it does have a significant impact (art 22(3), the 'Dutch clause'); equally, a concentration which technically has a Community dimension but has disproportionate impact in one member state may be referred by the Commission to the competition authorities of the state (art 9, the 'German clause').
3 Regulation 4064/89, art 2(2)-(3).
4 Decision 92/553 (*Nestlé/Perrier*), OJ L356, 5.12.92, p 1, [1993] 4 CMLR M17.
5 Regulation 2367/90, OJ L219, 25.7.90, p 5; [1990] 4 CMLR 683.
6 Regulation 2367/90, Annex 1.
7 Notice regarding Restrictions Ancillary to Concentrations, OJ, C203, 14.8.90, p 5, [1990] 4 CMLR 714; Notice regarding Concentrative and Co-operative Operations under Regulation 4064/89, OJ, C203, 14.8.90, p 10, [1990] 4 CMLR 721. These notices are soon to be amended.
8 Regulation 4064/89, art 2(1).
9 Ibid, art 10.
10 Ibid, art 10(6).
11 Decision 91/619 (*Aerospatiale-Alenia/de Havilland*), OJ L334, 5.12.91, p 42, [1992] 4 CMLR M2.

- public undertakings and undertakings to which member states grant special or exclusive rights[1], and
- undertakings entrusted with the operation of services of general economic interest or having the character of a revenue-producing monopoly[2].

Article 90(1) is concerned with the duties of member states in relation to measures taken by them, article 90(2) with the conduct of the undertakings themselves. Article 90(3) empowers the Commission to address directives or decisions to member states to ensure compliance with article 90. This power, though limited, has been used, for example, to require member states to separate the commercial and regulatory activities of public telecommunications undertakings[3]. Article 90 has assumed particular importance in the context of recent trends towards privatisation and deregulation.

250. State measures (article 90(1)). In relation to public and 'privileged' undertakings, member states may 'neither enact nor maintain in force any measures contrary to the rules contained in [the] Treaty'[4], especially the rule against discrimination upon grounds of nationality and the rules on competition, including state aids. Article 90(1) is therefore to be read with other articles of the Treaty, the issue being whether the state measure in question brings about a situation in conflict with another Treaty rule[5]. The grant or maintenance of monopoly or special rights must be justified by considerations of general interest (eg the need for universal supply at reasonable cost) and the scope of the rights conferred must be limited to what is necessary and proportionate to achieve that objective[6].

251. Conduct of undertakings (article 90(2)). Undertakings to which special tasks have been assigned must comply with the rules of the Treaty, especially the competition rules, except 'in so far as the application of such rules does not obstruct the performance, in law or in fact, of the particular tasks assigned to them. The development of trade must not be affected to such an

---

1 EC Treaty, art 90(1). This category covers essentially state monopolies, nationalised undertakings and private or privatised undertakings which have been granted, or have retained, a privileged position in the market.

2 Ibid, art 90(2). This category covers universal suppliers (water, gas, electricity, etc) and undertakings charged with running monopolies from which the state derives revenue (eg, national lotteries or tobacco monopolies).

3 Case 202/88 *France v Commission* [1991] ECR I-1223; Cases C-46/90 & 93/91 *Procureur du Roi v Lagauche* [1993] ECR I-5267.

4 EC Treaty, art 90(1).

5 In Case C-41/90 *Höfner v Mactroton* [1991] ECR I-1979 and Case C-323/93 *Société Civile Agricole du Centre d'Insémination de la Crespelle v Co-opérative d'Elevage et d'Insémination Artificielle du Département de la Mayenne*, judgment of 5 October 1994, not yet reported, the test applied was whether the rights conferred were such as *necessarily* to cause the privileged undertaking to breach the rules on competition. In Case C-260/89 *Elliniki Radiophonia Tileorassi v Dimotiki Etairia Pliroforissis* [1991] ECR I-2925 and Case C-179/90 *Merci Convenzionali Porto di Genova SpA v Siderurgica Gabrielli SpA* [1991] ECR I-5889, it was whether the undertaking was 'led' or 'induced' to do so.

6 Case C-230/91 *Criminal Proceedings against Corbeau* [1993] ECR I-2533.

extent as would be contrary to the interests of the Community.'[1] The test is whether the restriction of competition is necessary to enable the undertaking to perform its particular task, having regard to the economic conditions in which it must operate, the costs it must bear and the legislation, especially environmental legislation, with which it must comply[2].

252. Competition rules and the EEA. The Treaty establishing the European Economic Area (EEA) contains provisions identical *mutatis mutandis* to articles 85 and 86 of the EC Treaty. Undertakings ought to be aware that their conduct is now susceptible to the application of the competition rules of both treaties. Those of the EEA Treaty are discussed below[3].

(B) STATE AIDS

253. State aids (articles 92-94). The section of the Treaty on state aids opens with a general prohibition of 'any aid granted by a Member State *or through State resources in any form whatsoever* which distorts or threatens to distort competition by favouring certain undertakings or the production of certain goods'[4]. Thus, assistance provided by, for example, a local authority or a public development agency may constitute a prohibited state aid. The aid must affect trade between member states in order to fall within the prohibition[5]; the effect must be real but need not be appreciable[6]. Having stated the general prohibition, the Treaty then specifies types of aid which are always permissible[7] and other types of aid which may be permissible[8].

254. Commission supervision of state aids. Like the competition rules of articles 85 and 86, the Treaty provides for the adoption of legislation in order to give effect to the rules on state aids[9]. No such legislation has been adopted. The monitoring of state aids continues to rest upon Treaty authority in article 93, and depends upon whether the aid in question is an existing aid or a new aid.

Existing aids. The Commission is required to keep under constant review any existing state aids[10]. If it determines that an existing state aid is incompatible with the criteria of article 92 it may require that the member state abolishes or alters it[11]. As this is an adversarial procedure, the member state

---

1 EC Treaty, art 90(2).
2 Case C-393/92 *Municipality of Almelo v Energiebedrijf IJsselmij NV* [1994] ECR I-1477.
3 See Appendix I.
4 EC Treaty, art 92(1); emphasis added.
5 Ibid, art 92(1).
6 Case 102/87 *France v Commission* [1988] ECR 4067; Case 142/87 *Belgium v Commission* [1990] ECR I-959.
7 EC Treaty, art 92(2).
8 Ibid, art 92(3).
9 Ibid, art 94.
10 Ibid, art 93(1).
11 Ibid, art 93(2).

has a right to be heard. If a member state fails to comply with an order to terminate or alter a state aid, the Commission may raise enforcement proceedings before the Court of Justice without having to comply with the procedural requirements of article 169[1].

New aids. Any new aid (which includes alteration to an existing aid) must be notified to the Commission[2]. The Treaty provides that a member state may not introduce the aid until the Commission has decided upon its compatibility with article 92[3]. However, the Commission is required to respond to a notification 'without delay', and the Court of Justice has said that this means within a two-month period[4]; otherwise the member state may grant it, and it becomes an existing aid subject to the supervision of article 93(1).

255. Direct effect of articles 92 and 93. In the absence of implementing legislation, the enforcement of the state aid rules remains a matter for Commission discretion. There is no provision governing state aids equivalent to article 85(2), and articles 92 and 93 are not directly effective. The one exception is the requirement that new state aids be notified to the Commission. Failure to comply with the procedure of article 93(3), and *a fortiori* failure to notify the Commission at all of a proposed aid, will render that aid unlawful with direct effect. The Commission may also require that it be repaid[5]. In present practice the Commission also requires repayment of the interest deemed to have been earned since disbursement of the unlawful aid.

256. Judicial review and state aids. Whilst it is in general very difficult for a natural or legal person to challenge a Community act under article 173 of the Treaty[6], the Court of Justice adopts a lenient view of 'direct and individual concern' in the area of state aids. So, where the Commission adopts a decision approving or refusing to approve the grant of an aid, the intended recipient of the aid and even third (competitor) parties have been held to have title and interest to raise an action of annulment of the decision directly before the Court of First Instance[7]. This may be the only avenue of judicial review: where the intended recipient of a state aid was informed in writing by its government of a Commission decision refusing to authorise it and that

---

1 EC Treaty, art 93(2); on art 169 see paras 97ff above.
2 Ibid, art 93(3).
3 Ibid, art 93(3), final sentence.
4 Case 120/73 *Lorenz v Germany* [1973] ECR 1471; Case 84/82 *Germany v Commission* [1984] ECR 1505.
5 The requirement of repayment was approved by the Court of Justice in Case 70/72 *Commission v Germany* (Kohlegesetz) [1973] ECR 813, [1973] CMLR 741. For an example see Decision 93/359, OJ L143, 15.6.93, p 7, requiring British Aerospace to repay the £44.4 million in unlawful 'sweeteners' by which the United Kingdom government had persuaded it to buy the Rover Group. This was a re-adoption of an earlier Decision which was annulled by the Court of Justice for procedural impropriety; Case C-294/90 *British Aerospace & Rover Group Holdings v Commission* [1992] ECR I-493.
6 See para 101 above.
7 See eg Case C-313/90 *CIRFS v Commission* [1993] ECR I-1125, also recognising the *locus standi* of a trade association.

it could seek annulment under article 173 but failed to do so, it could not subsequently plead the invalidity of the decision in national proceedings[1].

(C) TAXATION

257. Rules as to taxation (articles 95–98). The Treaty does not seek to deprive the member states of power to levy taxes for the purpose of raising public revenues. However, Community trade could clearly be affected if a national taxation scheme favoured domestic production at the expense of imported goods. The first paragraph of article 95 of the Treaty therefore prohibits the imposition 'directly or indirectly, on the products of other Member States, [of] any internal taxation of any kind in excess of that imposed directly or indirectly on similar domestic products'. The second paragraph of article 95 extends this prohibition to taxation which affords 'indirect protection' to domestic production. Notwithstanding the apparent limitation of article 95 to 'products of other Member States', the Court of Justice has held that it applies its application to discriminatory taxation upon *any* products, whatever their origin, which are in free circulation[2].

258. Application of rules as to taxation. Clearly there may be argument, in any particular case, whether products are 'similar' or whether a difference in the rate of tax constitutes 'indirect protection'. The product need not be the same, and the best test is probably whether the ordinary consumer, faced with a free choice, might choose one product or the other for the particular purpose he or she has in mind. Thus, for example, British excise duties upon wine were held by the Court of Justice to be unfairly high in comparison with those imposed upon a more typically, and competing, British product (beer) and therefore constituted a breach of article 95(2)[3]. Care is also necessary in considering article 95 alongside article 12, as application of the two are mutually exclusive; a charge upon an imported good at point of entry may in fact be part of a non-discriminatory (and hence permissible) tax scheme, whilst, conversely, under certain conditions a measure which is on its face one of internal taxation may consitute a charge having equivalent effect to a customs duty[4].

259. Harmonisation of tax law (article 99). The Cockfield White Paper[5] identified tax disequilibrium and the frontier controls and equalisation charges necessary to deal with it as a fiscal barrier to trade and a serious impediment to the completion of the internal market. Article 99 provides for the

---

1 Case C-188/92 *TWD Textilwerke Deggendorf v Germany* [1994] ECR I-833. There could have been no doubt in this case of the undertaking's *locus standi* under art 173.
2 Case 193/85 *Co-operativa Co-Frutta v Amministrazione delle Finanze dello Stato* [1987] ECR 2085.
3 Case 170/78 *Commission v United Kingdom* [1980] ECR 417, [1980] 1 CMLR 716; [1983] ECR 2265, [1983] 3 CMLR 512.
4 See eg Case 105/76 *Interzuccheri v Ditta Rezzano e Cavassa* [1977] ECR 1029.
5 See para 26 above.

harmonisation of legislation regarding turnover taxes, excise duties and other forms of indirect taxation to the extent necessary to ensure the establishment and functioning of the internal market. Such harmonisation measures require unanimity in the Council. Much of the work necessary in approximating national law, particularly on turnover taxes, capital duty and (to a lesser extent) excise duties, was achieved by 1993, and only limited problems remain.

260. Direct taxation. The Treaty is almost silent as to direct taxation, and the area continues to be governed largely by bilateral double taxation agreements between member states. The Treaty requires only that the member states should negotiate with a view to concluding such agreements[1] and prohibits arbitrary discrimination when taxing the movement of capital and payments[2]. Some directives in the field of company law have a bearing upon direct taxation[3] but that is not their primary purpose. The Commission has adopted a recommendation on taxation of foreign income[4]. Discrimination in the taxation of companies based upon residence of the company is inconsistent with articles 52 and 58 of the Treaty[5].

(c) Other Common Policies

261. General. Titles VI to XVII of the Treaty cover a number of areas in which the member states are bound to pursue common policies. Many of them were added to the Treaty and/or refined by the Single European Act and the Treaty on European Union. Some of them are of great significance.

(A) ECONOMIC AND MONETARY POLICY

262. General. As discussed above, the Treaty now provides that the achievement of economic and monetary union (EMU) is a 'task' (article 2) and an 'activity' (article 3a) of the Community. The general principles are laid down in article 3a and given flesh by subsequent provisions. EMU is to be achieved, over a transitional period of three stages, in accordance with the 'Delors Plan' by 1999 at the latest. The Treaty provisions addressing EMU

---

1 EC Treaty, art 220.
2 Ibid, art 73d(3).
3 See eg Directive 90/434 (the mergers directive), OJ L225, 20.8.90, p 1; Directive 90/435 (the parent-subsidiary directive), OJ L225, 20.8.90, p 6; Directive 90/463 (arbitration convention), OJ L225, 20.8.90, p 10. See also the 1992 Report of the Ruding Committee which recommended further steps to be taken in order to eliminate remaining distortions to competition resulting from variations in direct taxation.
4 Recommendation 94/79, OJ L39, 10.2.94, p 22.
5 Case C-330/90 *R v Inland Revenue Commissioners, ex parte Commerzbank* [1993] ECR 4017, [1993] 3 CMLR 357.

and the institutional machinery intended to achieve it are extraordinarily complex, and they will be considered here only briefly.

263. Economic and monetary union. Economic and monetary union is not a common economic policy. Rather it requires the 'close coordination of Member States' economic policies'[1], which are 'a matter of common concern'[2], within the framework of broad guidelines established by the Council upon the basis of a 'conclusion' established by the European Council[3]. It envisages the irrevocable fixing of exchange rates leading to the introduction of a single currency (the ECU) and of a single monetary and exchange rate policy[4]. Both the Community and the member states are required to conduct their policies in a manner which complies with the 'guiding principles' of stable prices, sound public finances and monetary conditions and a sustainable balance of payments[5]. Member states are obliged to avoid excessive government deficits, and the Community institutions may intervene with significant powers of sanction to correct a failure to do so[6].

264. The three stages. The first stage required member states simply to comply with the Treaty provisions on the free movement of capital[7], to open up (if necessary) their financial institutions[8] and to work towards lasting convergence in economic policy[9]. The second stage started on 1 January 1994[10]. During it the member states are required to adopt financial discipline[11] and ensure by the end of the second stage (if necessary) that national legislation relating to central banks is compatible with the Treaty and the ESCB/ECB Statute[12]. The European Monetary Institute (EMI) was established and is required to assist in and monitor the development of and progress towards a high degree of sustainable convergence as defined by the Treaty[13]. The Council meeting as heads of State and government is required before the end of December 1996 to decide whether a majority of member states fulfil the necessary conditions for the adoption of a single currency, whether it is appropriate to enter the third stage, and, if so, to set a date for the beginning of the third stage[14]. The third stage is in any event to start by 1 January 1999[15].

---

1 EC Treaty, art 3a(1).
2 Ibid, art 103.
3 Ibid, arts 102a and 103(2); guidelines have now been established by Recommendation 94/480, OJ L200, 3.8.94, p 38.
4 EC Treaty, art 3a(2).
5 Ibid, art 3a(3).
6 Ibid, art 104c and Protocol on the Excessive Deficit Procedure. See also Regulation 3605/93, OJ L332, 31.12.93, p 7.
7 See para 220 above.
8 EC Treaty, arts 104 and 104a; see also Regulation 3603/93, OJ L332, 31.12.93, p 1 and Regulation 3604/93, OJ L332, 31.12.93, p 4.
9 EC Treaty, art 109e(1).
10 Ibid, art 109e(2).
11 Ibid, art 104c.
12 Ibid, art 108.
13 Ibid, art 109j(1) and Protocol on Convergence Criteria Referred to in Article 109j.
14 Ibid, art 109j(3).
15 Ibid, art 109j(4).

265. The third stage. Immediately upon the setting of the date for the third stage the European Central Bank and the European System of Central Banks are to be established and exercise their powers, in accordance with procedures established by the Council, from the first day of the third stage[1]. At the start of the third stage the Council is to adopt by unanimity of participating states[2] the conversion rates at which the ECU is to replace the national currencies at an irrevocably fixed rate and become a currency in its own right[3]. Thereafter the financial institutions (the ESCB and the ECB) will, through their legislative and enforcement powers, direct and control EMU in accordance with the Treaty and their Statute[4]. Like the German Bundesbank, the primary objective of the ESCB is price stability[5], within which it is to contribute to the achievement of the objectives of EMU and define and implement monetary policy, foreign exchange and payment systems[6]. The ECB is to enjoy the exclusive right to authorise the issue of banknotes[7]; the minting and issue of coinage will be for the member states but is subject to ECB approval of the volume[8].

266. Derogation. The third stage applies automatically but only to those member states which fulfil the necessary convergence criteria. Other member states – 'member states with a derogation'[9] – will not take part. They and their national central banks are excluded from rights and obligations within the ESCB and their voting rights within the Council on third stage matters are suspended[10]. How many member states will meet the rigorous criteria remains to be seen. The Council will 'abrogate' the derogation of a 'member state with a derogation' which subsequently fulfils the criteria for sustainable economic convergence[11] and will fix the rate at which the ECU is to be substituted for its currency[12], after which that member state will assume full rights and obligations of EMU.

267. United Kingdom and Danish exemption. By virtue of a Protocol attached to the Treaty[13], even if it fulfils the necessary convergence criteria the United Kingdom is not bound to enter the third stage. It may do so, and is obliged to notify the Council if it intends to do so – ie, unlike the Social

---

1 EC Treaty, art 109l(1).
2 See para 266 below.
3 EC Treaty, arts 109g and 109l(4).
4 See para 122 above.
5 EC Treaty, art 105(1) and ESCB/ECB Statute, art 2.
6 EC Treaty, art 105(1)–(2) and ESCB/ECB Statute, art 3.
7 EC Treaty, art 105a(1) and ESCB/ECB Statute, art 16.
8 EC Treaty, art 105a(2).
9 Ibid, art 109k(1).
10 Ibid, art 109k(3)-(5).
11 Ibid, art 109k(2). For these purposes the Council is required to meet as heads of State and government.
12 Ibid, art 109l(5).
13 Protocol on Certain Provisions relating to the United Kingdom of Great Britain and Northern Ireland.

Agreement[1] it may 'opt in' to EMU – but there is no obligation. If it does not, it will be accorded in effect the status of a permanent 'member state with a derogation'. In giving effect to the Treaty on European Union within the United Kingdom, Parliament enacted a statutory bar restraining the government from submitting notification without the approval of an Act of Parliament[2]. Denmark enjoys a similar right under the Treaty[3], and although it was drafted in a manner which permits Denmark to 'opt out' of the third stage (as opposed to the drafting of the United Kingdom Protocol which presumes non-participation but permits 'opting in'), the Danish government has already submitted notification that Denmark will not participate in the third stage[4]. Whilst it is not envisaged in the Treaty, the German Federal Constitutional Court said that it would be unconstitutional for Germany to proceed to the third stage without further approval from the German parliament[5].

(B) COMMERCIAL POLICY

268. The Common Commercial Policy (articles 110–115). The creation of a single market requires not only a Common Customs Tariff[6] but also a common commercial policy in trade with third states. The Common Commercial Policy (CCP) is one of the 'activities' of the Community[7]. It is closely bound to, and needs to be considered in conjunction with, the rules on the customs union. It is based upon 'uniform principles' in external Community trade[8]. Unlike the Common Customs Tariff, the CCP is not yet complete. Under article 113 the Community has sole competence to enter into bilateral or multilateral agreements regulating trade in all goods, including those subject to the ECSC and Euratom Treaties[9]. Cross-frontier services not involving the movement of natural or legal persons fall within the CCP, otherwise the Community shares competence with the member states in trade in services[9]. But as it is evolutionary the CCP may come to cover more in the future. Where trade agreements have been negotiated the Community rules occupy the field. Where they have not, the member states enjoy residual competence, which can be exercised only in accordance with framework legislation concerning common rules for imports[10].

269. Agreements between the Community and third countries. The Community has entered into a number of multilateral and bilateral

---

1 See para 273 below.
2 European Communities (Amendment) Act 1993, s 2.
3 Protocol on Certain Provisions relating to Denmark.
4 European Council in Edinburgh, Conclusions of the Presidency, Bull EC 12-1992, p 25.
5 Judgment of the Bundesverfassungsgericht of 12 October 1993, [1994] 1 CMLR 57.
6 See para 182 above.
7 EC Treaty, art 3(b).
8 Ibid, art 113(1).
9 Opinion 1/94 *re the World Trade Organisation*, opinion of 15 November 1994, not yet reported.
10 Regulation 518/94, OJ L67, 10.3.94, p 77 and Regulation 519/94, OJ L67, 10.3.94, p 89.

agreements with third countries which regulate trade amongst or between them[1]. Some ('association agreements') are comprehensive, involving the participation of both the Community and the member states, and implied is a gradual move towards eventual accession to the Community; others are less so. They may be grouped as follows:

(a) the agreement on the European Economic Area (EEA) with Iceland, Liechtenstein, Norway, Austria, Finland and Sweden[2];

(b) the Lomé Agreement with 68 African, Caribbean and Pacific (ACP) countries, most of them erstwhile colonies of the various member states[3];

(c) the 'Europe Agreements' with Poland, Hungary, the Czech Republic, Slovakia (the 'Visegrad countries'), Romania and Bulgaria, which provide for the progressive development of free trade and envisage (distant) accession to the Community[4];

(d) other association agreements with individual third countries;

(e) other agreements with individual third countries;

(f) agreements with international organisations, such as the GATT 1994 agreement and the agreement creating the World Trade Organisation[5].

All these agreements are capable of conferring direct effect depending upon their terms[6].

270. Safeguard measures (anti-dumping). Safeguard and retaliatory measures taken against imports from third countries which benefit from unfair subsidies or are dumped on the Community market fall within the Common Commercial Policy and are governed by Community legislation[7], not by article 91. The Commission and/or Council may impose upon imported goods countervailing or anti-dumping duties designed to eliminate or equalise the unfair advantage. It is an area of highly complex economic analysis and political sensitivity, and was the last subject area in which power of judicial supervision was transferred from the Court of Justice to the Court of First Instance[8].

(C) SOCIAL POLICY

271. General. The Treaty numbers amongst Community activities a policy in the social sphere and the strengthening of economic and social cohesion[9].

---

1 EC Treaty, arts 113(3) and 228.

2 See Annex I. The EEA Agreement displaced 'free trade agreements' entered into with each EFTA state; as Switzerland did not join the EEA relations between it and the Community continue to be governed by the 1972 Community-Switzerland Free Trade Agreement, JO L300, 31.12.72, p 191.

3 The Lomé Agreement (formerly the Yaoundé Agreement) is renegotiated every five years; for the current agreement (Lomé IV) see OJ L229, 17.8.91, p 3.

4 See eg the Europe Agreement with Hungary of 16 December 1993, OJ L347, 31.12.93, p 2.

5 See Opinion 1/94 *re the World Trade Organisation*, opinion of 15 November 1994, not yet reported.

6 See para 284 below.

7 Regulation 2423/88, OJ L209, 2.8.88, p 1.

8 Decision 94/149, OJ L66, 10.3.94, p 29.

9 EC Treaty, arts 3(i) and 3(j).

Social policy is now addressed in Title VIII of the Treaty, which also includes provisions on education, vocational training and youth. The Treaty considers the harmonisation of social systems 'to promote improved working conditions and an improved standard of living for workers'[1] as a necessary component of, or complement to, the common and internal markets. It charges the Commission with the task of promoting 'close co-operation between Member States' in the fields of employment, labour law and working conditions, vocational training, social security, prevention of occupational accidents and diseases, occupational hygiene and collective bargaining[2]. The Commission is also to 'endeavour to develop the dialogue between management and labour'[3]. Harmonisation directives may be adopted in relation to the working environment and health and safety of workers[4]. The Treaty also established a European Social Fund to assist in worker mobility, and adaptation to industrial change and training[5]. Implicit throughout is a presumption of the pre-eminence of national policies[6], which may in any event now be a Treaty requirement in the light of subsidiarity[7]. However, one area included in the Chapter on social provisions – the rules on sex discrimination – has had a very substantial impact within the national legal systems[8].

272. The Social Charter. In 1989 the heads of state and government of all member states but the United Kingdom adopted the Community Charter of the Fundamental Social Rights of Workers, commonly called the Social Charter[9], in the belief that 'social consensus . . . is an essential condition for ensuring sustained economic development' and that 'in the context of the establishment of the single European market, the same importance must be attached to the social aspects as to the economic aspects'[10]. The Social Charter is not a legislative act, but a blueprint for the development of social legislation within the Community. At the same time the Commission adopted an Action Programme containing more specific guidelines and draft proposals for legislation[11]. The Social Charter and the Action Programme address areas such as freedom of movement, rights in employment, living and working

---

1 EC Treaty, art 117, 1st para.
2 Ibid, art 118, 1st para.
3 Ibid, art 118b. This provision grew out of the 'social dialogue' begun in 1985 at Val Duchesse between the 'social partners' represented by the *Union des Industries de la Communauté Européenne* (UNICE) and the European Trade Union Confederation (ETUC), and led in turn to certain provisions of the Social Agreement, as to which see para 274 below.
4 EC Treaty, art 118a. An example of a measure adopted by authority of art 118a is Directive 93/104, OJ L307, 13.12.93, p 20 (the 'working time' Directive), which was challenged immediately by the United Kingdom for lack of competence; see Case C-84/94 *United Kingdom v Council* (pending).
5 EC Treaty, arts 123-125.
6 See eg Case 167/73 *Commission v France* [1974] ECR 359.
7 See para 157 above.
8 See paras 275-280 below.
9 For the text see Social Europe 1/90.
10 Social Charter, Preamble, recitals 5 and 2.
11 COM(89)568 fin.

conditions, social protection, freedom of association and collective bargaining, training, worker participation, health and safety and protection of children, adolescents, the elderly and the disabled. But both stress the pre-eminence of the member states rather than collective Community policy[1], and here again subsidiarity plays an important role.

273. The Social Protocol. At the intergovernmental conference which led to the adoption of the Treaty on European Union, eleven (of the then twelve) member states signalled a willingness to agree to more far-reaching provisions in the social sphere. Since the United Kingdom government did not agree, they could not be incorporated into the general social provisions of the Treaty. The result was the adoption of a Protocol on Social Policy attached to the EC Treaty, sometimes (wrongly) referred to as the 'Social Chapter'. The Protocol authorised the member states other than the United Kingdom to pursue a social policy and to use Community institutions and procedures to adopt legislation to that end, *but* the measures adopted are not to apply to or in the United Kingdom. The substantive rules to be pursued by means of this framework are laid down in an Agreement annexed to the Protocol (hence occasional reference to 'the Social Protocol and Agreement'). The United Kingdom was (necessarily) a party to the Social Protocol but is *not* a party to the Agreement. It does not take part in Council deliberations within the sphere of the Agreement[2], where there is a special system of weighted voting in the Council[3], and any financial consequences other than administrative costs entailed for the institutions do not apply to the United Kingdom[4]. The Social Protocol and Agreement are phrased in such a way that the United Kingdom is permanently outside the structure: there is no possibility, in the absence of treaty amendment, of 'opting in' to the Agreement. The Social Protocol is not recognised, and has no force, in British law[5]. There may however be legal difficulties in differentiating between the Treaty chapter on social provisions and the Social Agreement.

274. The Agreement on Social Policy. The Agreement on Social Policy provides a framework for substantive rules following the objectives of the Social Charter but including also adequate social protection[6], dialogue between management and labour (the 'social dialogue') and the development of human resources[7]. The member states acting under the Agreement are to support and complement national activities, and may adopt directives for

---

1 Social Charter, Preamble, recital 15 and point 27.
2 But UK MEPs take part in debates and in voting in the European Parliament in the sphere.
3 The Corfu Accession Treaty amends the system of weighted voting under the Protocol, presumably to take account of the accession to the Agreement of Austria, Finland and Sweden. But there seems to have been no formal act of accession by these three states to the Agreement.
4 Protocol on Social Policy, arts 2–3.
5 European Communities Act 1972, s 1(2)(k) as amended.
6 The English text reads 'proper social protection', which is a poor translation of *protection sociale adéquate*.
7 Agreement on Social Policy, art 1.

minimum standards in the fields of working environment and health and safety, working conditions, worker participation, sex equality, integration into the labour market, social security and protection, redundancy, collective representation, employment of non-Community citizens and financial subvention[1]. The most innovative provisions address arrangements for collective bargaining at European level[2] and toleration of positive discrimination in favour of women in the vocational and professional spheres[3]. An example of a measure enacted under the Social Protocol is the Directive establishing a European Works Council to promote worker information and participation[4]. In 1994 the Commission adopted a (not very ambitious) White Paper on the future development of social policy[5].

275. Sex discrimination. As a facet of social policy, article 119 of the Treaty prohibits discrimination upon the basis of sex in the area of pay. The original purpose of the rule was to ensure that undertakings in those member states (particularly France) which already had equal pay rules did not suffer through being required to compete with undertakings in other member states which permitted pay differential based upon sex. The effect of article 119 has however gone well beyond this original purpose.

276. Article 119. Article 119(1) of the Treaty provides, in the English text, that:

'Each Member State shall during the first [transitional] stage ensure and subsequently maintain the application of the principle that men and women should receive equal pay for equal work'.

Unfortunately, the word 'pay' is too narrow a translation of terms used in the original language texts (*Entgelt, rémunérations, retribuzioni, beloning*) and has given rise to much misunderstanding. 'Pay' is defined by article 119 in very broad terms. It means: 'the ordinary or basic minimum wage or salary *and any other consideration, whether in cash or in kind, which the worker receives, directly or indirectly, in respect of his employment from his employer*'[6]. 'Consideration' is also too narrow a translation of the original language texts which use words meaning advantage or recompense. This explains why favourable rates for railway travel for family employees[7], pensions paid under a contracted-out private occupational scheme and any benefits paid by an employer to an employee in connection with his compulsory redundancy[8] have been held to be 'pay'.

277. Implementing legislation. The basic rule of the Treaty, which relates only to the consideration received from an employer in respect of employment, has

---

1 Agreement on Social Policy, art 2.
2 Ibid, arts 3 and 4.
3 Ibid, art 6(3).
4 Directive 94/45, OJ L254, 30.9.94, p 64.
5 European Social Policy – A Way Forward for the Union, COM(94)333 fin.
6 EC Treaty, art 119(2); emphasis added.
7 Case 12/81 *Garland v British Rail Engineering Ltd* [1982] ECR 359, [1982] 1 CMLR 696.
8 Case 262/88 *Barber v Guardian Royal Exchange* [1990] ECR I-1889, [1990] 2 CMLR 513; see para 280 below.

been refined and expanded by a number of directives, each of which requires that there be adequate judicial protection for the rights conferred[1]:

- Directive 75/117 on equal pay for men and women[2]. This directive defines the scope of article 119 and introduces the principle of equal pay for work of equal value.
- Directive 76/207 on equal treatment for men and women as regards access to employment, vocational training and promotion, and working conditions[3]. This directive prohibits discrimination, both direct or indirect, based upon sex unless the sex of the employee constitutes a 'determining factor' in employment[4]. Discrimination based upon pregnancy constitutes direct discrimination[5].
- Directive 79/7 on equal treatment for men and women in matters of social security[6].
- Directive 86/378 on equal treatment in occupational social security schemes[7]. This directive has had far reaching effects upon social security schemes, particularly in the United Kingdom, Ireland and the Netherlands. It was required to be implemented by mid-1989 but it was 'frozen' by controversy resulting from the *Barber* judgment[8].
- Directive 86/613 on equal treatment in self-employed occupations[9].

278. Application of the sex discrimination rules. Article 119 prohibits both direct and indirect discrimination in the field of pay[10]. Direct discrimination is never justified. Where there is pay differential to the disadvantage of one sex disproportionately (eg as between full and part-time workers[11]), a *prima facie* case of discrimination is established and the onus shifts to the employer to show that there are objective grounds for the scheme unrelated to sex[12]. Article 119 has both vertical and horizontal direct effect[13]. So, rights arising from article 119 are enforceable before any competent national court or

---

1 See Case 14/83 *von Colson and Kamann v Land Nordrhein-Westfalen* [1984] ECR 1891, [1986] 2 CMLR 430 and Case 222/84 *Johnston v Chief Constable of the RUC* [1986] ECR 1651, [1986] 3 CMLR 328.
2 OJ L45, 19.2.75, p 19.
3 OJ L39, 9.2.76, p 40.
4 Ibid, art 2(2); see eg Case 222/84 *Johnston v Chief Constable of the RUC* [1986] ECR 1651, [1986] 3 CMLR 328.
5 Case 177/88 *Dekker v Stichting Vormingscentrum voor Jong Volwassenen Plus* [1990] ECR I-3941; Case C-32/93 *Webb v EMO Air Cargo Ltd* [1994] ECR I-3567, [1994] 2 CMLR 729. For limitations to the protection afforded pregnant women see Case 179/88 *Hertz v Dansk Arbejdsgiverforening* [1990] ECR I-3979.
6 OJ L6, 10.1.79, p 24.
7 OJ L225, 12.8.86, p 40.
8 See paras 279-80 below.
9 OJ L359, 19.12.86, p 56.
10 Case 96/80 *Jenkins v Kingsgate (Clothing Productions) Ltd* [1981] ECR 911, [1981] 2 CMLR 24; Case 170/84 *Bilka-Kaufhaus v Weber von Hartz* [1986] ECR 1607, [1986] 2 CMLR 701.
11 See *R v Secretary of State for Employment, ex parte Equal Opportunities Commission* [1995] 1 AC 1.
12 Case 170/84 *Bilka-Kaufhaus*, above; Case C-127/92 *Enderby v Frenchay Health Authority* [1993] ECR I-5535. Where the differential is a product of legislation the onus is borne by the member state to justify it; Case 171/88 *Rinner-Kühn v FWW Spezial-Gebäudereinigung* [1989] ECR 2743.
13 Case 43/75 *Defrenne v SABENA* (No 2) [1976] ECR 455, [1976] 2 CMLR 98. On vertical and horizontal direct effect see para 148 above.

tribunal and against any public or private person. Directive 75/117 on equal pay merely restates the principles of article 119 and in no way alters its content or scope[1]. The practical effect is that the provisions of the directive, including the principle of equal pay for work of equal value, also have vertical and horizontal direct effect. The other directives do not have horizontal direct effect; an employee of a public authority or an 'emanation of the state'[2] may invoke them[3] but an employee of a private undertaking may not. As against a private employer the employee must rely upon the national legislation implementing the directives – in the United Kingdom primarily the Equal Pay Act 1970, the Sex Discrimination Act 1975 and the Employment Protection (Consolidation) Act 1978, all as amended – although national courts and tribunals must, 'if at all possible', interpret and apply them in the light of the directives[4]. If it is not possible, a remedy for injury may, by applying *Francovich*, lie in damages against the state[5].

279. Pensions: application of article 119. A distinction is drawn between pensions paid under statutory social security schemes and those paid under occupational pension schemes. Social security pensions do not fall under article 119[6]. They are governed by Directive 79/7, which permits member states to maintain differential retirement ages for men and women, together with consequential discriminatory elements[7]. By contrast, pension payments under occupational schemes, whether contributory or non-contributory, fall under article 119[8]. The decisive test is, in terms of article 119 itself, whether the pension is paid directly or indirectly by the employer (ie funded wholly or partly by the employer) as part of the consideration in respect of the employment relationship[9].

280. Occupational pension schemes. Men and women must have equal access to occupational pension schemes[10]. They must be treated equally in relation to retirement ages and pension benefits (but only in relation to

---

1 Case 96/80 *Jenkins v Kingsgate (Clothing Productions) Ltd* [1981] ECR 911, [1981] 2 CMLR 24.
2 See para 148 above.
3 Case 152/84 *Marshall v Southampton and Southwest Hampshire Area Health Authority (No 1)* [1986] ECR 723, [1986] 1 CMLR 768, which confirmed that the state is bound by unimplemented directives not only in discharging its public functions but also in its private law relations as an employer.
4 See para 148 above. For an example of how far uniform interpretation may apply in this area see Case 177/88 *Dekker v Stichting Vormingcentrum voor Jong Volwassenen Plus* [1990] ECR I-3941.
5 See paras 141, 148 above.
6 Case 80/70 *Defrenne v Belgium* [1971] ECR 445.
7 Directive 79/7, art 7(1)(a); See Case C-9/91 *R v Secretary of State for Social Security, ex parte Equal Opportunities Commission* [1992] ECR I-4297.
8 Case 262/88 *Barber v Guardian Royal Exchange* [1990] ECR I-1889, [1990] 2 CMLR 513.
9 Case C-7/93 *Bestuur van het Algemeen Burgerlijk Pensioenfonds v Beune* [1994] ECR I-4471,
10 Case 170/84 *Bilka-Kaufhaus GmbH v Weber von Hartz* [1986] ECR 1607 and, applying *Bilka*, Case C-57/93 *Vroege v NCIV Instituut voor Volkshuisvesting* [1994] ECR I-4541 (exclusion of part-time workers) and Case C-128/93 *Fisscher v Voorhuis Hengelo* [1994] ECR I-4583 (exclusion of married women).

periods of service after 17 May 1990[1]). It is the prospective periodic pension payments that constitute 'pay' for the purposes of article 119, not the employer's contributions (actuarially calculated according to the needs of the scheme) nor the employee's transfer benefits or lump-sum options (actuarially calculated upon the basis of accrued rights)[2]. Article 119 applies to pensions paid to the spouses of deceased employees[3], to 'top-up' schemes (supplementing the state pension)[4] and to 'contracted-out' schemes (in substitution for the state pension)[5], but not to single sex schemes[6]. Pension scheme trustees must, so far as is possible, administer their scheme in compliance with article 119 and, if necessary, have recourse to the employer and/or the courts in order to do so[6]. Employees and the surviving spouses and representatives of deceased employees can invoke the direct effect of article 119 against employers and trustees[6].

(D) OTHER POLICIES

281. The policies. The Single European Act introduced into the Treaty provisions authorising Community activities in a number of new fields. The Treaty on European Union amended some of these and introduced still more, not all of which are primarily economic. They are now included amongst the activities of the Community in article 3 and addressed in greater detail in subsequent provisions. These are:

- education, vocational training and youth[7];
- culture[8];
- public health[9];
- consumer protection[10];

1 Ie, the date of the judgment in Case 262/88 *Barber v Guardian Royal Exchange* [1990] ECR I-1889, [1990] 2 CMLR 513. See Case C-109/91 *Ten Oever v Stichting Bedrijfspensioenfonds voor het Glazenwassers- en Schoonaakbedrijf* [1993] ECR I-4879 and Case C-7/93 *Bestuur van het Algemeen Burgerlijk Pensioenfonds v Beune* [1994] ECR I-4471, decided respectively before and after the entry into force of the Protocol concerning Article 119 (the 'Barber Protocol'), annexed to the EC Treaty by the Treaty on European Union. This limitation in time does *not* apply to equality of access to pension schemes; Case C-57/93 *Vroege* and Case C-128/93 *Fisscher*, above.
2 Case C-152/91 *Neath v Hugh Steeper Ltd* [1993] ECR I-6935.
3 Case C-109/91 *Ten Oever v Stichting Bedrijfspensioenfonds voor het Glazenwassers- en Schoonaakbedrijf* [1993] ECR I-4879.
4 Case C-110/91 *Moroni v Firma Collo GmbH* [1993] ECR I-6591.
5 Case 262/88 *Barber v Guardian Royal Exchange* [1990] ECR I-1889, [1990] 2 CMLR 513.
6 Case C-200/91 *Coloroll Pension Trustees Ltd v Russell* [1994] ECR I-4389.
7 EC Treaty, arts 126, 127.
8 Ibid, art 128.
9 Ibid, art 129.
10 Ibid, art 129a.

- trans-European networks[1];
- industry[2];
- economic and social cohesion[3];
- research and technological development[4];
- environment[5];
- development co-operation[6].

Article 3 also mentions measures in the spheres of energy, civil protection and tourism[7], but there are no subsequent operative provisions in the EC Treaty addressing these areas[8]. A declaration attached to the Treaty[9] states that, in the view of the Commission, action in these spheres may be pursued under other Treaty provisions.

282. Community competences. Article 3 provides that under the foregoing new heads of competence the Community is, variously, to adopt policies, to strengthen, to promote and/or to contribute to the field in question. In all of them the Community shares competence with the member states, necessitating close co-operation between national and Community authorities. The extent of the Community's powers varies widely. It is, for example, given substantial competences in the field of the environment, whilst in education and culture, Community action is restricted to incentive measures and recommendations[10], and even then only 'if necessary' in support of and supplementing national action whilst 'fully respecting' the responsibilities of the member states[11]. Harmonisation legislation in the fields of education, vocational training, culture and public health is expressly excluded[12]. The parameters of these new or amended competences are still to be worked out. Their importance lies in establishing a legal basis for Community interest and action and providing express authority to treat with third countries in these areas[13]. Where the Community acts in some of these areas (education, public health, consumer protection and the environment) it is required to be mindful of a 'high level' of protection[14]. The Treaty prescribes a variety of

1 EC Treaty, arts 129b-129d.
2 Ibid, art 130.
3 Ibid, arts 130a-130e.
4 Ibid, arts 130f-130p.
5 Ibid, arts 130r-130t.
6 Ibid, arts 130u-130y.
7 Ibid, art 3(t).
8 Energy is of course a prime concern of the ECSC and Euratom Treaties.
9 Declaration on Civil Protection, Energy and Tourism.
10 EC Treaty, arts 126(4) and 128(5).
11 Ibid, arts 126(1) and 128(1).
12 Ibid, arts 126(2), 127(4), 128(5) and 129(4).
13 Ibid, arts 126(3), 127(3), 128(3), 129(3), 129c(3), 130r(4), 130x-y. These provisions merely codify for sake of certainty an international personality which exists in any event by virtue of the judgment of the Court of Justice in Case 22/70 *Commission v Council* (ERTA) [1971] ECR 263, [1973] CMLR 335; see para 284 below.
14 EC Treaty, arts 126(1) ('quality' education), 129(1), 129a(1) and 130r(2). Single market legislation adopted by authority of art 100a (see para 193 above) is subject to a similar constraint by virtue of art 100a(3), the purpose of which is to ensure that standards are not whittled down by qualified majority vote.

legislative procedures[1], and there has already been a significant rise in litigation before the Court of Justice challenging the legal base of legislation[2].

283. Integration clauses. In six of these subject areas (culture, public health, industry, economic and social cohesion, environment and development co-operation) the Treaty provides 'integration clauses', which require, in varying terms, that the interests of these areas must be taken into account when the Community acts under other provisions of the Treaty[3]. So, for example, agricultural legislation which fails to take sufficient account of the interests of public health, the environment or development co-operation may be liable to annulment or invalidation as an infringement of the Treaty within the meaning of article 173[4]. However, these integration clauses are a new device not yet considered by the Court of Justice[5]; their meaning, breadth, application and justiciability have therefore yet to be tested.

(5) THE GENERAL AND FINAL PROVISIONS OF THE EC TREATY

284. International personality and external competence of the Community. Article 210 of the Treaty provides simply:

'The Community shall have legal personality'.

Article 238 of the Treaty explicitly accords to the Community the authority to enter into treaties with third states, groups of states or other international organisations with a view to creating association agreements with the Community. It was under this provision that the Community entered into the Agreement establishing the European Economic Area, the Lomé Agreement and other international agreements[6]. It is also expressly and exclusively competent to conclude tariff and trade agreements as a function of the Common Commercial Policy[7] and formal agreements on an exchange rate system for the ECU with non-Community currencies as a function of economic and monetary union[8]. The Community can also enter into international agreements with third states in any area in which it enjoys rule-making competences within the Community[9]. A special 'treaty making power' is

---

1 The article conferring legislative authority in the field of the environment, for example, contains no fewer than four different legislative procedures; see EC Treaty, art 130s.
2 See para 144 above.
3 EC Treaty, arts 128(4), 129, 130(3), 130b, 130r(2) and 130v.
4 See para 100 above.
5 The first integration clause was incorporated into the Treaty by the Single European Act in 1987 in the field of the environment (EEC Treaty, art 130r(2)), all the others were introduced into the Treaty (and the provisions on the environment were significantly amended) only with the entry into force of the TEU in 1993.
6 See para 269 above.
7 See para 268 above.
8 EC Treaty, art 109(1).
9 Case 22/70 *Commission v Council* (ERTA) [1971] ECR 263, [1973] CMLR 335; Opinion 1/92 *re the EEA Treaty (No 2)* [1993] ECR I-1061, [1992] 2 CMLR 217.

now written into the Treaty in a number of areas[1]. In some areas Community competence may be exclusive[2]. In 'mixed agreements' whose subject matter falls partly within Community competence and partly within that of the member states, the Community and the member states must collaborate, each within their respective spheres, in order to arrive at a mutually acceptable result[3]. The Court of Justice has held that international agreements into which the Community has entered, as well as acts of autonomous institutions created by such agreements and charged with their implementation, can of themselves be relied upon before national courts provided that their provisions are such as to confer direct effect[4]. If they are not they must be implemented by appropriate Community legislation.

285. Contractual liability of the Community. The non-contractual liability of the Community is discussed above[5]. The Treaty provides that the contractual liability of the Community is to be governed by the law applicable to the contract in question[6]. The Court of Justice may be awarded jurisdiction to give judgment pursuant to an arbitration clause contained in such a contract[7].

286. Extraordinary derogation from the Treaty. Member states are permitted to adopt measures derogating from Treaty rules which are necessary for the protection of the essential interests of their security connected with production and trade in arms, munitions and war materials[8], in the event of serious internal disturbance affecting the maintenance of law and order or of serious international tension constituting a threat of war[9] or in the event of a sudden balance of payments crisis[10]. In each such case a member state is required to operate closely with the Community institutions so as to ensure that it cannot make improper use of these powers, and the Commission may bring before the Court of Justice a member state it alleges is so doing[11].

---

1 See para 282 above.
2 See eg Case 22/70 *Commission v Council* (ERTA) [1971] ECR 263, [1973] CMLR 335; Cases 3, 4 & 6/76 *Cornelius Kramer* [1976] ECR 1279, [1976] 2 CMLR 440; Ruling 1/78 *re Draft Convention on the Physical Protection of Nuclear Materials* [1978] ECR 2151, [1979] 1 CMLR 131; Case 127/87 *Commission v Greece* [1988] ECR 3333 at 3348.
3 See eg Opinion 1/94 *re the World Trade Organisation*, opinion of 15 November 1994, not yet reported.
4 See eg Case 181/73 *Haegemann v Belgian State* [1974] ECR 449, [1975] 1 CMLR 515; Case 104/81 *Hauptzollamt Mainz v Kupferberg* [1982] ECR 3641, [1983] 1 CMLR 1; Case C-192/89 *Sevince v Staatssecretaris van Justitie* [1990] ECR I-3461, [1992] 2 CMLR 57; Case C-432/92 *R v Minister for Agriculture, Fisheries and Food, ex parte Anastasiou (Pissouri) Ltd* [1994] ECR I-3087.
5 See para 105 above.
6 EC Treaty, art 215(1).
7 Ibid, art 181.
8 Ibid, art 223(1).
9 Ibid, art 224.
10 See para 220 above.
11 EC Treaty, art 225, 2nd para. At the time of writing such a case is before the Court regarding Greece's closing of its frontier with the former Yugoslav Republic of Macedonia; see Case C-120/94 *Commission v Greece* (pending). Uncertainty as to the interpretation of these provisions was cited by the Court as a ground for refusing the Commission's application for interim measures; see Case C-120/94R *Commission v Greece* [1994] ECR I-3037.

287. The general power: article 235. The Treaty could not provide for all eventualities in which it would be appropriate for the Community to act. It therefore provided in article 235 a general or residual power for the Council, acting by unanimity, to adopt measures in the event that

> '. . . action by the Community should prove necessary to attain, in the course of the operation of the common market, one of the objectives of the Community and this Treaty has not provided the necessary powers. . .'.

Article 235 confers a very broad legislative competence: all that is necessary is that Community action is 'necessary to attain [an] objective of the Community'. Article 235 was used extensively in the early days as the Community institutions came to adopt legislation in areas not clearly within other Treaty authority but which was nevertheless deemed 'necessary'. Its use has decreased with express extension of Community legislative authority under the Single European Act and the Treaty on European Union. The legislative authority of article 235 is residual only: an act based upon article 235 either alone or in tandem with another legal base for which a sufficient legal base exists elsewhere in the Treaty is liable to annulment or invalidation by the Court of Justice[1].

---

1 See eg Case 165/87 *Commission v Council* (Generalised Tariff Preferences) [1987] ECR 1493, [1988] 2 CMLR 131.

5. THE TREATY ON EUROPEAN UNION

288. General. As is discussed above[1], the constitutional structure of the European Union is based upon three so-called pillars. The Communities and their law are the central pillar. The two other pillars are outside the scope of Community law: common foreign and security policy and co-operation in the fields of justice and home affairs (Titles V and VI respectively of the Treaty on European Union). But all three pillars, including the Community, are part of, and subject to, the constitutional order of the Union[2]. The effect of Titles V and VI is to bring within the single institutional framework of the Union areas which were already the subject of co-operation amongst the member states: 'political co-operation' in foreign affairs under the Single European Act[3] and co-operation in the fields of justice and home affairs under, for example, the Schengen Agreement on the elimination of border controls (to which the United Kingdom is not party)[4], and the Dublin Convention on asylum[5]. The TEU contains general and final provisions applicable to all three pillars, again including the Community.

289. The law of the European Union in the United Kingdom. Because Titles V and VI of the TEU are, in effect, traditional intergovernmental treaty agreements governed by public international law and their subject matters fall within prerogative powers in the United Kingdom, they were not incorporated into, and form no part of, United Kingdom law[6]. Indeed, the European Union is not, as such, recognised by United Kingdom law.

290. Institutions of the European Union. According to the Treaty on European Union

> 'The Union shall be served by a single institutional framework which shall ensure the consistency and the continuity of the activities carried out in order to attain its objectives while respecting and building upon the *acquis communautaire*. . . .

---

1 See para 37.
2 The 'Common Provisions' of the TEU (arts A–F) provide very little in the way of constitutional norms which bind the Union and its institutions in their conduct. They do, however, require that 'the Union shall respect the national identities of its Member States' and 'the Union shall respect fundamental rights, as guaranteed by the [ECHR] and as they result from the constitutional traditions of the Member States' (arts F(1)–(2)). Note that articles of the TEU are identified by letters rather than numbers in order to distinguish them from articles of the Community treaties.
3 See para 29 above.
4 Convention of 14 June 1985 concerning the Gradual Elimination of Controls at External Frontiers, [1990] CLE F271. The parties to the Schengen Agreement are the Community member states other than Ireland, Austria, the three Scandinavian member states and the UK.
5 Convention of 15 June 1990 Determining the State Responsible for Examining Applications for Asylum lodged in one of the Member States of the European Communities (1991) 30 ILM 425; Cmnd 1623. The Convention is not yet in force.
6 See the European Communities (Amendment) Act 1993, which expressly excludes Titles V and VI (and the Social Protocol; see para 273 above) from the ambit of those treaties recognised as having force in UK law.

The European Parliament, the Council, the Commission and the Court of Justice shall exercise their powers under the conditions and for the purposes provided for, on the one hand, by the provisions of the Treaties establishing the European Communities ... and, on the other hand, by the other provisions of this Treaty'[1].

The Union therefore adopts, or 'borrows', the institutions established by the Community treaties in order to carry out the tasks of the non-Community pillars of the Union. The one exception is the European Council, which is hardly mentioned in the Community treaties. It is probably best seen as an institution of the European Union rather than of the Community.

291. Decision making in the European Union. The principal institution competent to act by authority of Titles V and VI is the Council (of Ministers). The Commission is to be 'fully associated' with the work carried out under both Titles[2] and may propose joint positions, joint action and multilateral Conventions under Title VI[3], but is otherwise accorded no specific powers. Where any institution acts under these Titles, its conduct and activities are of a qualitatively wholly different nature from those pursued under the Community treaties. The Council may adopt 'decisions'[4] and other measures under both Titles, but they are *not* decisions in the sense of article 189 of the EC Treaty[5]: they are acts adopted autonomously, without formal input from the other institutions, by unanimous vote[6] within the Council meeting inter-governmentally; they bind the parties to the TEU as a matter of international law but have, and can produce, no internal legal effect, at least in the United Kingdom[7]. The status of these rules has yet to be defined, but they seem to constitute a new, emergent category of legal norm, that of 'intergovernmental law'. Decisions adopted by the Council, particularly under common foreign and security policy, are frequently accompanied or followed up by Community action in order to give effect to them.

292. Political and judicial control of the European Union. The European Parliament has no formal right to influence activities undertaken within Titles V and VI. In the area of common foreign and security policy the Presidency of the Union is required to consult the Parliament 'on the main aspects and the basic choices'[8], and in both areas the Parliament is entitled to be informed regularly of discussions and developments, to have its views 'duly taken into consideration' and to ask questions of, and make

1 TEU, arts C and E.
2 Ibid, arts J.9 and K.4(2).
3 Ibid, art K.3(2).
4 Ibid, arts J.3, J.11, K.8(2), K.9.
5 See paras 142ff above.
6 TEU, arts J.8(2) and K.4(3). The Council may by unanimity decide that certain procedural matters are to be decided by qualified majority; TEU, arts J.3(2), J.8, K.3 and K.4(2). A Declaration on voting in the field of common foreign and security policy attached to the TEU provides that member states will 'to the extent possible' avoid preventing the adoption of a unanimous decision where a qualified majority exists in favour of its adoption; the declaration has no legal force.
7 This may not be so in other, 'monist' member states the constitutions of which recognise general treaty law as a source of law directly effective within the national legal system.
8 TEU, art J.7.

recommendations to, the Council[1]. It has no formal role to play in the adoption of measures under either Title. With one minor exception[2], jurisdiction of the Court of Justice to consider these provisions is expressly excluded[3]. So, measures adopted by the institutions under Titles V and VI are not subject to judicial review before the Court; and if they are adopted without reference to the (minimal) prerogative powers of the Parliament the Court cannot interfere. The two Titles therefore fall almost entirely outwith the political and judicial supervisory control of Community machinery.

293. International personality of the European Union. The Treaty on European Union contains no provisions equivalent to articles 210 and 238 of the EC Treaty[4]. The Union therefore has no international personality and no treaty making power; third countries may treat only with the Community *qua* Community (where the subject matter falls within Community competence) and/or with the member states.

(1) COMMON FOREIGN AND SECURITY POLICY

294. Common foreign and security policy. The provisions on common foreign and security policy are contained in Title V of the TEU, comprising articles J to J.11. The common foreign and security policy is 'established' by the TEU[5] and defined and implemented by the Union and its member states[6]. Its objectives are: to safeguard the common values, fundamental interests and independence of the Union, to strengthen its security, to preserve peace and strengthen international security, to promote international co-operation and to develop and consolidate democracy and the rule of law and respect for human rights and fundamental freedoms[7]. They are to be pursued by establishing systematic co-operation and gradually implementing joint action[8] within principles and general guidelines established by the European Council[9]. The member states have a general obligation of loyalty and mutual solidarity to Union policy and to refrain from any action contrary to its interests[10]. They must inform and consult one another on any matter of foreign and security policy of general interest[11]. The Council defines common

---

1 TEU, arts J.7 and K.6.
2 Ibid, art K.3(2)(c), 3rd para.
3 Ibid, art L. Art L also excludes from the jurisdiction of the Court the Preamble and the Common Provisions (arts A-F) of the TEU. However, as these provisions form constitutional rules of the Union to which all three pillars (including the Community) are subject, some aspects of their interpretation fall within the Court's legitimate jurisdiction. Arts J.11 and K.8 also refer to matters falling within the Court's jurisdiction.
4 See para 284 above.
5 TEU, art J.
6 Ibid, art J.1(1).
7 Ibid, art J.1(2).
8 Ibid, art J.1(3).
9 Ibid, art J.8(1).
10 Ibid, art J.1(4).
11 Ibid, art J.2(1).

positions 'whenever it deems it necessary'[1], and the member states are bound to uphold them and ensure that their national policies conform to them[2]. The Council may also decide when joint action is appropriate[3], which then commits the member states in the positions they adopt and in the conduct of their activities[4]. Diplomatic and consular missions of the member states and Commission delegations have a duty to co-operate[5]. There are special provisions for co-operation with the Western European Union (of which all member states are full members or observers) and NATO and for consultation with member states, members (permanent or otherwise) of the UN Security Council[6]. The Council is assisted by a Political Committee, with responsibilities analogous to those of COREPER in the Community sphere[7]. In matters coming within foreign and security policy the Union is represented by the Presidency[8].

(2) JUSTICE AND HOME AFFAIRS

295. General. The provisions on co-operation in justice and home affairs are contained in Title VI of the TEU, comprising articles K to K.9. Title VI deals with areas which are, if anything, more sensitive than those of common foreign and security policy, embracing immigration, residence, asylum and refugee policies and judicial and police co-operation in the detection, pursuit and punishment of crime. Hence, Title VI provides for 'co-operation' in these fields, not, as in Title V, the creation and implementation of a 'policy'. Any action is firmly within the control of the member states, which 'inform and consult one another within the Council with a view to coordinating their action'[9].

296. Fields subject to Title VI. Title VI declares the following matters to be of 'common interest': asylum policy, external border controls, immigration policy and policy on third country nationals, drug addiction, fraud, customs co-operation, judicial co-operation in civil matters and judicial and police co-operation in criminal matters[10]. The Council may adopt joint positions,

---

1 TEU, art J.2(2).
2 Ibid, arts J.2(2)-(3).
3 Ibid, art J.3.
4 Ibid, art J.3(4).
5 Ibid, art J.6.
6 Ibid, arts J.4(2)-(5), J.5(4). See also the Declaration on Western European Union attached to the TEU.
7 Ibid, art J.8(5). The Political Committee was first established to assist in the process of EPC under the Single European Act; SEA, art 30(10). As to COREPER, see para 60 above. A Declaration on practical arrangements in the field of common foreign and security policy attached to the TEU provides for the examination of the division of work between the Political Committee and COREPER, and implicitly a degree of merging of their functions.
8 TEU, art J.5(1).
9 Ibid, art K.3(1).
10 Ibid, art K.1.

promote co-operation and, subject to a subsidiarity test, adopt joint action[1]. A Co-ordinating Committee, again analogous to COREPER, was established in order to assist the Council[2]. The member states are bound (although in language less mandatory than that of Title V) to defend in international fora any common position adopted[3] and are required to establish collaboration amongst their relevant government departments[4]. All activities under Title VI must be dealt with in compliance with the European Convention on Human Rights and the 1951 Convention on the Status of Refugees[5].

297. Complementary Community competences. The provisions on justice and home affairs are not hermetically sealed from Community competences. The EC Treaty empowers the Community to determine the third countries whose nationals require a visa to enter the Community[6] and a uniform format for visas is to be adopted by the (EC) Council by 1996[7]. A number of the fields of activity addressed by Title VI may, without Treaty amendment, be transferred to Community competences[8] by unanimous decision of the Council followed by ratification by all member states[9] - a 'double lock' in the view of the United Kingdom government[10].

298. Complementarity with the Community. As was mentioned above[11], the internal market was not fully achieved by the end of 1992. This is particularly so for the free movement of persons. Co-operation between the member states pursued under Title VI may therefore assist, if indirectly, the completion of the internal market.

(3) FINAL PROVISIONS OF THE TREATY ON EUROPEAN UNION

299. Amendment to the Treaties. The EC Treaty provides relatively simple mechanisms for amendment in certain minor 'housekeeping' areas[12].

---

1 TEU, art K.3(2).
2 Ibid, art K.4(1).
3 Ibid, art K.5.
4 Ibid, art K.3(1).
5 Ibid, art K.2(1).
6 EC Treaty, arts 3(d) and 100c. For a Commission proposal see COM(93) 684 (II).
7 Ibid, art 100c(3).
8 Ibid, art 100c(6); TEU, art K.9.
9 TEU, art K.9.
10 HC Debates, 27 January 1993, col 1112.
11 See para 170.
12 Eg a unanimous Council may alter the composition of the Commission (art 157(1)) and of the Court of Justice (art 165, 4th para; art 166, 3rd para) and may amend the Statute of the Court of Justice (art 188) and the ESCB/ECB Statute (art 106(5)). Certain provisions of the ECSC Treaty may be amended by a relatively simple procedure usually called '*petit révision*'; see ECSC Treaty, art 95. The EC and Euratom Treaties have no equivalent provision.

Otherwise, it may be amended only in accordance with the procedures laid down by the Treaty on European Union[1]. The Commission or a member state must first submit to the Council a proposal for amendment 'of the Treaties on which the Union is founded', ie, the TEU and the Community treaties. The Council may by simple majority, after consulting the Commission, the Parliament, and the European Central Bank if the proposals address monetary issues, convene an intergovernmental conference to determine 'by common accord' the appropriate amendments to be made to the Treaty. If the conference is successful in reaching unanimous agreement upon a text, it is submitted to the member states to be ratified in accordance with their own constitutional procedures and requirements[2]. If ratified, the amendments then enter into force in accordance with the terms of the amending treaty. In all cases hitherto this has been in the month following deposit of the last ratification. The EEC Treaty was amended by analogous, now repealed[3], procedures on eight occasions, most significantly by the Single European Act and the Treaty on European Union. The latter now itself provides that another intergovernmental conference is to be convened in 1996 in order to consider further amendments to the Treaties[4].

300. Accession to the European Union. Accession of new member states is possible only to the European Union as a whole, and no longer to the Community alone[5]. Any European state may apply for accession to the Union. An application must be approved by a unanimous Council and have the assent of the Parliament[6], after which the existing member states and the applicant state(s) agree the conditions of accession and the necessary adjustments to the treaties. This agreement, or treaty, is then submitted for parliamentary ratification by all member states and the applicant state(s), and enters into force following ratification and in accordance with its terms. There have been three accession treaties accommodating the enlargements of the Community in 1973 (Denmark, Ireland and the United Kingdom), 1981 (Greece) and 1986 (Spain and Portugal) and one accession treaty accommodating enlargement of the Union in 1995

---

1 TEU, art N.
2 In the United Kingdom ratification is normally accompanied by legislation in order to give effect in UK law to the changes. For important amending treaties this is done by statute (see eg the European Communities (Amendment) Acts 1986 and 1993, which gave the force of law to the provisions of the Single European Act and the Treaty on European Union respectively). However, the same result may be, and on occasion has been, achieved by Order in Council following a positive resolution of both Houses of Parliament by authority of the European Communities Act 1972, s 1(3).
3 EEC Treaty, art 236, repealed by TEU, art G(B)(83).
4 TEU, art N(2).
5 Ibid, art O, which replaces equivalent, repealed provisions in each of the Community treaties, eg EEC Treaty, art 237.
6 Parliamentary assent to accession requires - uniquely - an affirmative vote cast by an absolute majority of MEPs.

(Austria, Finland and Sweden)[1]. The reunification of Germany in 1990 and the consequent 'accession' to the Community of the five Eastern *Länder* did not require recourse to this procedure, or indeed any treaty amendment, as the former German Democratic Republic was dissolved and its territory deemed to revert to the Federal Republic. At the time of writing, formal applications for accession have been received from Turkey, Cyprus, Malta, Hungary and Poland. At the Essen Summit in December 1994 it was agreed in principle that Bulgaria, the Czech Republic, Hungary, Poland, Romania and Slovakia ought to be admitted to the Union, but no date was set.

301. Secession from the European Union. The Treaty on European Union does not address secession of a member state. Most treaties establishing international organisations include provisions for withdrawal or denunciation, usually requiring only a period of notice. The EC, Euratom and European Union treaties do not; rather they are concluded for 'an unlimited period'[2]. Secession of Greenland from the Communities was brought about in 1985 by formal amendment to the treaties in accordance with the then existing procedures. It was universally accepted at the time that treaty amendment was necessary to give effect to the wishes of Greenlanders to secede, and that it was beyond the power of Greenland and/or Danish authorities to do so unilaterally. It is submitted that, owing to the nature of the treaties as now interpreted and applied, any purported unilateral secession from the Union of a member state or part of a member state would be unlawful without negotiated amendment to the treaties. This is of course contrary to the conventional United Kingdom view of the supremacy of Parliament. Whether or not United Kingdom courts would give effect to an Act of Parliament purporting to amend or repeal the European Communities Act 1972 in order unilaterally to take the United Kingdom out of the Union is a question of theological nicety beyond the scope of this book.

1 For the texts see the (Brussels) Accession Treaty of 1972 (OJ L73, 27.3.72, p 1; Cmnd 7462); the (Athens) Accession Treaty of 1979 (OJ L291, 19.11.91, p 1; Cmnd 7650); the Accession Treaty of 1985 (OJ L302, 15.11.85, p 1; Cmnd 9634); and the (Corfu) Accession Treaty of 1994 (OJ C241, 29.8.94, p 9 as amended by the Adaptation Decision of 1 January 1995). Each treaty includes an Act of Accession which sets out the conditions and a transitional period for accession.
2 EC Treaty, art 240; Euratom, art 208; TEU, art Q. The exception is the ECSC Treaty, which is concluded for a period of fifty years (art 97). The ECSC is therefore scheduled to come to an end in the year 2002. The option now most seriously considered is that, rather than renewing it, the ECSC ought to be allowed to die a natural death, all coal and steel activity thereafter to be subsumed within the EC Treaty, either as it stands or with special new provisions.

APPENDIX I

THE EUROPEAN ECONOMIC AREA

1. Introduction. In January 1994 the Treaty between the Community and its member states on the one part and the European Free Trade Association (EFTA) states of Iceland, Liechtenstein[1], Norway, Austria, Finland and Sweden on the other establishing the European Economic Area (EEA) entered into force[2]. With the accession of Austria, Finland and Sweden to the European Union in January 1995 changes to the EEA Treaty will be necessary but are, at the time of writing, still awaiting agreement. Since Switzerland, the seventh EFTA state, opted to stay out of the EEA, in what follows 'EFTA states' refers to those EFTA states party to the EEA Treaty.

2. The purpose and nature of the EEA. The purpose of the EEA is

> 'to promote a continuous and balanced strengthening of trade and economic relations between the Contracting Parties with equal conditions of competition, and the respect of the same rules, with a view to creating a homogenous European Economic Area . . .'[4].

The EEA is not otherwise defined in the Treaty, and its nature is difficult to define. It is a sophisticated free trade area, but includes also provisions on free movement of persons, services and capital, with a view to economic integration less profound than that of the Community but deeper than that of the EFTA. Its institutions are not competent to legislate in the same way as the Community institutions under the EC Treaty. The EEA Treaty implies no cession of sovereignty.

3. The institutions of the EEA. The EEA Treaty creates an EEA Council, an EEA Joint Committee, an EEA Parliamentary Committee and an EEA Consultative Committee. The EEA Council comprises the members of the European Council plus one member from the government of each of the EFTA states[5]. Its function is, for the EEA, broadly similar to that of the European Council for the Community. The EEA Joint Committee consists of a representative from each of the contracting states, and acts by agreement between the Community representatives on the one hand and those of the

---

1 Owing to the closeness of its economic ties with Switzerland, the Protocol of March 1993 which amended the EEA Treaty to recognise the refusal of Switzerland to take part (OJ L1, 3.1.94, p 572) also recognised a temporary, special status for Liechtenstein.
2 For the text see OJ L1, 3.1.94, p 3.
3 See para 300 above.
4 EEA Treaty, art 1.
5 Ibid, art 90; for the Rules of Procedure see OJ L138, 2.6.94, p 39.

EFTA states, speaking with one voice, on the other[1]. Its purpose is to ensure the effective implementation and operation of the EEA Treaty[2], to which end it is granted the power to adopt binding acts[3] and significant powers of dispute settlement[4]. The EEA Joint Parliamentary Committee consists of members drawn equally from the European Parliament and members of the parliaments of the EFTA states[5], with the task of contributing, through dialogue and debate, to a better understanding between the Community and EFTA of the issues covered by the Treaty[6]. The EEA Consultative Committee has functions broadly similar to those of the Community's Economic and Social Committee[7]. The EEA Treaty also required the establishment of the EFTA Surveillance Authority and the EFTA Court. All decisions of these authorities are published in the Official Journal of the Community.

4. The EFTA Surveillance Authority. The EEA Treaty required the EFTA states to create an independent surveillance authority, the EFTA Surveillance Authority[8], which came into being on 1 January 1994[9]. It consists of five members, chosen upon grounds of general competence and whose independence is beyond doubt[10]. They are appointed by the common accord of the EFTA governments for a four-year renewable term[11], and are wholly independent in the performance of their duties[12]. It is assisted by an executive secretariat, five directorates, a legal service and administration[13]. Its task is to ensure on the part of the EFTA states the fulfilment of the obligations arising under the EEA Treaty[14]. It therefore co-operates closely with the Commission, which performs a similar task on the Community side[15]. Like the Commission, the EFTA Surveillance Authority is competent to adopt binding measures which impose pecuniary sanctions and are enforceable by civil process[16].

---

1 EEA Treaty, art 93. Procedures for adopting a common Community position within the EEA Council and Joint Committee are laid down in an EC regulation; see Regulation 2894/94, OJ L305, 30.11.94, p 6.
2 EEA Treaty, art 92.
3 Ibid, art 7.
4 Ibid, art 111.
5 Ibid, art 95(1) and Protocol 36.
6 Ibid, art 95(3).
7 Ibid, art 96.
8 Ibid, art 108(1).
9 EFTA Surveillance Agreement of 2 May 1992 establishing a Surveillance Authority and an EFTA Court of Justice, [1992] 1 *Commercial Laws of Europe* 277 (hereinafter 'EFTA Surveillance Agreement'). For the Rules of Procedure of the Surveillance Authority see OJ L113, 4.5.94, p 19.
10 EFTA Surveillance Agreement, art 7.
11 Ibid, art 9.
12 Ibid, art 8.
13 Rules of Procedure of the EFTA Surveillance Authority, art 2.
14 EEA Treaty, art 109.
15 Ibid, art 109 and Protocol 23.
16 Ibid, art 110.

5. The EFTA Court. The EEA Agreement also required the EFTA states to create an EFTA Court[1], which was created with effect from 1 January 1994[2]. It consists of five judges appointed for a six-year renewable term. It sits only in plenary session, although it could request the EFTA states to permit it to establish chambers. There are no Advocates-General. The sole working language is English except where the Court directs otherwise and where national courts refer questions for interpretative opinions[3]. Its seat is in Geneva.

6. The jurisdiction of the EFTA Court. The forms of process before the EFTA Court fall into five categories:

(a) Infringement proceedings raised by the EFTA Surveillance Authority against an EFTA state[4], analogous to article 169 of the EC Treaty.

(b) Settlement of disputes between EFTA states relating to the EEA[5], analogous to article 170 of the EC Treaty.

(c) Actions to annul a decision of the EFTA Surveillance Authority[6], analogous to articles 173 and 174(1) of the EC Treaty. The first such action was raised in April 1994[7].

(d) Actions against the EFTA Surveillance Authority for failure to act[8], analogous to article 175 of the EC Treaty.

(e) Advisory opinions to national courts of EFTA states[9]. But it is important to note that there are significant differences between this procedure and article 177 of the EC Treaty. First, because the EEA Treaty does not require the transfer of legislative authority to any EEA institution[10], advisory opinions of the EFTA Court are, unlike preliminary rulings from the Court of Justice, non-binding. Second, an advisory opinion may be sought only upon the interpretation of the EEA Treaty, and not upon the interpretation or validity of acts of the institutions. Further, there is no obligation to seek an advisory opinion, even for courts of last instance, and national rules may restrict access to the procedure to courts of last instance[11]. The first request for an advisory opinion, from a Finnish customs appeal committee, was lodged in April 1994 and decided in December 1994[12].

---

1 Ibid, art 108(2).
2 EFTA Surveillance Agreement; the Statute of the Court is contained in Protocol 5. For the Rules of Procedure see OJ L278, 27.10.94, p 1; [1994] 1 CMLR 832.
3 See para 6 of this Appendix.
4 EFTA Surveillance Agreement, art 31.
5 Ibid, art 32.
6 Ibid, art 36.
7 Case E-2/94 *Scottish Salmon Growers Association v EFTA Surveillance Authority* (pending).
8 EFTA Surveillance Agreement, art 37.
9 Ibid, art 34.
10 EEA Treaty, Protocol 35.
11 Only Austria adopted such a rule.
12 Case E-1/94 *Ravintoloitsijain Liiton Kustannus Oy Restamark v Helsingin Piiritullikamari*, judgment of 16 December 1994.

7. Relationship between the Court of Justice and the EFTA Court. The original EEA Treaty envisaged an EEA Court of Justice, comprised of judges drawn from the Court of Justice and the EFTA member states, to which the entire EEA - both the Community and EFTA – would be subject. This mechanism was declared by the Court of Justice to be incompatible with the EEC Treaty (as it then was)[1], and the amended text of the Treaty provides for no EEA Court and no direct co-operation between the Court of Justice and the EFTA Court. However, a judgment of the Court of Justice is binding upon the EFTA Court in so far as it addresses a Community rule which is identical in substance to an EEA provision and was decided prior to the signature of the EEA Treaty[2]. A judgment delivered after that date must be given 'due consideration' by the EFTA Court[3]. The contracting states have power to agree to request from the Court of Justice a ruling on the interpretation of a provision of the EEA Treaty identical in substance to an EC provision[4], and an EFTA state can permit its national courts to seek from the Court of Justice an advisory opinion on the interpretation of such a provision[5]. However, there would be political difficulties in activating the latter jurisdiction, and no EFTA state has done so. In the interests of harmonious interpretation of the Treaty the EEA Joint Committee is obliged to keep the developments of the case law of the Court of Justice and the EFTA Court under constant review[6] and to establish a system for the exchange of information between them[7].

8. Substantive rules of the EEA. In order to create the 'homogeneous European Economic Area' the EEA Treaty establishes a regime governing the free movement of goods, persons, services and capital, most of which is drawn verbatim from the equivalent rules of the EC Treaty. The rules on the free movement of goods[8] therefore abolished customs duties upon imports and exports and all charges having equivalent effect, quantitative restrictions upon imports and exports and all measures having equivalent effect[9] and discriminatory taxation. The major difference between the Community and the EEA is that these rules apply generally only to products originating in the territory of the contracting states[10]. The EEA therefore constitutes a (very sophisticated) free trade area, and not a customs union. The rules also apply only to certain named agricultural products[11]. The provisions on the

---

1 Opinion 1/91 *re the Draft EEA Treaty* [1991] ECR I-6079, [1992] 1 CMLR 245.
2 EEA Treaty, art 6. In this manner the *acquis communautaire* (as at the signature of the EEA Treaty) became part of the law of the EEA.
3 EFTA Surveillance Agreement, art 3(2).
4 EEA Treaty, art 111(3).
5 Ibid, art 107 and Protocol 34.
6 Ibid, art 105.
7 Ibid, art 106.
8 Ibid, arts 8-27.
9 Subject to considerations identical to those of art 36; see EEA Treaty, art 13.
10 Ibid, art 8(2). A very detailed set of rules of origin is provided in Protocol 4.
11 Ibid, art 8(3)(b) and Protocol 3.

free movement of persons and services[1] are essentially identical to those of the EC Treaty, whilst those on the free movement of capital[2] are similar to those in force within the Community prior to 1988[3].

9. The EEA and competition law. Article 53 of the EEA Treaty is identical *mutatis mutandis* to article 85 of the EC Treaty, prohibiting restrictive practices 'between Contracting Parties' which distort competition 'within the territory covered by [the EEA] Agreement'. The block exemptions adopted by the Commission and existing prior to signing of the Treaty apply to article 53[4]. Article 54 of the EEA Treaty is identical to article 86 of the EC Treaty except that it applies to a dominant undertaking 'within the territory covered by this Agreement' in so far as it may affect trade 'between Contracting Parties'. Restrictive practices and potentially abusive conduct within the Community but with wider effects are therefore to be assessed in the light of articles 85 and 86 of the EC Treaty *and* of articles 53 and 54 of the EEA Treaty. The Merger Regulation applies, the thresholds intact but turnover criteria to include that in the territories of the EFTA states, to a concentration 'with a Community or EFTA dimension'[5]. The Treaty provides further rules governing public undertakings and state aids analogous to articles 90 and 92–94 of the EC Treaty[6].

10. Enforcement of the competition rules. The competition rules of the EEA Treaty are enforced by the Commission within the territory of the Community and by the EFTA Surveillance Authority within the territory of the EFTA states, in which it enjoys 'equivalent powers to those of the EC Commission, at the time of the signature of the Agreement, for the application of the competition rules of the [EEC] Treaty'[7]. The EFTA Surveillance Authority has established its own competition Directorate, with its seat in Brussels. The two institutions are required to co-operate closely[8], and the Treaty provides rules governing which of them ought to be competent to determine situations which fall within the territorial jurisdiction of both[9]. Parties wishing to notify a restrictive agreement are required to determine which of the two is, by virtue of these rules, the 'competent surveillance

---

1 EEA Treaty, arts 28-39.
2 Ibid, arts 40-45.
3 See para 220 above.
4 EEA Treaty, art 60 and Annex XIV. So, all the block exemptions enumerated in para 245 above apply except the block exemption in the insurance sector and the block exemption on computer reservation systems in air transport. Annex XIV also directs enforcement authorities to 'take due account' of the various Commission Notices on the block exemptions and on other matters.
5 EEA Treaty, art 57 and Annex XIV.
6 Ibid, arts 59 and 61-64. On state aids see the Surveillance Authority's (extensive) Procedural and Substantive Rules in the Field of State Aid, [1994] 2 CMLR 7.
7 EEA Treaty, Protocol 21, art 1; for the detail see EFTA Surveillance Agreement, Protocol 4.
8 EEA Treaty, art 58 and Protocols 23 and 24.
9 Ibid, art 56.

authority'; if the wrong authority has been notified, it is required to transfer the case 'without delay' to the other[1]. A decision of the EFTA Surveillance Authority is subject to judicial review by the EFTA Court[2]. As articles 53 and 54 are identical *mutatis mutandis* to articles 85 and 86 of the EC Treaty and therefore ought to be interpreted in the same manner[3], they *ought* to have direct effect within the territory of the EEA and so be enforceable in national courts.

1 EEA Treaty, Protocol 23, art 10.
2 See para 6 of this Appendix.
3 EEA Treaty, art 6.

APPENDIX II

GUIDE TO COMMUNITY SOURCES AND MATERIALS

(1) PRIMARY MATERIALS

The Treaties

The Treaties and other primary sources of European Union and Community law are indicated in the text at para 124. The Treaties themselves are available in a number of editions, of which the most authoritative are those published by the Office for Official Publications of the European Communities, L-2985 Luxembourg. The Treaty on European Union, the EC Treaty and many other important texts are published by the Office in a very useful compendium, *European Union: Selected Instruments taken from the Treaties, Book I, Volume 1.*

Basic Community Laws (ed Rudden & Wyatt, 5th edn, OUP, 1994) and *EEC Legislation* (ed Foster, 5th edn, Blackstone's, 1994) are abridged student editions which also include some of the most important legislation adopted by the Community institutions. Other primary sources of Community law may be found in collections published by the Office for Official Publications.

Legislation

Official Journal of the European Communities

The Official Journal is the official gazette of the Community, containing the legislation and a wide range of other important texts adopted by the Community institutions. It is produced daily in two series, the 'L' series (legislation) and the 'C' series (*communications* in French, information and notices in English). Each contains a section for decisions of the EEA and EFTA institutions, which are consolidated in an EEA Supplement. There is also a Supplement which reproduces notices and other information on public procurement contracts (see text, para 195). The Official Journal is published in all eleven Community languages.

The English language Official Journal is cited 'OJ'. But since English was not an official language of the Community prior to 1973, the original pre-1973 Official Journals are usually cited 'JO' (*Journal officiel*). All Community laws still in force at the time of British and Irish accession were consolidated in an English language Special Edition of the Official Journal ('S Edn'). It is nevertheless sometimes necessary to go back to the original texts.

A Community act is formally cited by the type of instrument (Regulation, Directive, Decision, Recommendation, Opinion); its number and year of promulgation; and the number, date, and page reference in the Official Journal.

So, Regulation 4064/89, OJ L395, 30.12.89, p 1 signifies the 4064th regulation adopted in 1989, published in the Official Journal on 30 December 1989, in Number 395 (of 1989) of the L series, at page 1. A simpler and more common form of citation is Regulation 4064/89 OJ 1989 L395/1. In the case of directives, decisions, recommendation and opinions the year precedes the number - so Directive 75/117 is the 117th directive of 1975. The English language Special Edition of the Official Journal is normally cited by year, volume and page number. So: Regulation 1612/68, JO L257, 19.10.68, p 2; S Edn 1968 (II) p 475.

Encyclopedia of European Community Law

The Encyclopedia (ed KR Simmonds), produced by Sweet & Maxwell and W Green & Son, is published in three series: United Kingdom sources, primary sources and legislation of the Community institutions. It is a substantial consolidation of most Community law and legislation (it excludes most of the agricultural legislation) in loose-leaf form, classified by subject matter, with commentary, and updated regularly.

Guide to Legislation

Abstracting and indexing guides to Community legislation are published periodically by the Community as an adjunct to the Official Journal (*Directory of Community Legislation in Force and other Acts of the Community Institutions*), by Butterworths (*European Community Legislation: Current Status*), by Europe Data (*EC-Index* or *Ellis*) and by the TMC Asser Institute in the Hague (*Guide to EC Legislation*). Some of the more important legislative acts, decisions and draft legislation in the field of competition law are now reproduced in CMLR (see below). A most useful compendium of legislation in the competition field is Jones, Van der Woude and Lewis, *EC Competition Law Handbook* (see below).

Law Reports

European Court Reports

The *European Court Reports* ('ECR') are the official reports of the European Court of Justice. They contain all judgments of the Court of Justice and the Court of First Instance in chronological order of the date of judgment. ECR is in two parts: reports of judgments of the Court of Justice (Part I) and reports of judgments of the Court of First Instance (Part II). Since January 1994 judgments of the Court in staff cases (see text, para 104) are reported in ECR only if they are of general interest or establish principles of law; otherwise they are reported separately as *Reports of European Community Staff Cases* (ECR-SC).

Until 1994, with the exception of 1985 and 1986, the report of a case in ECR contained the Judge Rapporteur's Report for the Hearing (prior to 1985 as the 'Facts and Issues' part of the report), the opinion of the Advocate-General and the judgment of the Court. The Report for the Hearing is no longer published except in exceptional cases where the Court so directs, but it can be obtained directly from the Court in the language of the case.

Judgments of the Court of Justice and the Court of First Instance are normally cited in English by reference to case number (which is assigned sequentially by the Registrar), the names of the parties and the page reference in ECR. So: Cases C-6 & 9/90 *Francovich and Bonifaci v Italy* [1991] ECR I-5357; Case T-24/90 *Automec v Commission* [1992] ECR II-2223 (the 'I' and 'II' indicating Parts I and II of the ECR). Citation in other languages varies with their traditions, but usually includes the date of judgment. Since judgments are published in ECR in strict chronological order, it is not difficult to trace the report of a case from its date.

ECR are published in all eleven Community languages and since 1973 have been printed in such a way that the pagination is the same for all languages. For many years the French version of ECR (*Recueil de la Jurisprudence de la Cour de Justice et de la Tribunal de Premier Instance – Recueil* for short) was available many months – often more than a year – before other language versions. Since January 1994 the time lag has been sharply reduced, but at the cost of delaying publication of ECR in English and other languages for 1992 and 1993. Judgments in ECR-SC are in the language of the case only, although summaries are provided in each of the other languages.

Copies of individual judgments and opinions of Advocates-General can be obtained promptly and at reasonable price directly from the Court. It is also possible to receive copies of all judgments and opinions as issued in one or more languages. The Court also publishes a very useful weekly summary of its judgments, called *Proceedings of the Court of Justice and the Court of First Instance*. Information can be obtained from The Information Service, Court of Justice of the European Communities, L-2925 Luxembourg.

Common Market Law Reports

A most helpful series of reports is the Common Market Law Reports ('CMLR'), produced by the European Law Centre in London. CMLR contains not only reports of selected judgments of the Court of Justice but also selected decisions of national courts (primarily but not exclusively British) in which the application of Community law is considered. CMLR is now issued weekly and in five volumes per year, the fourth and fifth (the Antitrust Supplement) specialising in competition matters. Judgments from CMLR are usually cited in normal English fashion, for example Cases C-6 & 9/90 *Francovich and Bonifaci v Italy* [1993] 2 CMLR 66. Care should be taken to note where CMLR has made its own translation of a judgment or opinion (especially prior to 1973 when *all* translations into English were unofficial); where possible, ECR (or, until publication of ECR, the text issued by the Court) should be consulted for the authentic text or approved translation.

Other Sources

Judgments of the Court of Justice appear from time to time in a number of other reports. From 1995 the All England Law Reports publish a separate series of reports of selected judgments of the Court (All ER (European Cases)) in ten parts per year. The Industrial Relations Law Reports ('IRLR') frequently report very promptly judgments of the Court in employment law matters. The standard British reports of British court judgments following a preliminary ruling under article 177 invariably include a report of that ruling. All judgments of the Court are also available on CELEX and LEXIS databases.

Other Primary Materials

Annual Reports and the Bulletin

The Commission publishes an annual report on the activities of the Communities and developments over the preceding year in policy formulation and legislative programmes. It also publishes a monthly bulletin ('Bull EC'). Some important documents are issued as Supplements to the Bulletin.

Reports on Competition Policy

The Commission also publishes an annual Report on Competition Policy. This includes a survey of relevant case law of the Court of Justice and the Court of First Instance and decisions of the Commission. It also contains a number of important policy statements by the Commission as to how it will apply the competition rules of the Treaty.

Parliamentary Papers

The proceedings of the Parliament are published in the C series of the Official Journal. Reports of the various committees of the Parliament, some of them excellent, are published from time to time by the Parliament itself.

(2) SELECTED SECONDARY SOURCES

(This list is far from comprehensive and aims only to point the way to the next step in a search. It includes only recent or updated texts, omitting good but dated works, for materials in Community law enjoy a brief shelf-life. For the linguistically adroit, there are several very valuable encyclopaedias and similar works in other Community languages not mentioned here.)

KR Simmonds (ed) *Encyclopedia of European Community Law* (Sweet & Maxwell); see above.

C Jones, M van der Woude and X Lewis *EC Competition Law Handbook* (Sweet & Maxwell). This handbook, updated annually, contains all documents and case references necessary for a competition practitioner's daily work.

D Vaughan (ed) *Law of the European Communities* (Butterworths); first published in 1986 as a two-volume treatise on Community law (also published as volumes 51 and 52 of *Halsbury's Laws of England* (4th edn)); since 1990 published in loose-leaf, updated form.

CW Bellamy and GD Child *Common Market Law of Competition* (Sweet & Maxwell, 4th edn, 1993).

M Brealey and M Hoskins *Remedies in EC Law: Law and Practice in the English and EC Courts* (Longmans, 1994).

LN Brown and T Kennedy *The Court of Justice of the European Communities* (Sweet & Maxwell, 4th edn, 1994).

CS Kerse *Antitrust Procedure* (Sweet & Maxwell, 3rd edn, 1994).

KPE Lasok *The European Court of Justice: Practice and Procedure* (Butterworths, 2nd edn, 1994).

D O'Keeffe and PM Twomey *Legal Issues of the Maastricht Treaty* (Chancery Law Publishing, 1994).

HG Schermers and M Waelbroeck *Judicial Protection in the European Community* (Kluwer, 5th edn, 1992).

D Wyatt and A Dashwood *European Community Law* (Sweet & Maxwell, 3rd edn, 1993).

The leading specialist journals published in English are:

Common Market Law Review (CMLRev) (Europa Instituut of the University of Leiden);
European Law Review (ELRev) (European Law Centre);
Legal Issues of European Integration (LIEI) (Deventer); and
Yearbook of European Law (YEL) (Oxford University Press).
Important articles in English also appear in *Cahiers de Droit Européen* (CDE) (Emile Bruylant).

The Reports of the House of Lords Select Committee on the European Communities, with important documents not otherwise available reproduced as appendices, are known throughout the Community as 'Red Books' and are greatly respected.

Index

Acquis communautaire, 131, 290
Acquisitions. *See* MERGERS
Advocates-General, 85, 88, 89, App I, 5
See also COURT OF JUSTICE
Agreement on Social Policy, 267, 273, 274
See also PROTOCOL ON SOCIAL POLICY
Agriculture, 65, 198, 221, App I, 8
Annulment, Action of. *See* COURT OF JUSTICE, FORMS OF PROCESS
Anti-dumping, 223, 270
Appeals. *See* COURT OF JUSTICE, FORMS OF PROCESS
Approximation of laws, 223
See also HARMONISATION
Assembly. *See* EUROPEAN PARLIAMENT
Austria,
accession, 42, 300

Barriers, trade. *See* TRADE BARRIERS
Belgium, 9, 56
Bridge, Lord, 136
Brussels Judgments Convention, 109, 124
Budget,
Court of Auditors, 116
European Communities, 19
European Parliament, 19, 53

Capital, free movement of. *See* FOUR FREEDOMS, FREE MOVEMENT OF CAPITAL
CCT. *See* COMMON CUSTOMS TARIFF
Citizenship. *See* EUROPEAN COMMUNITY TREATY, CITIZENSHIP; EUROPEAN UNION, CITIZENSHIP
Cockfield White Paper,
general, 26, 32, 170
Single European Act, 32
taxation, 259
trade barriers, 195
Co-decision procedure. *See* LEGISLATION
Comfort letters, 244
Comité des Représentants Permanents, 60
Commission,
Commissioners. *See* MEMBERSHIP *below*
committees, 65
establishment, 14
European Economic Area, 67, App I, 10
European Parliament, 22, 69
general, 2
Legal Service, 72
legislative process, involvement in, 74, 76, 80
membership, 61, 62, 68
organisation,
general, 70
Secretariat-General. *See* SECRETARIAT-GENERAL *below*

Commission—*contd*
powers,
competition. *See* COMPETITION, ENFORCEMENT, COMMISSION
general, 65, 66, 67, 74, 75, 76, 80
state aids. *See* COMPETITION, STATE AIDS
Presidency, 63
Rules of Procedure, 45, 67
Secretariat-General, 71
See also EUROPEAN COMMUNITY, INSTITUTIONS
Committee of the Regions, 76, 118
See also EUROPEAN COMMUNITY, POLICIES
Committees of Inquiry, 54
Common Agricultural Policy, 198, 283
See also EUROPEAN COMMUNITY, POLICIES
Common Commercial Policy, 165, 183, 223, 268, 270, 284
See also EUROPEAN COMMUNITY, POLICIES
Common Customs Tariff, 182, 268
Common market, 163, 170, 287
See also EUROPEAN COMMUNITY TREATY, PRINCIPLES
Common Transport Policy, 221
See also EUROPEAN COMMUNITY, POLICIES
Community Charter of Fundamental Social Rights of Workers. *See* SOCIAL CHARTER
Community Customs Code, 177, 182
Community law. *See* EUROPEAN COMMUNITY LAW
Company law, 219
Competition,
agreements, 225, 232, 237, 243, 244, 245, 246
comfort letters, 244
Common Agricultural Policy, 198
concentrations, 247, 248
concerted practices, 225, 232, 237, 244
dominant position, 225, 233, 234, 235, 236, 237, 243, 247, App I, 9
abuse of, 225, 233, 235, 236, 237, 243, 247, App I, 9
dumping, 223, 270
enforcement,
Commission, 229, 238, 240, 242, 243, 244, 245, 246, 248, 254, App I, 10
national courts, 229, 239, 240, 246, 255, App I, 10
European Economic Area, 252, App I, 9, 10
exemption, 230, 240, 241, 242, 243, 244, 245, 246
block, 245, 246, App I, 9
general, 65, 90, 165, 196, 197, 198, 222-225
intellectual property rights, 196, 237
mergers. *See* CONCENTRATIONS *above*
Merger Regulation, 248, App I, 9

Competition—*contd*
monopolies, 236, 249-251
negative clearance, 243
notification, 242, 243, 244, 245, 246
obligations,
    member states, 227
    undertakings, 226
oligopolies, 236
relevant market, 231
restrictive practices, 196, 225, 228, 232, 240,
    App I, 9
rule of reason, 232
state aids, 197, 223, 250, 253-256, App I, 9
taxation. *See* TAXATION, RULES
undertakings, 226, 232, 233, 234, 235, 236, 237,
    238, 239
    public, 197, 249-251, App I, 9
Concentrations. *See* COMPETITION,
    CONCENTRATIONS
Co-operation procedure. *See* LEGISLATION
COREPER, 60, 294, 296
Corfu Accession Treaty, 42, 300
Council,
composition. *See* MEMBERSHIP *below*
COREPER, 60
general, 20
legislative process. *See* LEGISLATION, COUNCIL
membership, 56
organisation, 58
powers, 46, 55, 75–81, 291
Presidency, 59
Rules of Procedure, 45, 58
voting, 77, 78. *See also* VETO; LUXEMBOURG
    COMPROMISE
See also EUROPEAN COMMUNITY LAW; EUROPEAN
    COMMUNITY, INSTITUTIONS
Council of Europe, 2, 7, 8, 20
See also EUROPEAN CONVENTION ON HUMAN
    RIGHTS
Council of Ministers. *See* COUNCIL
Council of the European Union. *See* COUNCIL
Court of Auditors, 116
See also EUROPEAN COMMUNITIES, BUDGET
Court of First Instance,
establishment, 84
jurisdiction, 90, 104, 137
membership, 89
organisation, 89
procedures, 90
Rules of Procedure, 45, 90
See also COURT OF JUSTICE
Court of Justice,
Advocates-General, 85, 88, 89, App I, 5
appeals from Court of First Instance, 86, 90,
    111, 113
chambers, 87
Court of First Instance. *See* COURT OF FIRST
    INSTANCE
direct actions. *See* FORMS OF PROCESS *below*

Court of Justice—*contd*
Economic and Monetary Union, 114
enforcement of Community rights, 132-134,
    137, 140, 141
European Economic Area, 115, App I, 7
European Monetary Institute, 121
forms of process,
    general, 94-114
        annulment, 100-102
        appeals, 90, 111
        failure to act, 103
        failure to fulfil obligation, 97-99
        interveners in actions, 96
        non-contractual liability, 105
        opinions, 112
        parties to actions, 96
        plea of illegality, 110
        preliminary rulings, 106-110
        staff cases, 104
        summary procedure, 111, 113
interim measures, 86, 111, 113
jurisdiction, 83, 93, 115, 137, 292
languages, 91
membership, 85
orders, 95, 111, 113
organisation, 87
Presidency, 86
procedures, 87, 97
Rules of Procedure, 45, 83
sanctions, 98
Treaty on European Union, 93, 292
See also COURT OF FIRST INSTANCE; EUROPEAN
    COMMUNITY LAW; LEGISLATION
Customs duties. *See* FOUR FREEDOMS, FREE
    MOVEMENT OF GOODS
Customs Union. *See* FOUR FREEDOMS, FREE
    MOVEMENT OF GOODS

***Dassonville* test,** 187
de Gaulle, Charles, 15
Decisions. *See* LEGISLATION, DECISIONS
Delors, Jacques, 26, 34, 262
Delors Commission, Committee and Plan.
    See DELORS, JACQUES
Denmark,
accession, 16, 300
Economic and monetary union, 267
secession, 301
Direct effect. *See* EUROPEAN COMMUNITY LAW,
    DIRECT EFFECT
Directives. *See* LEGISLATION, DIRECTIVES
Discrimination,
nationality, 156, 168, 207
See also EUROPEAN COMMUNITY LAW, PRINCIPLES;
    EUROPEAN COMMUNITY TREATY, GENERAL
    PRINCIPLES
sex. *See* SEX DISCRIMINATION
Dominance, market. *See* COMPETITION,
    DOMINANT POSITION

Dooge Committee, 25, 26
Dublin Convention, 288
Dumping, 223, 270

EAEC. *See* EUROPEAN ATOMIC ENERGY
    COMMUNITY
ECB. *See* EUROPEAN CENTRAL BANK
EC. *See* EUROPEAN COMMUNITY
EC Treaty. *See* EUROPEAN COMMUNITY TREATY
ECHR. *See* EUROPEAN CONVENTION ON HUMAN
    RIGHTS
Economic and monetary union,
Court of Justice, 114
Denmark, 267
exemptions, 267
general, 34, 38, 164, 262-267
Germany, 267
institutions, 44
obligations of member states, 263, 264, 266
United Kingdom, 267
See also EUROPEAN MONETARY INSTITUTE;
    EUROPEAN MONETARY SYSTEM; EUROPEAN
    SYSTEM OF CENTRAL BANKS; EUROPEAN
    CENTRAL BANK
Economic and Social Committee, 76, 117,
    118
See also EUROPEAN COMMUNITY, INSTITUTIONS
Economic and Social Policy. *See* EUROPEAN
    COMMUNITY, POLICIES
ECSC. *See* EUROPEAN COAL AND STEEL
    COMMUNITY
ECU. *See* EUROPEAN CURRENCY UNIT
Edinburgh Summit, 45
Education, 204, 281, 282
free movement of services, 218
See also FOUR FREEDOMS, FREE MOVEMENT OF
    SERVICES
EEA. *See* EUROPEAN ECONOMIC AREA
EEC. *See* EUROPEAN ECONOMIC COMMUNITY
EEIG. *See* EUROPEAN ECONOMIC INTEREST
    GROUPING
EIB. *See* EUROPEAN INVESTMENT BANK
EMI. *See* EUROPEAN MONETARY INSTITUTE
EMS. *See* EUROPEAN MONETARY SYSTEM
EMU. *See* ECONOMIC AND MONETARY UNION
Environment, 189, 281, 282, 283
EPC. *See* EUROPEAN POLITICAL CO-OPERATION
Equal pay. *See* SEX DISCRIMINATION, EQUAL PAY
Equivalence, 214
ERM. *See* EXCHANGE RATE MECHANISM
ESCB. *See* EUROPEAN SYSTEM OF CENTRAL BANKS
Essen Summit, 300
Euratom. *See* EUROPEAN ATOMIC ENERGY
    AUTHORITY
Europe, Council of. *See* COUNCIL OF EUROPE
Europe Agreements, 269
European Atomic Energy Community,
establishing treaty. *See* TREATY *below*
general, 3

European Atomic Energy Community—
    contd
treaty, 3, 11, 13
See also EUROPEAN COMMUNITIES
European Central Bank, 100, 101, 122, 265
See also ECONOMIC AND MONETARY UNION;
    EUROPEAN SYSTEM OF CENTRAL BANKS;
    EUROPEAN MONETARY INSTITUTE; EUROPEAN
    MONETARY SYSTEM; EUROPEAN COMMUNITY,
    INSTITUTIONS
European Coal and Steel Community,
establishing treaty. *See* TREATY *below*
general, 3, 10
institutions, 10, 13
signatory states, 9
treaty, 3, 9, 10, 12, 13
See also EUROPEAN COMMUNITIES
European Commission. *See* COMMISSION
European Communities (the three
    communities), 3, 12, 43
See also EUROPEAN COMMUNITY; EUROPEAN COAL
    AND STEEL COMMUNITY; EUROPEAN ATOMIC
    ENERGY COMMUNITY
European Community (formerly EEC),
agreements with international organisations,
    269
agreements with third countries, 269, 284
budget, 19
See also COURT OF AUDITORS
change of name from EEC, 3, 38, 43
development, 7-43
institutions, 13, 14, 44-45, 84, 123
See also COMMITTEE OF THE REGIONS;
    COMMISSION; COUNCIL; COURT OF JUSTICE;
    ECONOMIC AND SOCIAL COMMITTEE;
    EUROPEAN CENTRAL BANK; EUROPEAN
    INVESTMENT BANK; EUROPEAN MONETARY
    INSTITUTE; EUROPEAN PARLIAMENT;
    EUROPEAN SYSTEM OF CENTRAL BANKS
international personality, 284
law. *See* EUROPEAN COMMUNITY LAW
liability, 105, 285
policies,
    agriculture. *See* COMMON AGRICULTURAL
        POLICY *below*
    commercial policy. *See* COMMON
        COMMERCIAL POLICY *below*
    Common Agricultural Policy, 198
    Common Commercial Policy, 165, 183, 223,
        268, 270, 284
    See also FOUR FREEDOMS, FREE MOVEMENT OF
        GOODS
    Common Rules on Competition, Taxation
        and Approximation of Laws, 222-
        260
    See also COMPETITION
    Common Transport Policy, 221
    economic and monetary policy. *See*
        ECONOMIC AND MONETARY UNION

European Community (formerly EEC)— *contd*
economic and social policy. *See* ECONOMIC AND SOCIAL COMMITTEE; COMMITTEE OF THE REGIONS
financial policy. *See* EUROPEAN INVESTMENT BANK; EUROPEAN INVESTMENT FUND; EUROPEAN MONETARY INSTITUTE; EUROPEAN SYSTEM OF CENTRAL BANKS; EUROPEAN CENTRAL BANK
free movement of capital. *See* FOUR FREEDOMS
free movement of goods. *See* FOUR FREEDOMS
free movement of persons. *See* FOUR FREEDOMS
free movement of services. *See* FOUR FREEDOMS
general, 165, 172, 261, 281-283
harmonisation, 271, 282
integration clauses, 283
social policy, 271-280
See also SOCIAL CHARTER; EUROPEAN SOCIAL FUND; PROTOCOL ON SOCIAL POLICY; AGREEMENT ON SOCIAL POLICY; SEX DISCRIMINATION
transport policy. *See* COMMON TRANSPORT POLICY *above*
See also EUROPEAN UNION, POLICIES
political aims, 12
treaty. *See* EUROPEAN COMMUNITY TREATY
See also EUROPEAN ATOMIC ENERGY AUTHORITY; EUROPEAN COAL AND STEEL COMMUNITY
European Community law,
Acquis communautaire, 131, 290
agreements, 124
autonomy, 130
direct effect, 133, 135, 136, 138, 140, 145, 146, 148, 169, 185, 202, 212, 220, 229, 239, 255
enforcement, 133-141
Court of Justice, 97-110
damages, rights, 141
national courts, 138
establishing treaties. *See* TREATIES *below*
general, 3, 31, 73, 131
general principles,
equality of treatment. *See* NON-DISCRIMINATION *below*
general, 152, 158
identifiability, 154
language, understandability, 154
legal certainty, 102, 154
legitimate expectation, 102, 154
natural justice. *See* RIGHTS, NATURAL JUSTICE *below*
non-discrimination, 156, 194, 207
prescription, 154
proportionality, 155, 166, 189, 191, 192, 217

European Community law—*contd*
rights,
acquired, 154
fundamental, 153
See also EUROPEAN CONVENTION ON HUMAN RIGHTS
natural justice, 153
subsidiarity, 157
interpretation, 127-130, 132
languages, 126, 130
legislation. *See* LEGISLATION
legislative process, 74-82
precedent, 132, 135
primacy, 134, 135, 136, 301
sources, 124, 125, 127
supremacy. *See* PRIMACY *above*
treaties, 3, 124, 128, 129
United Kingdom,
damages, rights, 141
enforcement, 3, 132, 136, 139
status, 136
See also COURT OF JUSTICE; EUROPEAN COMMUNITY TREATY
European Community Treaty,
agricultural products, 198
amendment, 299
annexes, 160
citizenship, 38, 171
See also EUROPEAN UNION, CITIZENSHIP
declarations, 160
effects, 174
general, 44-46, 159-161, 287
legislative process. *See* LEGISLATION
obligations,
European Community, 166
member states, 167
policies. *See* EUROPEAN COMMUNITIES, POLICIES
preamble, 159, 161
principles, 159, 161, 162-170
results (national differences), 175, 192, 286
rights, 171
transitional period, 169, 170, 180
protocols, 160
structure, 159
See also EUROPEAN COMMUNITY LAW; TRADE BARRIERS
European Company, 219
European Convention for the Protection of Human Rights and Fundamental Freedoms. *See* EUROPEAN CONVENTION ON HUMAN RIGHTS
European Convention on Human Rights,
Council of Europe, 2
general, 2, 124, 153
United Kingdom,
enforcement, 2, 153
ratification, 7
See also EUROPEAN COMMUNITY LAW
European Council, 20, 46, 263, 290

European Court. *See* COURT OF JUSTICE
European Court of Human Rights, 2
European Court Reports, 92, App II
European Currency Unit, 21, 265
European Economic Area,
Commission, 67
competition rules, App I, 9, 10
Court of Justice, 115
establishment, 40
European Free Trade Association, 5, 40,
    App I, 4-7
general, 5, 269, App I, 1
institutions, App I, 2, 3
purpose, 41, App I, 2
rules, App I, 8
scope, 41
treaty, 40, 115, App I, 1-5
United Kingdom, 5
See also FOUR FREEDOMS; EUROPEAN FREE TRADE
    ASSOCIATION
European Economic Community. *See*
    EUROPEAN COMMUNITY (FORMERLY EEC);
    EUROPEAN COMMUNITIES
European Economic Interest Grouping, 219
European Free Trade Association,
Court,
    Court of Justice, App I, 7
    jurisdiction, App I, 6
European Economic Area, 5, 40, App I, 4-7
Surveillance Authority, App I, 4, 10
European Investment Bank, 119
See also EUROPEAN INVESTMENT FUND; EUROPEAN
    COMMUNITY, INSTITUTIONS
European Investment Fund, 120
See also EUROPEAN INVESTMENT BANK
European law,
scope, 1
European Monetary Institute,
Court of Justice, 121
general, 121, 264
See also ECONOMIC AND MONETARY UNION;
    EUROPEAN MONETARY SYSTEM; EUROPEAN
    CENTRAL BANK; EUROPEAN SYSTEM OF
    CENTRAL BANKS
European Monetary System, 20
See also ECONOMIC AND MONETARY UNION;
    EUROPEAN MONETARY INSTITUTE; EUROPEAN
    CENTRAL BANK; EUROPEAN SYSTEM OF
    CENTRAL BANKS
European Parliament,
budget, 19, 53
Bureau, 51
Committees of Inquiry, 54
consultation, 79, 292
elections, 22, 48
European Commission, 22, 69
European Union, 292
legislative process, involvement in. *See*
    LEGISLATION; EUROPEAN PARLIAMENT

European Parliament—*contd*
membership, 48
officers, 51
Ombudsman, 54
organisation, 51
political groups, 50, 51
powers, 19, 22, 52-54, 79, 292
procedures, 49
rights of citizens, 55
Rules of Procedure, 45, 49
See also EUROPEAN COMMUNITY, INSTITUTIONS;
    EUROPEAN UNION
European Political Co-operation, 29
European Social Fund, 271
See also EUROPEAN COMMUNITY, POLICIES
European System of Central Banks, 122, 265
See also ECONOMIC AND MONETARY UNION;
    EUROPEAN CENTRAL BANK; EUROPEAN
    MONETARY INSTITUTE; EUROPEAN MONETARY
    SYSTEM
European Union,
accession, 300
See also under names of individual countries
citizenship, 38, 171
See also EUROPEAN COMMUNITY TREATY, CITIZENSHIP
decision making, 291
European Parliament, 292
general, 4, 37, 43
institutions,
    general, 290
international personality, 293
judicial control, 292
policies,
    foreign and security policy, 294
    general, 292
    justice and home affairs, 295-298
    See also EUROPEAN COMMUNITY, POLICIES
political control, 292
scope, 4, 37
secession, 301
United Kingdom, 37, 289
See also EUROPEAN UNION, TREATY ON
European Union, Treaty on,
amendment, 39, 299
general, 3, 20, 25, 26, 36, 37, 288
See also EUROPEAN UNION
Exchange Rate Mechanism,
general, 21
United Kingdom, 21
Exports,
restrictions. *See* TRADE BARRIERS

Finance,
policy. *See* EUROPEAN INVESTMENT BANK;
    EUROPEAN INVESTMENT FUND; EUROPEAN
    MONETARY INSTITUTE; EUROPEAN SYSTEM OF
    CENTRAL BANKS; EUROPEAN CENTRAL BANK;
    EUROPEAN COMMUNITY, POLICIES, FREE
    MOVEMENT OF SERVICES

Finance—*contd*
See FOUR FREEDOMS, FREE MOVEMENT OF SERVICES
Financial services, 219
Finland,
accession, 42, 300
Fontainebleau Summit, 25
Foreign and security policy, 294
See also EUROPEAN UNION, POLICIES
Four Freedoms,
establishment. *See* FREE MOVEMENT OF PERSONS,
   RIGHT OF ESTABLISHMENT *below*
free movement of capital, 220, 264
free movement of goods,
   customs duties, 174, 178, 180-182
   customs union, 176, 177, 179, 182
   general, 174, 176
   non-tariff barriers, 179, 184-186
   quantitative restrictions. *See* NON-TARIFF
      BARRIERS *above*
   restrictions. *See* CUSTOMS UNION *and* NON-
      TARIFF BARRIERS *above*
   tariff barriers. *See* CUSTOMS UNION
free movement of persons,
   beneficiaries, 203-204
   definition, 199-201
   equivalence of qualifications. *See*
      HARMONISATION OF QUALIFICATIONS
      below
   harmonisation of qualifications, 213-215
   restrictions, 202, 210-212
   right of establishment, 199, 201, 209, 212
   rights, migrant workers, 205-209
   social security benefits, 208
free movement of services,
   definition, 199-201
   education, 218
   financial services, 219
   restrictions, 217
   scope, 216
general, 173
See also EUROPEAN COMMUNITY, POLICIES;
   EUROPEAN COMMUNITY TREATY, PRINCIPLES;
   TRADE BARRIERS; COMPETITION;
   UNDERTAKINGS; EUROPEAN ECONOMIC AREA,
   RULES
France, 9, 15, 62
Free movement of capital. *See* FOUR
   FREEDOMS, FREE MOVEMENT OF CAPITAL
Free movement of goods. *See* FOUR FREEDOMS,
   FREE MOVEMENT OF GOODS
Free movement of persons. *See* FOUR
   FREEDOMS, FREE MOVEMENT OF PERSONS
Free movement of services. *See* FOUR
   FREEDOMS, FREE MOVEMENT OF SERVICES
Free trade. *See* TRADE BARRIERS

General principles of Community law. *See*
   EUROPEAN COMMUNITY LAW, GENERAL
   PRINCIPLES

Genscher-Colombo Plan, 24
Germany, 8, 9, 56, 62, 267
Goods, free movement of. *See* FOUR
   FREEDOMS, FREE MOVEMENT OF GOODS
Great Britain. *See* UNITED KINGDOM
Greece,
accession, 23, 300
Greenland,
secession, 301

Hanover Summit, 34
Harmonisation,
policies, 271, 282
See also EUROPEAN COMMUNITY, POLICIES
qualifications. *See* FOUR FREEDOMS, FREE
   MOVEMENT OF PERSONS
Single European Act, 193
taxation, 259
trade barriers, 193
Heath, Edward, 16, 17
High Authority. *See* COMMISSION

Imports,
restrictions. *See* TRADE BARRIERS
Industrial property rights, 196, 237
Integration clauses, 283
See also EUROPEAN COMMUNITY, POLICIES
Intellectual property rights, 196, 237
Internal market, 165, 170
International personality, 284, 293
Ireland,
accession, 16, 300
Ioannina Compromise, 78
Italy, 9, 62, 134

Judicial review, 151
See also COURT OF JUSTICE, FORMS OF PROCESS;
   LEGISLATION
Justice and home affairs policy, 295-298
See also EUROPEAN UNION, POLICIES
Legal base, 82, 144
Legal certainty, 102, 154
See also EUROPEAN COMMUNITY LAW, GENERAL
   PRINCIPLES
Legal Service, 72
Legislation,
co-decision procedure, 81
co-operation procedure, 80
Commission, 74
Council, 75-81
decisions, 146
directives, 147
   direct effect. *See* ENFORCEMENT *below*
   enforcement, 148
   interpretation, 148
   uniform interpretation. *See* INTERPRETATION
      above
European Parliament, 74, 79-82
general, 142-144, 150

Legislation—*contd*
judicial review, 151
legal base, 82, 144
legislative process, 73-82
opinions, 149
recommendations, 149
regulations, 145
sex discrimination, 277
substantive requirements, 144
transport, 222
veto, 15, 78
See also COURT OF JUSTICE
Legitimate expectation, 102, 154
See also EUROPEAN COMMUNITY LAW, GENERAL
PRINCIPLES
Lomé Agreement, 269
Luxembourg, 9
Luxembourg Compromise, 15, 30, 78
See also EUROPEAN COUNCIL, VOTING; VETO
Luxembourg Conference, 26

Macmillan, Harold, 15
Maastricht, Treaty of. *See* EUROPEAN UNION,
TREATY ON
Mandatory requirements, 189, 193, 217
Market dominance. *See* COMPETITION,
DOMINANT POSITION
Markets,
equivalence, 231
relevant, 231
Merger Treaty, 14
Mergers. *See* COMPETITION, CONCENTRATIONS
Messina Conference, 11
Milan Summit, 26-28
Monopolies,
commercial, 197
competition rules, 236, 249-251
See also COMPETITION; TRADE BARRIERS
Mutual recognition of qualifications, 215

Netherlands, 9
Non-discrimination. *See* EUROPEAN
COMMUNITY LAW, GENERAL PRINCIPLES;
EUROPEAN COMMUNITY TREATY, PRINCIPLES
Non-existence, 102
Non-tariff barriers. *See* FOUR FREEDOMS, FREE
MOVEMENT OF GOODS
Norway, 16, 42

Oligopolies. *See* COMPETITION, OLIGOPOLIES
Ombudsman, 54
See also EUROPEAN PARLIAMENT

Paris, Treaty of, 3
Parliament. *See* EUROPEAN PARLIAMENT
Pensions (sex discrimination), 279, 280
Persons, free movement of. *See* FOUR
FREEDOMS, FREE MOVEMENT OF PERSONS
Plea of illegality. *See* COURT OF JUSTICE, FORMS
OF PROCESS

Policies. *See* EUROPEAN COMMUNITY, POLICIES;
EUROPEAN UNION, POLICIES
Portugal,
accession, 27, 300
Preliminary rulings. *See* COURT OF JUSTICE,
FORMS OF PROCESS
Prescription, 154
See also EUROPEAN COMMUNITY LAW, GENERAL
PRINCIPLES
Primacy. *See* EUROPEAN COMMUNITY LAW,
PRIMACY
Proportionality, 155, 166, 189, 191, 192, 217
See also EUROPEAN COMMUNITY LAW, GENERAL
PRINCIPLES
Protocol on Social Policy, 273
See also EUROPEAN COMMUNITY, POLICIES
Public procurement,
restrictions, 195
Public undertakings. *See* COMPETITION,
UNDERTAKINGS, PUBLIC

Referenda, 17, 36, 40, 42
Regulations. *See* LEGISLATION
Relevant market, 231
See also COMPETITION
Restrictive practices. *See* COMPETITION,
RESTRICTIVE PRACTICES
Reverse discrimination, 194
Right of establishment. *See* FOUR FREEDOMS,
FREE MOVEMENT OF PERSONS, RIGHT OF
ESTABLISHMENT
Rights. *See* EUROPEAN CONVENTION ON HUMAN
RIGHTS; EUROPEAN COMMUNITY LAW,
PRINCIPLES; EUROPEAN PARLIAMENT, RIGHTS
OF CITIZENS; EUROPEAN COMMUNITY TREATY,
RIGHTS; FOUR FREEDOMS, FREE MOVEMENT OF
PERSONS
Rome, Treaties of,
general, 3, 11
Rome Contracts Convention, 109, 124
Rule of reason, 189, 232
Rules of Procedure. *See under individual*
institutions

Safeguard measures, 270
Schengen Agreement, 288
Schuman Declaration, 9, 12
Secession. *See* EUROPEAN UNION, SECESSION
Services, free movement of. *See* FOUR
FREEDOMS, FREE MOVEMENT OF SERVICES
Sex discrimination,
equal pay, 275-276
legislation, 277
pensions, 279, 280
rules, 278
See also EUROPEAN COMMUNITY, POLICIES
Single European Act, 20, 28-32
Cockfield White Paper, 32
harmonisation, 193

Single European Act—*contd*
internal market, definition, 170
Social Agreement. *See* AGREEMENT ON SOCIAL
    POLICY
Social Charter, 33, 38, 272
See also EUROPEAN COMMUNITY, POLICIES;
    PROTOCOL ON SOCIAL POLICY
Social policy, 271-280
See also EUROPEAN COMMUNITY, POLICIES
Social Protocol. *See* PROTOCOL ON SOCIAL
    POLICY
Social Security benefits, 208
See also FOUR FREEDOMS, FREE MOVEMENT OF
    PERSONS
Solemn Declaration of Stuttgart, 24
Spaak, Paul-Henri, 11
Spaak II Committee, 25
Spain,
accession, 27, 300
commissioners, 62
State aids. *See* COMPETITION, STATE AIDS
State monopolies, 197, 249
See also COMPETITION, UNDERTAKINGS, PUBLIC
Students, 206, 218
Stuttgart, Solemn Declaration of, 24
Subsidiarity, 157, 166
See also EUROPEAN COMMUNITY LAW, GENERAL
    PRINCIPLES
Summits. *See under names of individual*
    summits, eg Milan Summit
Supremacy. *See* EUROPEAN COMMUNITY LAW,
    PRIMACY
Surveillance Authority, App I, 4, 10
See also EUROPEAN FREE TRADE ASSOCIATION
Sweden,
accession, 42, 300
Switzerland, 40, App I, 1

Tariff barriers, 176, 177, 179, 182
See also FOUR FREEDOMS, FREE MOVEMENT OF
    GOODS
Taxation,
direct, 260
general, 197, 223
harmonisation, 259
rules,
    application, 258
    general, 257
Trade barriers,
agricultural products, 198
Cockfield White Paper, 195

Trade Barriers—*contd*
general, 163, 170, 185, 187-191
harmonisation, 193
industrial property rights, 196
public procurement, 195
state monopolies, 197, 249
See also FOUR FREEDOMS, FREE MOVEMENT OF
    GOODS; EUROPEAN COMMUNITY LAW;
    EUROPEAN COMMUNITY TREATY;
    COMPETITION; UNDERTAKINGS
Transitional period, 169, 170, 180
See also EUROPEAN COMMUNITY TREATY
Transport,
legislation, 221
policy, 221
See also EUROPEAN COMMUNITY, POLICIES
Treaties. *See under names of individual treaties,*
    eg Paris, Treaty of and under names of
    institutions, eg European Community. See
    also EUROPEAN COMMUNITY LAW

Undertakings. *See* COMPETITION,
    UNDERTAKINGS
United Kingdom,
accession, 16, 300
commissioners, 62
Economic and Monetary Union, 267
European Community Law. *See* EUROPEAN
    COMMUNITY LAW, UNITED KINGDOM
European Convention on Human Rights. *See*
    EUROPEAN CONVENTION ON HUMAN RIGHTS,
    UNITED KINGDOM
European Economic Area, 5
European Union, 37, 289
Exchange Rate Mechanism, 21
financial contribution, 22, 25
membership, 15-17
Protocol on Social Policy, 273
Social Charter, 33

Variable geometry, 31
Veto, 15, 78
See also EUROPEAN COUNCIL, VOTING

Wilson, Harold, 16, 17
Workers,
definition, 200
rights, 205-209
See also FOUR FREEDOMS, FREE MOVEMENT OF
    PERSONS